Architecture of the Old South
MARYLAND

Architecture of the Old South
MARYLAND

MILLS LANE

Special Photography by VAN JONES MARTIN
Editorial Assistance by MICHAEL F. TROSTEL
Drawings by GENE CARPENTER

A BEEHIVE PRESS BOOK
Abbeville Press · Publishers · New York · London · Paris

Frontispiece: Bohemia, George Milligan House, Earlville vicinity, c. 1765.

This book was conceived, edited, and designed by The Beehive Press of Savannah, Georgia.

Library of Congress Cataloging-in-Publication Data

Lane, Mills.
    Architecture of the Old South. Maryland / Mills Lane : special photography by Van Jones Martin ; editorial assistance by Michael F. Trostel ; drawings by Gene Carpenter.
        p.   cm.
    "A Beehive Press book."
    Includes bibliographical references and index.
    ISBN 1-55859-040-4
    1. Architecture, Colonial—Maryland. 2. Architecture, Modern—19th century—Maryland. 3. Architecture—Maryland. I. Title.
    NA730.M3L36   1991
    720'.9752—dc20   91-17344
                                                                            CIP

Copyright © 1991 Mills Lane. All rights reserved under international copyright conventions. No part of this book may be reproduced or utilized in any form or by any means, electronic or mechanical, including photocopying, recording, or by any information storage and retrieval system, without permission in writing from the publisher. Inquiries should be addressed to Abbeville Press, Inc., 488 Madison Avenue, New York, N.Y. 10022. Printed and bound in Italy.

All photographs, unless otherwise credited, are by Van Jones Martin.

Contents

	Foreword	8
I.	The Colony	12
II.	The Federal Era	74
III.	The Greek Revival	142
IV.	Romantic Styles	166
	Notes	234
	Index	243

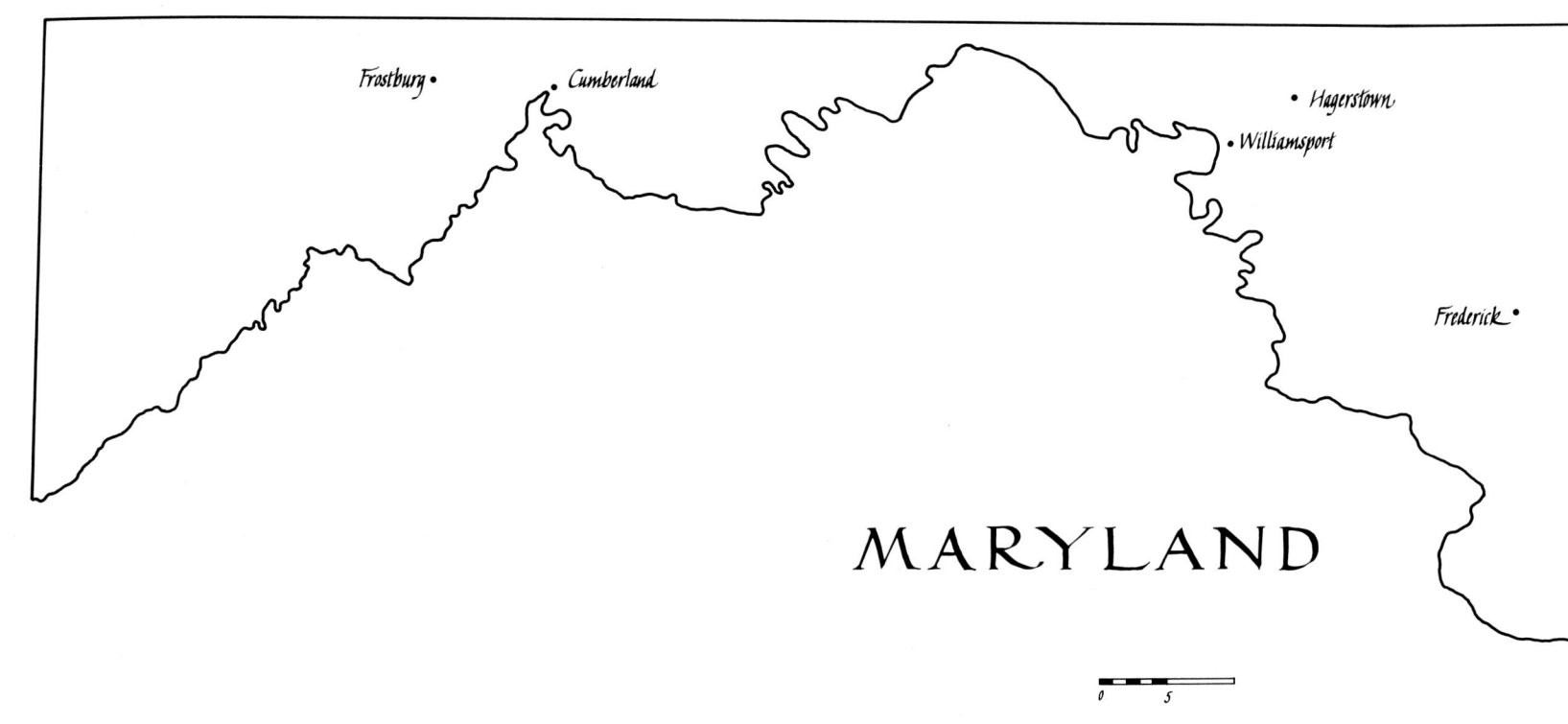

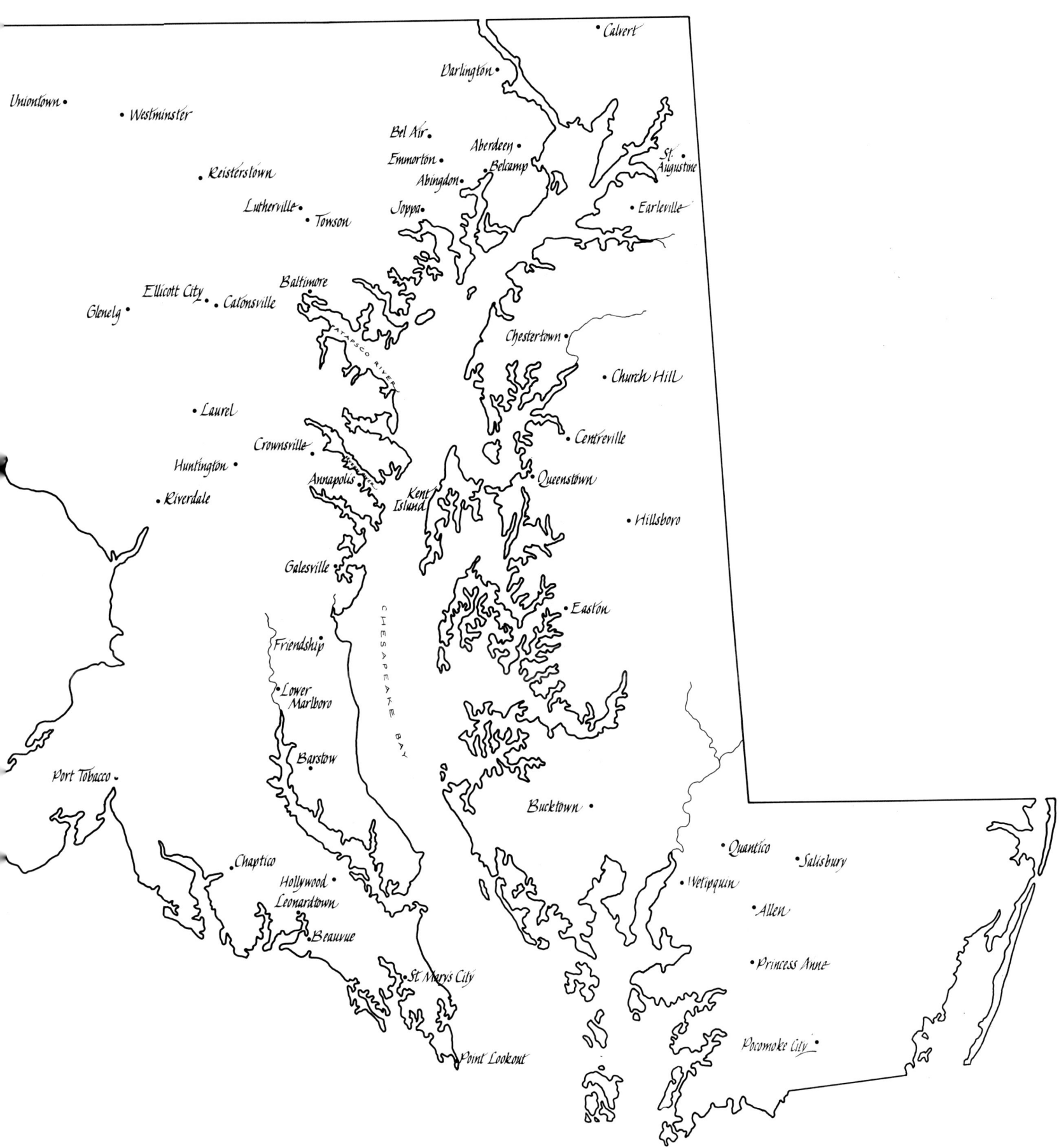

Foreword

This volume continues a series of books about the historic buildings of the Old South. Each volume illustrates and describes the important and beautiful buildings—restored, unrestored, demolished and sometimes designs that were never executed—in one or two states, arranged in a sensible chronological and stylistic order and set in a brief cultural and social background. This seventh volume of the series is devoted to Maryland, a state that did not join the Southern Confederacy despite the ownership of many slaves and much sympathy for the Southern cause. The northern border of Maryland is the famed Mason-Dixon Line, laid out in the 1760's by two English mathematicians, Charles Mason and Jeremiah Dixon, to resolve a long-standing territorial dispute with Pennsylvania. In fact, a cultural geographer might more accurately draw the North-South divide perhaps thirty miles below the Mason-Dixon, for the influence of Pennsylvania and the North was important along the border.

There have been many books about American architecture in general, but these surveys too often illustrate the same famous buildings, select didactic examples and impose a grand, though artificial, orderliness on the subject. Except for this series, there have been few recent serious studies about the historic buildings of individual states. Many people know the most famous buildings of Maryland—the colonial mansions of Annapolis and Latrobe's great Catholic Cathedral in Baltimore top the list—but even determined enthusiasts find it hard to explore the isolated enclaves of the Eastern Shore of the Chesapeake Bay. Undoubtedly, the greatest treat in this volume is the lost public architecture of Baltimore during the early 19th century, when the city was one of the largest, richest and most cosmopolitan cultural centers in the young republic. Baltimore's greatest architects, Benjamin Latrobe and Maximilian Godefroy, introduced a simple but revolutionary concept to America: the idea that public architecture should be different from domestic architecture. This concept was grandly represented by a succession of noble public buildings: the Cathedral, an Exchange, the Unitarian Church, a proposed library and the almost abstract Washington Monument, a gigantic Doric column supporting a statue of the first president, by Latrobe's pupil Robert Mills.

Another important theme that emerges in this volume, more than in any of the other volumes in the Architecture of the Old South series, is the struggle to establish the profession of architecture in young America. Implicitly, if not explicitly, we observe the role of rich planters and merchants and how buildings, however brilliant the designers, are never built without appreciative patrons. The great plantation houses of the Eastern Shore, the villas surrounding Baltimore and the cities' imposing public buildings were equally the result of money as well as imagination. We will survey in detail many of Latrobe's trials and tribulations in Baltimore. Of the taste of the city, Latrobe once complained: "I believe anything that can be said of the vandalism of the Baltimoreans in the arts, provided it is exceedingly absurd and ridiculous." Born and educated a gentleman, at least by American standards, Latrobe resented the condescension of the Maryland planters and merchants who looked down on him as a common workman. Latrobe quarreled with hard-headed, old-fashioned local builders, with professional friends like Godefroy—ending a long and fruitful friendship when egos clashed—and with his students.

Despite Latrobe's criticisms, Baltimore was an exciting city in the early 19th century that nurtured considerable architectural talent. We might say that his mentor, Thomas Jefferson, was the "grandfather" of the architecture profession in America and that Jefferson's architectural grandchildren were the Latrobe pupils who became the first professionally trained, native-born American architects. Robert Mills was the most famous of these, but probably more gifted was William F. Small, the son and grandson of Baltimore builders, whose career was cut short by an early death. Only three Southern cities produced important native-born architects: Charleston, the great 18th-century city, Baltimore, the great Federal-era city, and New Orleans, the great mid-19th-century city. Baltimore's greatest native-born talent was Robert Cary Long, Jr., a skilled designer of both Greek and Romantic buildings who was the son of a well-established local architect.

Buildings are three-dimensional history books that reflect the comings and goings, successes and failures of real people. An early start and the cultivation of tobacco made Maryland a well-established and rich colony, with 18th-century architecture second only to Virginia and South Carolina in the South. Along with wigmakers and staymakers, Maryland planters and merchants imported builders and stucco artists from England, who brought with them the latest fashions from London. However, after a burst of prosperity between the Revolution and the War of 1812, Maryland suffered economic problems in the 1820's and 1830's, the heyday of the Greek Revival, and thus produced relatively few important buildings in that style. However, the foundations for future prosperity were laid by railroads and manufacturing, whose iron furnaces also produced cast-iron decoration for Romantic architecture in the 1850's. Actually, it will be in our next volume, *Kentucky and Tennessee,* where we learn more about buildings as history books by recognizing important buildings that record the contributions made to the Kentucky and Tennessee scene by settlers from Maryland.

The Civil War marks the triumph of industrialization in America, homogenizing the nation's cultural life and beginning the end of regionalism. Despite the name of this series, *Architecture of the Old South*, we have found that buildings throughout America were probably more alike than they were different. The great architectural styles—Adamesque Federal, the Greek Revival, the Gothic Revival and, earlier, colonial Georgian—were all international movements. Professional architects from England, Philadelphia and New York designed the most important buildings, or provincial builders copied designs from pattern books published in London, Philadelphia or New York. The great names in Maryland architecture are the English-born Latrobe, the Frenchman Godefroy, and Alexander Jackson Davis of New York City. The bustling city of Baltimore was located south of the Mason-Dixon line, but, except for slavery and a climate that was a little warmer, how was its culture different from cities to the North? In unsettled 19th-century America, a land of on-the-move, on-the-make entrepreneurs and professionals who were often relocating to find new careers and opportunities, the same observation could be made of Savannah, Mobile or New Orleans. Except for an inevitable accommodation to the climate, it seems evident that much of what some experts have described as Southern architecture is an accident of geography and exists mostly in the preconceptions of the beholder.

Paradoxically, upon a close look at the architecture of one state, the forces of localism seem to be stronger than regionalism. The isolated Eastern Shore, rather like Ireland's relationship with England, developed its own slightly eccentric version of colonial Georgian architecture. Baltimore, prosperous port during the Federal era and a bustling industrial city in the 1850's, produced its particular interpretations of current styles—for example, the distinctive Baltimore fondness for the use of advancing and receding planes for building façades. The 19th-century Baltimore row house is easily distinguished from its counterparts in Charleston, Savannah or Mobile. Actually, thanks to proximity, Baltimore's row houses most closely resemble those of Philadelphia. The five-part plan (a center block flanked by wings connected to the center by hyphens) became a distinctive favorite of Marylanders during the Federal era. The popularity of the five-part plan reflects not only the influence of 18th-century England but also that of climate, for Maryland is hot in summer and cold in winter. It was convenient to have kitchens separated from dwellings but still connected by covered passageways, or hyphens.

We have seen in previous volumes how Virginia had been the largest, richest and most populous English colony in the South, with early architecture of unsurpassed richness and variety. South Carolina was also a well-established and prosperous colony with important buildings, especially in Charleston, the metropolis of the 18th-century South. But both Virginia and South Carolina began to suffer a relative decline in growth and quality of architecture by the late 1820's, when people began moving from the old, exhausted tobacco and cotton lands of the upper and coastal South to the fertile new lands of the Mississippi River Valley. North Carolina was also an early colony, but, with treacherous coasts, poor harbors and shallow rivers, it was slow to develop.

Settlers from Virginia and North Carolina had begun to move into present-day Kentucky and Tennessee in the 1790's. Lexington, in Kentucky, and Nashville, in Tennessee, became important early centers of commerce and culture. These "frontier" states probably retain more early buildings than Georgia, an older state. Georgia was the last and poorest colony, and less than a handful of pre-Revolutionary buildings has survived there. The rich cotton port of Savannah experimented with the Greek Revival more than a decade before its full flowering in the South, and Georgia enjoyed its greatest prosperity during the heyday of the Greek Revival. Mississippi and Alabama, the two states carved from the historic Mississippi Territory, were settled by a wave of newcomers from the upper and coastal South in the late 1830's and produced a surprising variety and quality of buildings in the relatively brief period before the Civil War. Louisiana began as a French colony, and there French culture, language and law prevailed long after the Louisiana Purchase of 1803. Louisiana's architectural history is the story of clashing cultures—French, brought from France and the Caribbean, and English, brought from the Atlantic seaboard cities, notably New York, and by ambitious newcomers from the upper, older Southern states—and of New Orleans, the metropolis of the 19th-century South.

Now that our exploration of the South has traveled all the way from Maryland to Louisiana, we begin to appreciate the relationship between the history and buildings of the old, well-established coastal states—Virginia, Maryland, the Carolinas—and the rougher frontier states—Georgia, Alabama, Mississippi and Louisiana. In our two remaining volumes, we will learn more about the frontier states of Kentucky and Tennessee and survey at last the history and architecture of the Old South in general.

I. *The Colony*

In late 1633, some 140 colonists sailed from England for Maryland, the new proprietary colony established by George Calvert and his son Cecil, royal favorites despite their Catholic faith. Cecil, the second Lord Baltimore, directed the colonists to "build their houses in as decent and uniform a manner as their abilities and the place will afford," and instructed every five colonists to carry five broad hoes, five narrow hoes, two broad axes, five felling axes, two steel handsaws, one whipsaw set, two hammers, three shovels, three spades, two augers, six chisels, two piercers, two gimlets, two hatchets, two frows (wedge-shaped tools for splitting boards), two pick axes, nails of all sorts, glass and lead for windows and, if they could afford to hire one, "a Carpenter, of all others the most necessary" servant.[1] In March, 1734, these colonists reached the Chesapeake Bay and landed at the site of an Indian village on the western shore they renamed St. Mary's. It would remain the colony's capital for sixty-one years. The colonists hastily erected a wooden guard house, store house and a "pallizado of one hundred and twentie yarde square" around the camp.[2] Another settlement on the Eastern Shore of the Bay had already been made three years earlier by William Claiborne, a Virginian who established a trading post on Kent Island.

In 1638 Thomas Cornwallis, who supervised construction of the palisade fort and a water-powered corn mill at St. Mary's, was building "A house toe put my head in, of sawn Timber framed, A story and half hygh, with A sellar and Chimnies of brick toe Encourage others toe follow my Example, for hitherto wee Live in Cottages."[3] By "cottages" Cornwallis probably meant dwellings like those of yeomen farmers in England, one-room huts with dirt floors, thatch roofs supported by crucks (pairs of large curved timbers) and a hole in the ceiling through which smoke rose from an open fire in the center of the floor. In 1638 John Lewger, an Anglican clergyman who had come to Maryland with his wife and nine-year-old son to serve as the administrative and financial officer of the colony, also built a one-and-one-half-story timber-framed house at St.

Mary's. It was fifty-two feet long and twenty feet deep, with two rooms separated by a central chimney and a stone foundation.[4] Because this house had the largest room in Maryland, it was used as a meeting place for the colonial assembly for many years. Lewger's house was built by two indentured servants, Andrew Baker and Philip West, and a free carpenter, Francis Gray. The house of Leonard Calvert, the thirty-six-year-old brother of the proprietor of the colony who came to Maryland in 1633 and served as governor for more than a decade, also had timber-framed walls, two rooms with a simple board partition and "a stack of brick chimneys near about the middle of the house."[5] By 1640 there were at least ten houses, a forge, a mill, a chapel and some sixty people at St. Mary's, plus some six hundred other colonists along the Chesapeake Bay and the rivers running into it.

The houses of Cornwallis, Lewger and Calvert were boxlike frames of timbers that had been shaped into long rectangles with a broad axe and smoothed with an adze. It might take thirty great timbers, each fifteen by twelve inches thick, to build a small four-room, two-story house. The heavy timbers of the frame rested on a low foundation of logs, stone or brick. The timbers were fitted together with mortise-and-tenon joints and then, partially assembled and raised into place, held together with wooden pegs, a technique that would be used till the second quarter of the 19th century, when lightweight, machine-milled lumber and cheap, factory-made nails became available. The skeletal frame and roof of one of these buildings was much like the hull of a ship turned upside down, each timber fitted together with a chisel, mallet and auger, creating a mechanical structure that was a work of art by virtue of the care with which each part had to be carved and joined together. The roofs were covered with thatch or shingles; the spaces between the upright studs of the walls might be filled with straw, clay, brick, stone or marsh grass. Clapboards were split from logs about four or six feet long, and chimneys were made of brick, when available, or a combination of wood and clay.

The Rev. Hugh Jones, a Welshman who came to Maryland at the age of twenty-four and died there after only a few years, reported that the colony was plentifully supplied with "severall sorts of oake, viz. the red, white, black, chestnutt, water, Spanish, and live oaks," plus red cedar for posts and groundsills, white cedar for boards and poplar for planks.[6] Bricks were made in the colony from an early period, but they were soft and porous, and bricklayers were hard to find. In November, 1643, Thomas Gerrard of St. Clements agreed to give the bricklayer Cornelius Canedy food, drink, clothing, lodging, 200 acres of land, a house twenty-five by sixteen feet, two cows, two sows, two goats, five barrels of corn, a

Patuxent Manor, Lower Marlboro, Calvert County, c. 1730. *Photograph by Frances Benjamin Johnston, Library of Congress*

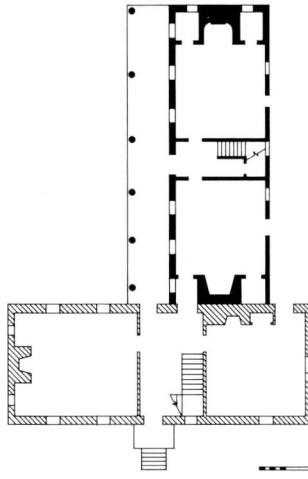

Holly Hill, Friendship vicinity, Anne Arundel County, 1698–c. 1730, an 18th-century overmantel painting of the house, a 20th-century photograph and the plan, showing additions.

feather bed, pillow, rug, two dishes, one pot and six spoons in return for three years of labor.[7] Ironware, tools, roof tiles, paving stones and lead casement windows were imported from England.

In 1653 the carpenter Thomas Wilford agreed to build a house for Paul Sympson, the house to be "fifteen foot square with a Welch chimney [clay and sticks], floored and lofted with Deale boards and lined with Riven Boards on the inside, with a handsome Joined Bedstead, one Small Joyned Table and Six Joined Stooles and three Wainscott Chaires."[8] Three years later, in 1656, John Hammond described houses in Maryland and Virginia as "for the most part . . . but one story besides the loft, and built of wood, the rooms large, daubed and whitelimed, glazed and floored, and if not glazed windows, shutters which are made very pretty and convenient." In 1657 there were 2,400 colonists in Maryland.

In 1665 the colonial assembly employed William Smith to build a State House at St. Mary's: "forty foot square, two storeys and a half high, the first story to be ten foot cleare, the second story to be Eight foot cleare, the half story four foot with a hip roofe . . . and underneath the said house a bricked sellar twenty-four foot square."[9] There were also to be brick chimneys, a roof of tile or shingles and glass windows. Two years later in 1667, Smith, unable to fulfill his contract, was dismissed.[10] In 1674 the assembly hired John Quigly to build the State House: "of brick or stone . . . Covered with Slate or tile laid in Morter . . . two Stories high and to Continue in length forty-five foote . . . with a porch in front . . . the said Porch to have an arch in front . . . the whole house to be well plaistered within . . . the windows of the Hall . . . Eight in number with double lights divided with a transome att two-thirds of the hight of the said windoes . . . two Iron Casements to every window . . . glazed with good cleer square glass."[11] This two-story, cruciform brick building with its iron casement windows was completed in 1676. Casement windows continued to be used into the first quarter of the 18th century, but colonists began adopting sash windows, a Dutch invention, about 1700.

But few Maryland colonists before 1725 could command the great skill, time and money to erect fine buildings of brick or timber frame. In 1678 it was reported that houses in Maryland were built "very mean and Little and Generally after the manner of the meanest farme houses in England."[12] In 1680 two Dutch travelers from New York, Jaspar Danckaerts and Peter Sluyter, complained: "The dwellings are so wretchedly constructed that if you are not so close to the fire as almost to burn yourself, you cannot keep warm, for the wind blows through them everywhere."[13] While the most common house in mid-17th-century records is a two-room timber-frame building, twenty to forty feet long and fifteen

Holly Hill, grained paneling in chamber, c. 1730.

Holly Hill, stair. *Library of Congress*

Bounds Lott, Allen vicinity, Wicomico County, c. 1740.

to twenty feet deep, with clapboard walls, a roof of thatch or boards, shutters in place of glazed windows and chimneys of wood and clay, surviving records do not always reflect the everyday reality of colonial Maryland.

Archaeological explorations have revealed the widespread use of a building technique that was cheaper and faster, though less permanent, than timber-frame construction.[14] We now know that most early Marylanders, including prosperous farmers, lived in one-story huts supported by puncheons, or upright logs, buried several feet apart in the ground, like those described by a Virginia colonist: "Their houses stand one from another, and are onlie made of wood; few or none of them being framed houses but punches [puncheons] sett into the Ground and covered with Boards."[15] Buildings of this primitive type are described as far away as Georgia and Louisiana. With posts taking the place of masonry foundations and complex timber-framing, these puncheon buildings saved labor, which was so scarce during an era of initial settlement. They were definitely considered temporary, and few have survived. Archaeological investigations have identified seven surviving 17th-century buildings in the Chesapeake region. Fragments of two small wooden houses in Anne Arundel County have survived within later brick walls. Holly Hill, now a T-shaped brick building near the hamlet of Friendship, began as a one-room house in 1698. Cedar Park, with brick additions of the mid-19th century, at Galesville, began as a two-room house built for Richard Galloway II about 1702. Both were timber-frame structures resting on buried cedar posts.

By the end of the 17th century, there were 30,000 colonists in Maryland, settled along both sides of the Chesapeake Bay.[16] Paradoxically, the English Civil War brought the colony into closer touch with England, for a new wave of well-to-do colonists came to Maryland in search of refuge, and in 1689 the Crown seized political control of the colony from the Catholic Calvert family. One of the first acts of the new royal governor was to make the Anglican Church the established faith of Maryland, an arm of government and a vehicle for the transmission of British culture.

The prosperous tobacco and wheat farmers of Maryland now had the means to erect more substantial buildings, though not especially large in scale or academically correct in their attempt at Classical details. Patuxent Manor, at Lower Marlboro, Calvert County, is not clearly documented, but it is representative of the more substantial Maryland houses of the second quarter of the 18th century: a one-and-one-half-story, gable-roof house with a slightly projecting watertable, Flemish-bond walls, segmental window arches and a denticulated cornice. An unusual

Parlor, Bounds Lott.

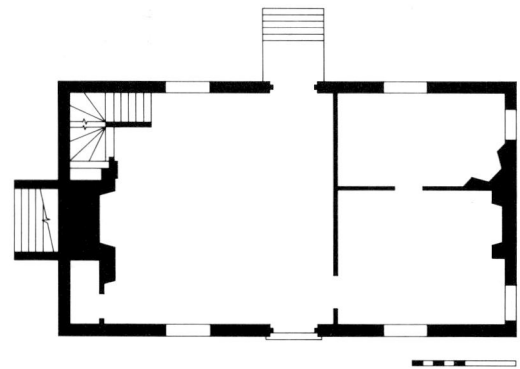

Pemberton Hall, Isaac Handy House, Salisbury vicinity, Wicomico County, c. 1741. *Enoch Pratt Free Library, Baltimore*

Readbourne, James Hollyday House, Centreville vicinity, 1733, an 18th-century sketch. *Private Collection of Thomas Hollyday, copyright and all rights reserved*

decorative detail is the recessed apron under each front window. By 1730, the house at Holly Hill, near Friendship, Anne Arundel County, had become a one-and-one-half-story brick house that looked much like Patuxent Manor. (As we have already noted, Holly Hill had begun as a small two-room wooden house in 1698, which was substantially rebuilt within new brick walls in 1704 and further enlarged with a new wing to create a T-shaped plan about 1730.) Of special interest at Holly Hill are early marbleized paneling and several over-mantel paintings from the second quarter of the 18th century, including the earliest-known painting of an American house.

Wicomico County, on the once bustling but now tranquil Eastern Shore, has several small houses distinguished by careful workmanship and flashes of naive ingenuity. Bounds Lott, four miles west of Allen, was probably built for Jonathan Bounds about 1740, though some experts believe it may be a remodeling of an earlier building. The interior features a large fireplace flanked by fluted pilasters and round-headed cupboards and surmounted by three diamond-shaped panels and a dentil cornice. Pemberton Hall, three miles southwest of Salisbury, is a one-and-one-half-story brick house built for Isaac Handy, a planter and lumber merchant, in 1741. Of special interest are the gambrel roof, with its characteristic double slope, the coved plaster cornice and walls laid in Flemish bond, featuring an elegant pattern of glazed headers alternating with stretchers in each brick course. The interior is divided by simple board partitions, but a large fireplace is flanked by pilasters and surmounted by paneling. Despite its great size, such a richly embellished fireplace would not have been used for cooking, which took place in a kitchen wing. Pemberton Hall is open to the public.

A house of the next generation in the county, Long Hill, near Wetipquin, was built for John Stewart about 1750 or perhaps at the time of his marriage in 1767. The interiors of this relatively modest house were enriched with a fully paneled fireplace wall (now removed) and fully paneled walls in the passage. The gable walls of this frame house are brick, with bands of glazed headers paralleling the eaves. These brick ends afforded some protection from fire that might spread from chimneys and open hearths, yet did not necessitate the trouble and expense of building a house entirely of brick.

Two-story brick houses first appear in number in the 1730's, often distinguished by pleasing proportions, elegant Flemish-bond brickwork, interior paneling and carved staircases. Paneling was practical as well as ornamental, for it helped control dampness within brick walls. Wide, flaring eaves kicked water away from walls and windows, and string-

Parlor, Pemberton Hall.

20

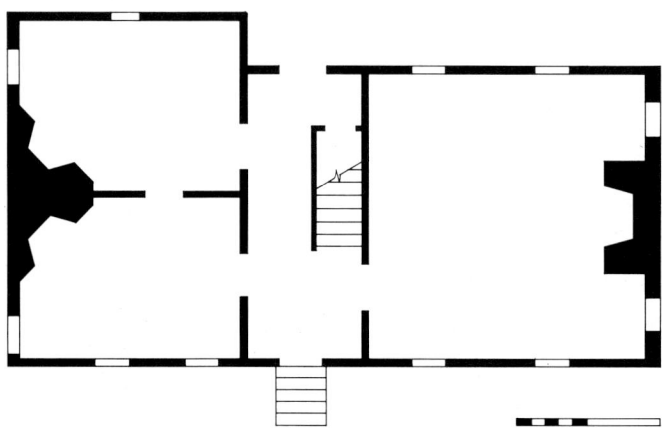

Long Hill, Wetipquin vicinity, Wicomico County, c. 1750.

Long Hill, stair.

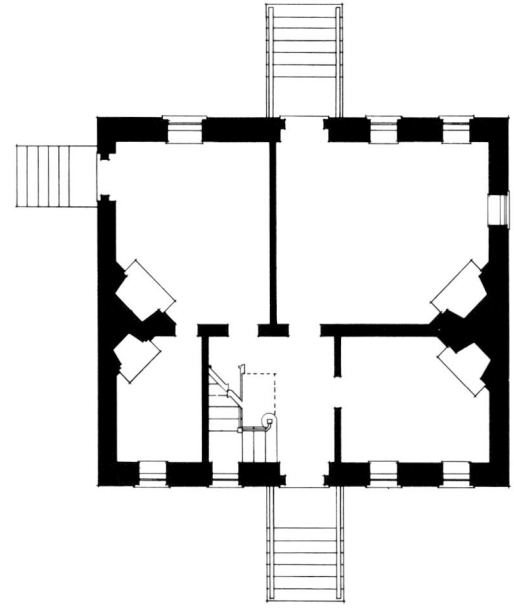

Yarmouth, John Eccleston House, Bucktown vicinity, c. 1735. *Elevation and plan by Michael Trostel and Peter Pearre*

courses strengthened walls where floor joists were inserted. The pure geometry of the walls was punctuated by modillion or dentil cornices, quoins of brick or stone at corners and window arches of rubbed or gauged brick, which gave them contrasting color and shaped them to form voussoirs.

Readbourne was built for the planter-merchant James Hollyday outside Centreville. In March, 1733, Hollyday recorded in his journal: "I agreed with Luke Breze to build my Dwelling house of brick at the rate of 8 per thousand for Laying and I am to give him 40 [more if] he make[s] the arches in front windows and door."[17] We can still see the original appearance of the house in a tiny sketch made about 1760: a two-story brick building with a hipped roof and cupola, modillion eaves cornice and a round-headed entrance. At the time of the 1798 tax, the mansion was flanked by two detached brick buildings, a kitchen and a storehouse. The mansion has been extensively remodeled and some paneling was removed in the late 1920's to the Henry Francis du Pont Winterthur Museum.

Yarmouth, two miles south of Bucktown, Dorchester County, was probably built for John Eccleston in the 1730's. A squarish two-story brick mansion with a tall gable, Yarmouth was another imposing house for its period, with Flemish-bond walls, a watertable, jack arches over the windows, a stringcourse between the first and second-story windows and a deep coved cornice of plaster. The elaborately finished interior, which appears to be intact except for some restorations at the bottom of the stair, features a carved staircase, molded chairrails, paneled window jambs and window seats and corner fireplaces with pilasters and paneling.

Meanwhile, different building traditions were being brought to north and west-central Maryland by German settlers from Pennsylvania. Before the Revolution, perhaps one-third of Pennsylvania's population was of German birth or descent, and about one-third of those later decided to move to the rich open lands of the South: Maryland, North Carolina and beyond. In the early 1660's, Augustin Hermann, a merchant-diplomat from Bohemia, came to Maryland by way of New York, prepared the first accurate and extensive map of the colony and received vast grants of land, some 25,000 acres, around the upper end of the Chesapeake Bay. Except for a small group of religious dissenters who settled on Hermann's land, few Germans came to eastern Maryland before the Revolution. But by 1730 a great migration of German settlers from the Rhineland, Moravia and Bohemia, having resided for a time in east-central Pennsylvania, began flooding into central Maryland toward the Susquehanna River and the Valley of Virginia.

Yarmouth, John Eccleston House, stair.

24

Yarmouth, John Eccleston House, parlor chimneypiece.

John Hager House, Hagerstown, 1739–40.

Schiefferstadt, Joseph Brunner House, Frederick, 1743.

John Churchman House, Calvert vicinity, 1745.

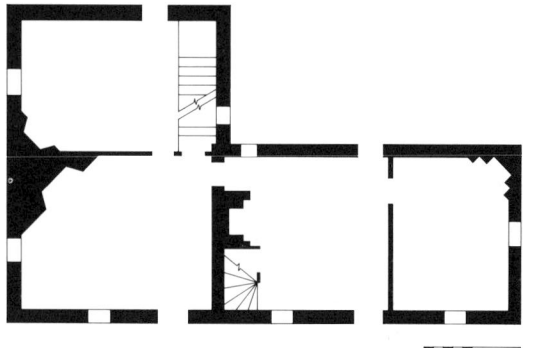

Plan of John Churchman House.

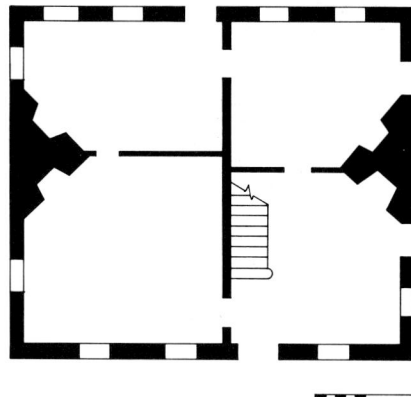

Great House, James Bayard House, St. Augustine, c. 1750–55.

These German settlers brought with them a tradition of stone construction and a fondness for highly functional plans built around central chimneys. John Hager, a colonist from Westphalia, reached the vicinity of present-day Hagerstown in the late 1730's and built a one-and-one-half-story stone house over a spring in 1739–40. Hager lived there for five years and then sold it to Jacob Rohrer, for whose descendants the house was enlarged to two stories. Hager House is open to the public. Another German settler from Pennsylvania, Joseph Brunner, came from Mannheim to present-day Frederick in 1743. There he built a substantial stone house, now known as Schiefferstadt, which is open to the public. After a slow start, western Maryland developed rapidly in the second and third quarters of the 18th century, and Frederick, with 1000 people, became, by the Revolution, one of the largest towns in the province.

In the meantime the northeastern corner of Maryland was long claimed both by Pennsylvania and Maryland until the Mason-Dixon Line was laid out in the 1760's, by which time many English colonists from Pennsylvania had already settled in present-day Maryland. John Churchman's house near Calvert, Cecil County, only a few miles south of the state line, bears the date of its construction, 1745, in glazed headers laid in a gable end. Churchman House features Flemish-bond walls, with their characteristic sparkling pattern of glazed headers, and the first-story pent eave that was common in Pennsylvania. A stone wing was added at the northern end for the builder's son, George Churchman, about 1785. Great House, at St. Augustine, Cecil County, was probably built shortly before the death of its first owner, James Bayard, in 1755. Great House has massive T-shaped chimneys and a pent eave. Also noteworthy is the mid-18th-century Rumsay House near the old town of Joppa, an important crossroads between Maryland and Pennsylvania. This building is incompletely documented and has suffered some jarring alterations, but its tall gambrel roof, massive cove cornice of plaster and first-story pent eave on two façades are further evidence of Pennsylvania influence in northeastern Maryland.

In 1694, a new royal governor, Francis Nicholson, reached Maryland. One of his first acts was to move the capital from St. Mary's to Annapolis, a settlement fifty miles to the north on the Severn River. The relocation of the capital signaled a shift in population and power from the areas of early Catholic settlement in southeastern Maryland to the more recently settled areas of Anglican influence along the northern end of Chesapeake Bay. A state house was built at Annapolis during 1696–98; after it burned in 1704, a second building rose immediately; this was de-

Great House, James Bayard House, view of stair and hall.

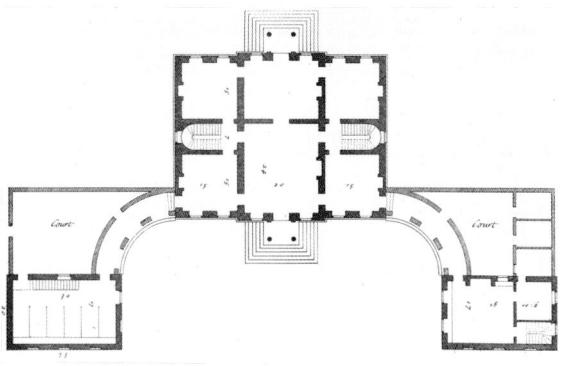

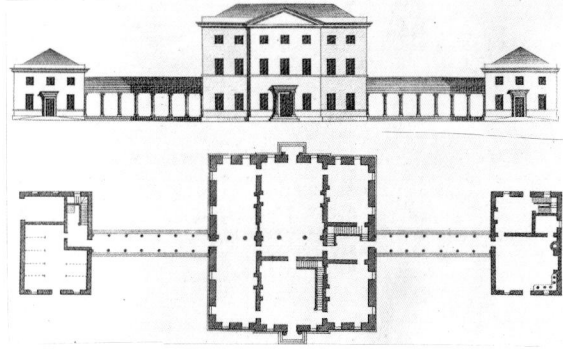

Palladian house designs from James Gibbs's *Book of Architecture* (London, 1728) and Robert Morris's *Select Architecture* (London, 1757). Houghton Library, Harvard University; Avery Architecture and Fine Arts Library, Columbia University

molished in 1772 to make way for the larger and grander edifice that stands today. Another of Governor Nicholson's initial acts was to establish the Anglican Church as the official faith of the colony, making it an extension of the provincial government, with authority to levy taxes, assist the poor and build churches at public expense. St. Anne's Church was begun at Annapolis in 1696; this was replaced by a second church, begun in the 1770's, completed in the 1790's and destroyed by fire in 1848. Symbolizing the triumvirate of church, state and trade, the plan of Annapolis was laid out with two circles surrounding the state house and church, built atop two hills, and streets radiating from these circles down to the harbor.

Governor Thomas Bladen began construction of a grand mansion at Annapolis in the early 1740's.[18] Though extraordinary in scale and richness for Maryland, this mansion would have been a fairly ordinary building in England, a handsome but academic Palladian country house, with two stories, hip-on-hip-roof and projecting pedimented pavilions on both principal façades. Andrea Palladio, the late 16th-century Italian architect, had introduced the use of ancient temples as models for domestic buildings. Palladio employed columns, pediments or projecting pavilions to suggest giant temple porticoes, as well as raised first stories and balanced wings or flankers, often connected to the main block by passageways or hyphens. Palladian architecture was known in England through Palladio's own *Four Books of Architecture,* first issued in an English translation by Giacomo Leoni in 1716–20, and the works of Palladio's principal English popularizers, James Gibbs, whose *Book of Architecture* was published in 1728, and Robert Morris, whose *Select Architecture* appeared in 1757.

After a few years of construction, the colonial assembly refused to appropriate additional money to complete Governor Bladen's mansion. In 1747 a legislative committee reported that the mansion was already badly deteriorated, with a crack in one corner of the wall running "from the Bottom almost to the Top" and an open roof, through which rain fell and rotted the beams.[19] In 1760 the Rev. Andrew Burnaby lamented that the Governor's Mansion was "unfinished . . . now going to ruin."[20] In the 1780's the decaying building was given to the newly chartered St. John's College, which resumed construction and added a third story. The present building was rebuilt within its standing walls after a fire in 1909. Another large monumental building of the 1740's was St. Thomas Manor, built at Port Tobacco, Charles County, for a religious order in 1741. Though smaller than Bladen's Folly, the Manor was another palace-like design with a projecting pedimented center pavilion and even finer brickwork, brick

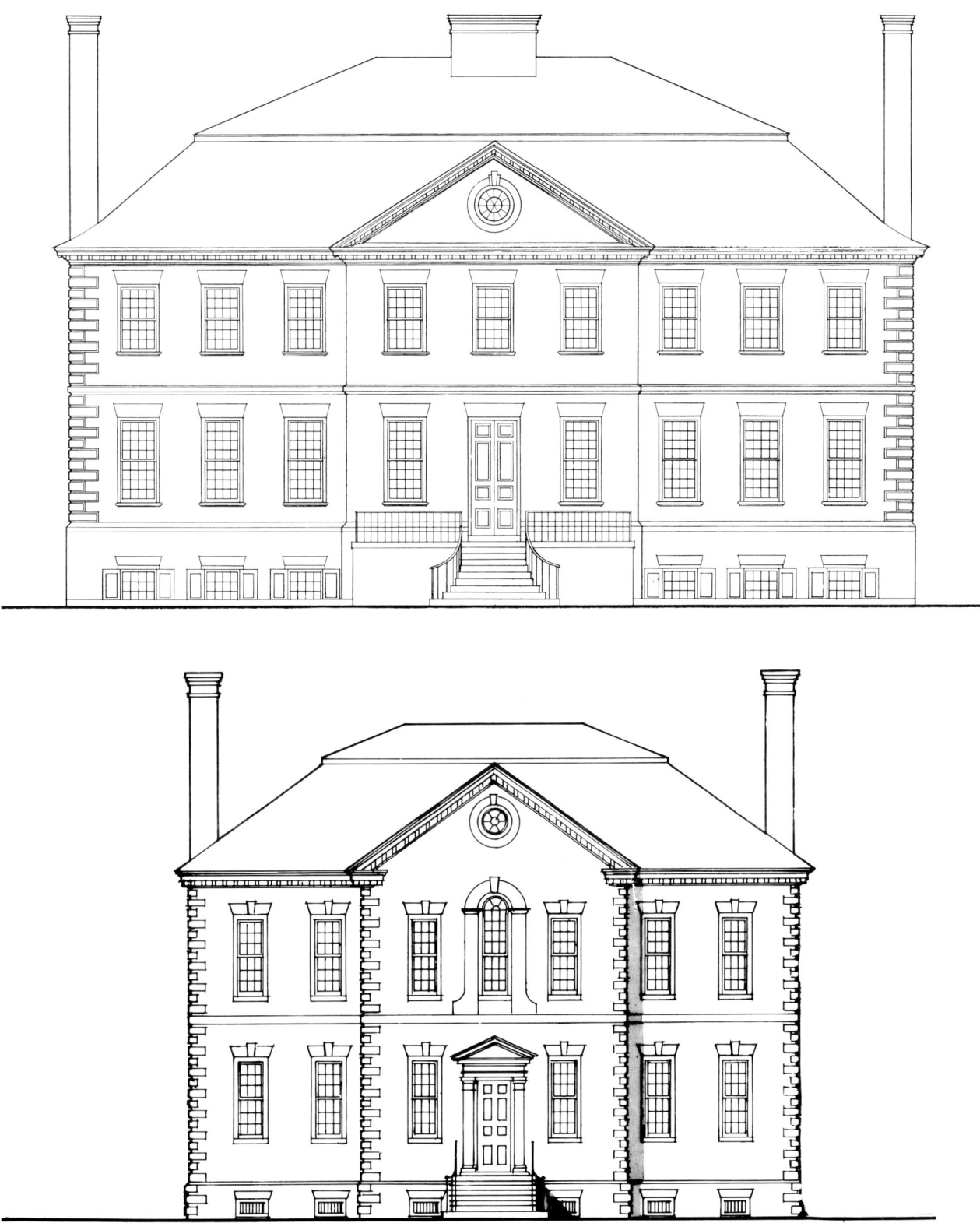

Top: Thomas Bladen House, Annapolis, begun c. 1740. Bottom: St. Thomas Manor, Port Tobacco, 1741. *Elevations by Michael Trostel and Peter Pearre*

quoins at the angles and gauged voussoirs with keystones. Rival Jesuit priests called St. Thomas Manor "a palace unbecoming a religious order."

By the third quarter of the 18th century, especially after the end of the French and Indian War in 1763, Maryland had grown more secure, richer and more populous. Tobacco exports increased from thirty million pounds a year in the 1720's to one hundred million pounds annually in the 1770's. The taste for fine architecture also flourished. Tulip Hill, overlooking the West River near the hamlet of Galesville, Anne Arundel County, was built in 1755–62 by the brickmaker and bricklayer John Deavour for the planter-merchant Samuel Galloway. The cupboard in the entrance hall suggests that this room may have been used for summer dining. Three years after his father's death and two years after his marriage to Sarah Chew of Philadelphia, John Galloway, Samuel's son, added the flanking wings and hyphens connecting them to the center block, creating a five-part plan, which became a favorite of Maryland builders in the late 18th century. In April, 1789, John Galloway wrote: "From all accounts our house is not inhabitable but we must make Mr. White patch up a room for us. Sally has such charming accounts of the improvements that she is very impatient to see them."[21] The portico of Tulip Hill probably dates from the early 19th century.

Mulberry Fields was built for John Attaway Clarke about 1755 near Beauvue, St. Mary's County, on a dramatic site, a high hillside overlooking the Potomac River.[22] The walls of the principal façades are laid in all-header bond, and the house is flanked by symmetrically arranged brick kitchen and weaving house. A two-story Tuscan portico on the river front and dormers were added about 1835. The passage and principal rooms of the first story are fully paneled with a molded chair rail; the chimney pieces are 19th-century replacements. Ratcliff Manor, outside Easton, Talbot County, was built in 1756–62 for the well-to-do planter-merchant Henry Hollyday, son of the builder of Readbourne. Two other notable country mansions of the third quarter of the 18th century are Beverly, built for Littleton Dennis about 1773–74 southwest of Pocomoke City, Worcester County, and Pleasant Valley, built for Howes Goldsborough about 1773 outside Easton, Talbot County. Beverly features a curiously small fanlight entrance and a second-story Palladian window. Pleasant Valley is adorned with extensive paneling and a magnificent stair.

Builders lavished their greatest ingenuity on stairs, so hard to build they were often executed by itinerant craftsmen who specialized in their construction. One of the finest surviving stairs from 18th-century Maryland is found in Sophia's Dairy, at Belcamp, near Aberdeen, Harford County. The house, built for Acquilla Hall and his bride Sophia in 1768,

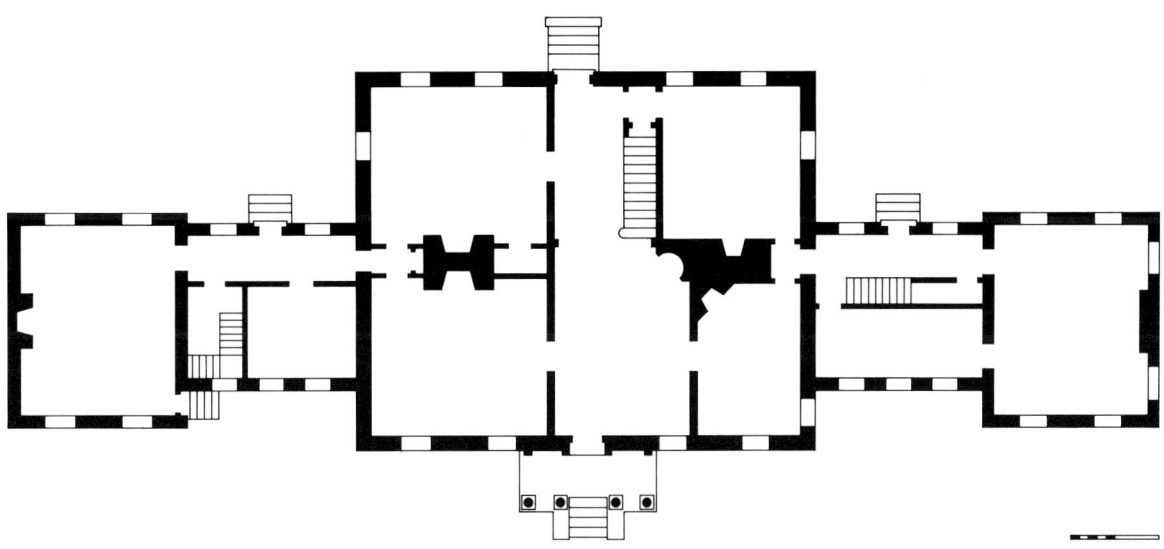

Bachelor's Hope, William Hammersley House, Chaptico vicinity, 1749–50.
Photograph by Frances Benjamin Johnston, Library of Congress

Tulip Hill, Samuel Galloway House, entrance passage.

Tulip Hill, Samuel Galloway House, stair detail.

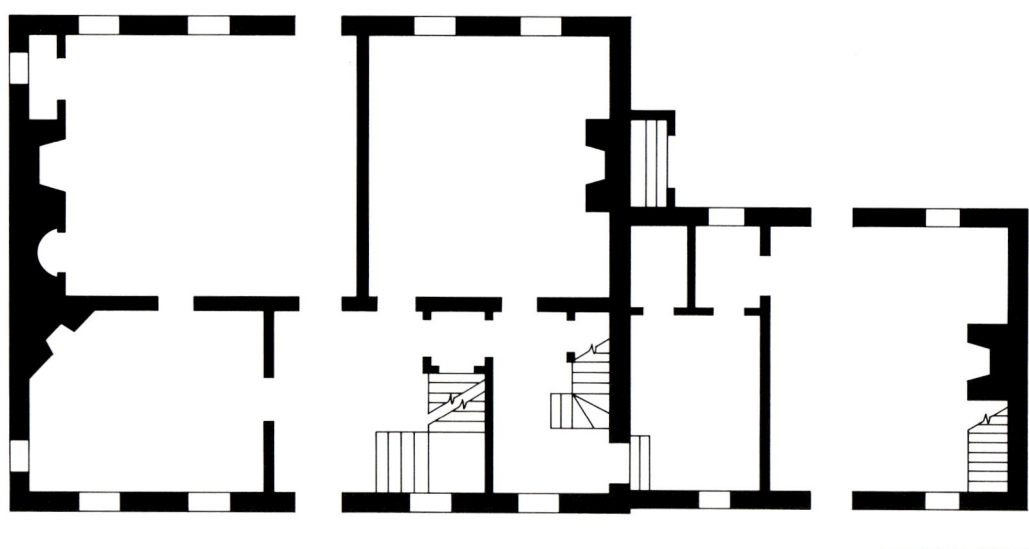

Ratcliff Manor, Henry Hollyday House, Easton vicinity, 1756–62.

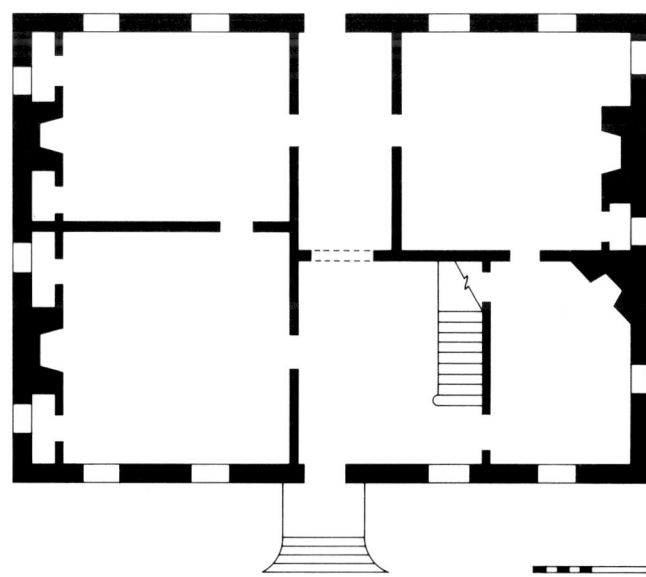

Beverly, Littleton Dennis House, Pocomoke City vicinity, 1773–74.

Pleasant Valley, Howes Goldsborough House, Easton vicinity, 1773–74, stair. *Photograph by Frances Benjamin Johnston, The Baltimore Museum of Art, Museum Purchase, BMA 1938.75*

Pleasant Valley, Howes Goldsborough House, interior paneling. *Photographs by Frances Benjamin Johnston, The Baltimore Museum of Art, Museum Purchase, BMA 1938.73/74*

Oxen Hill, Prince George's County, c. 1760, the magnificent stair of a demolished, undocumented house seen in a c. 1900 photograph. *Maryland Historical Society*

Sophia's Dairy, Acquilla Hall House, Belcamp, 1768, stair. *Photograph by Frances Benjamin Johnston, The Baltimore Museum of Art, Museum Purchase, BMA 1938.37*

is a rather awkwardly proportioned two-story brick structure with a gable roof; despite its unprepossessing exterior, the interior stair is a virtuoso effort by some highly skilled craftsmen, with two flights rising from the front and rear of the passage to meet at a landing, then ascending to another landing before turning to the second story. All of this complicated geometry is enriched with carved stepends, molded chair rail, turned balusters and paneled soffit.

Along with staymakers and perukemakers and other craftsmen from England, Marylanders also imported builders. At their best, these often obscure artisans benefitted from apprenticeship in England, study of English architecture books and flashes of native ingenuity. In May, 1751, John Ariss, a builder active in Virginia and Maryland, "lately from England," offered to design "Buildings of all Sorts and Dimensions . . . in the neatest Manner (and at the cheapest Rates) either of the Ancient or Modern Order of Gibb's Architect [James Gibbs, *Book of Architecture*]," with "a great Variety and sundry Draughts of Buildings in Miniature" ready for inspection.[23] Henry Crouch, a carver from London, reached Annapolis in January, 1760.[24] George White, a painter and glazier from London, was ready for work in November, 1764.[25] John Rawlings and James Barnes, plasterers and stucco workers from England, came to Annapolis in February, 1771, offering to do work "as neat as in London."[26]

The English-trained joiner Richard Boulton flourished in St. Mary's County during the 1760's, and there his finest surviving work can be seen at a curious house called Sotterley, near Hollywood. This informal, sprawling building was begun in the second quarter of the 18th century for John Bowles. In 1727 the house consisted of the present-day drawing room, passage, library, small parlor and kitchen, plus three chambers in the second story. In 1729 Bowles's widow, Rebecca, married George Plater II, whose son, George Plater III, inherited the property in 1753. It was George Plater III who hired Richard Boulton to add pedimented doorways, a long piazza and interior embellishments—a Chinese latticework stair in the passage and shell-backed cupboards and opulent overmantel in the drawing room. Sotterley is open to the public.[27]

To Boulton is also attributed a Chinese lattice-work stair and very similar drawing room cupboards and overmantel at Bushwood, a house which stood fifteen miles north of Leonardtown till it burned in 1934. Boulton also designed and built St. Andrew's Church, five miles east of Leonardtown, in 1766.[28] The visitor enters through a one-story loggia surmounted by a projecting pedimented pavilion with a Palladian window and flanked by two towers enriched with quoins and apsidal niches. The interior features a stone-paved floor, high box pews, Ionic columns

Sotterley, Hollywood vicinity, 1727, Chinese latticework stair added about 1760.

Bushwood, Leonardtown vicinity, c. 1760, Chinese latticework stair. *Private Collection*

Sotterley, parlor embellishments added about 1760.

This page and opposite: Exterior and interior views of St. Andrew's Church, Leonardtown, 1766.

45

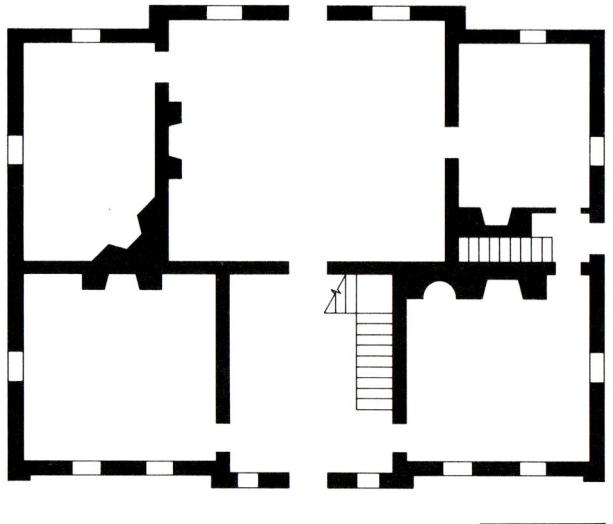

This page and opposite: Exterior and interior views of Bohemia, George Milligan House, Earleville vicinity, c. 1765.

supporting a barrel-vaulted ceiling and a massive reredos with a broken pediment. An upper gallery, at one time for slaves, is entered through a separate doorway and stair from the loggia. When the pews were sold in May, 1769, the first was purchased by Boulton's employer, George Plater III, a vestryman of the Church.

Another striking Chinese latticework stair from the 1760's survives at Bohemia, built for the Scots planter-merchant George Milligan, south of Earleville, Cecil County, scarcely twenty miles from the present-day Pennsylvania border on the upper Eastern Shore. This fine mansion, with its well-proportioned façade, laid in all-header bond, with pedimented projecting pavilion, molded brick watertable, a stringcourse, stone lintels with keystones, molded stone window sills and rich rococo plasterwork, as well as the sumptuous latticework stair, suggest the skills of sophisticated English-trained craftsmen from Philadelphia.

One of the idealized visions of English Palladianism was a two-story house with a templelike pediment and flanking one-story wings. Robert Morris's *Select Architecture* was one of many works that illustrated such houses, and William Halfpenny, another popularizer of Palladian architecture, whose books were intended for less ambitious builders, illustrated many small farm buildings with a two-story center and one-story wings in his *Useful Architecture* of 1752. An example of this form in Maryland, as charming as it is small, is Bachelor's Hope, probably built in 1749–50 for William Hammersley outside Chaptico, St. Mary's County. This elegant composition features a one-story loggia, sparkling Flemish-bond brickwork and an incongruously informal jerkinhead roof (a gable with the ends clipped).

In 1764–65 Governor Horatio Sharpe commissioned Whitehall, a much grander house of this same type, on the north bank of the Severn River outside Annapolis.[29] Sharpe had come to Maryland in 1753 at the age of thirty-five, after military service in the West Indies. In July, 1765, an anonymous French traveler reported that the Governor was then building "a pretty box of a house,"[30] a pleasure pavilion for boat trips from the capital, with an innovative monumental Corinthian portico, perhaps the earliest on any Southern house, and a two-story saloon. In December, 1768, when he was retiring as governor, Sharpe wrote to London: "I shall immediately remove my things to my Farm . . . on which I have a small elegant lodge."[31] During his retirement from public service, Sharpe extended the wings of his mansion, creating a magnificent façade two hundred feet long. Despite his devotion to the province, he was obliged to leave Maryland in 1773, and Whitehall later became the property of his secretary and friend, John Ridout, who, in the 1790's, demol-

Three-part Palladian houses illustrated in William Halfpenny's *Useful Architecture* (London, 1752) and Robert Morris's *Select Architecture* (London, 1757). *Avery Architecture and Fine Arts Library, Columbia University*

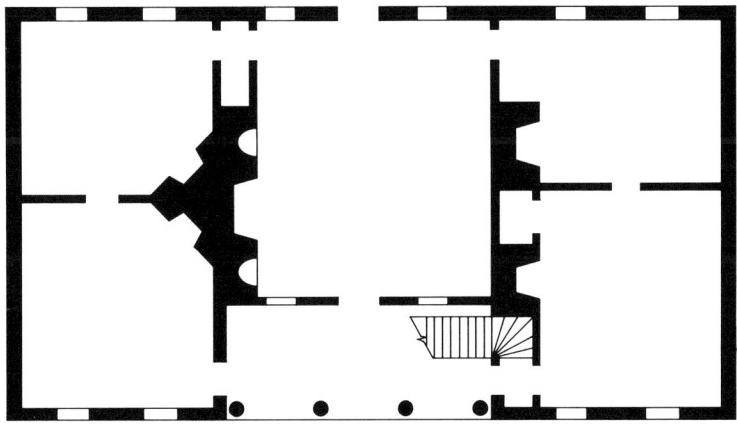

Bachelor's Hope, William Hammersley House, Chaptico vicinity, 1749–50.
Photograph by Frances Benjamin Johnston, Library of Congress

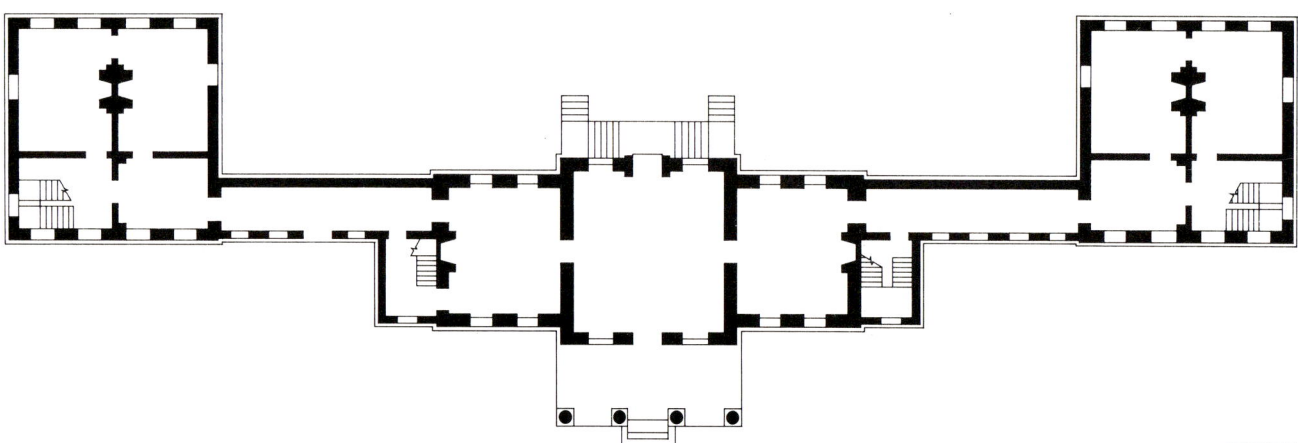

Whitehall, Horatio Sharpe House, Annapolis vicinity, 1765, wings added about 1770. The top photograph shows the mansion before its restoration, with the second story added in the 1790's by John Ridout. *Pre-restoration photograph from Enoch Pratt Free Library, Baltimore*

Whitehall, Horatio Sharpe House, view of the saloon.

52

Whitehall, Horatio Sharpe House, doorway in saloon.

ished the extreme ends of the wings and used the salvaged brick to add a second story over the rooms that flanked the saloon. This second story was removed during a 1957 restoration.

Upton Scott, an Irish-born army surgeon who came to Maryland with the entourage of Governor Sharpe in 1753, commissioned a mansion on Shipwright Street in Annapolis in 1762–65.[32] Its scale and finish were so grand that Scott was obliged to report to his father in December, 1765: "I am at present exceedingly hampered on account of the expense of building a house which is not yet finished, my workmen having pursued measures that have run away with more cash than I proposed." These "measures" included laying the front wall in all-header bond, with a Doric frontispiece set into a projecting center pavilion, and interior walls plastered to simulate wooden paneling.

In the same years, 1763–65, William Paca, the Philadelphia-educated, Annapolis-trained lawyer, commissioned a five-part brick mansion at 186 George Street. The large but plain exterior suggests the work of an unsophisticated brickmason, but other artisans embellished the interior with a Chinese latticework stair and overmantel carvings adapted from English architecture books.[33] Restored in 1970–76, Paca House is open to the public.

In 1767, only a few months after the death of his father, a wealthy Annapolis lawyer and landowner, twenty-year-old James Brice began construction of another five-part brick mansion nearby at 42 East Street. Brice personally supervised its construction and decoration for the next six years. In April, 1767, he purchased rum for his workers to celebrate the laying of the cornerstone of his new house. Though Brice paid a small amount to an unidentified person for "drawing the Plann," it is believed that Brice—whose interest in architecture was evidenced by purchasing a copy of Isaac Ware's edition of Palladio from his London factor in December, 1767—was probably his own architect. The awkward proportions of the façade, with tiny windows, large areas of blank wall surface and an out-of-scale Palladian window, suggest an amateur's eye. Brice, however, employed highly skilled craftsmen to complete the interior, including the carpenter Michael Mantle and his brother Frederick, the plasterer Thomas Harvey, the painter William Tuck, the joiner George Foster, who built the main stair, and William Brampton, an indentured carver who was hired to finish the carpenter's and joiner's work in "the largest room" but ran off after eight months' work.[34] Brampton selected as his model for the chimneypiece in the drawing room Plate LI of Abraham Swan's *The British Architect*. As at Upton Scott House, the plaster walls of Brice's house are molded to simulate wooden paneling.

William Paca House, 186 George Street, Annapolis, 1763–65.

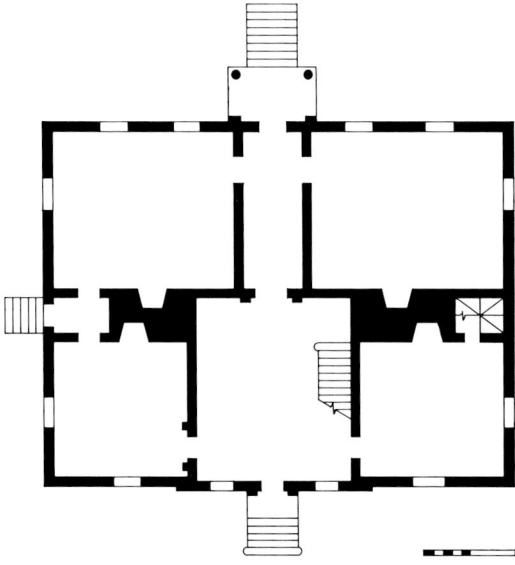

Upton Scott House, Shipwright Street, Annapolis, 1762–65. *Photograph from the Library of Congress*

Upton Scott House, view of hall and passage.

William Paca House, parlor.

William Paca House, view of stair at second-story.

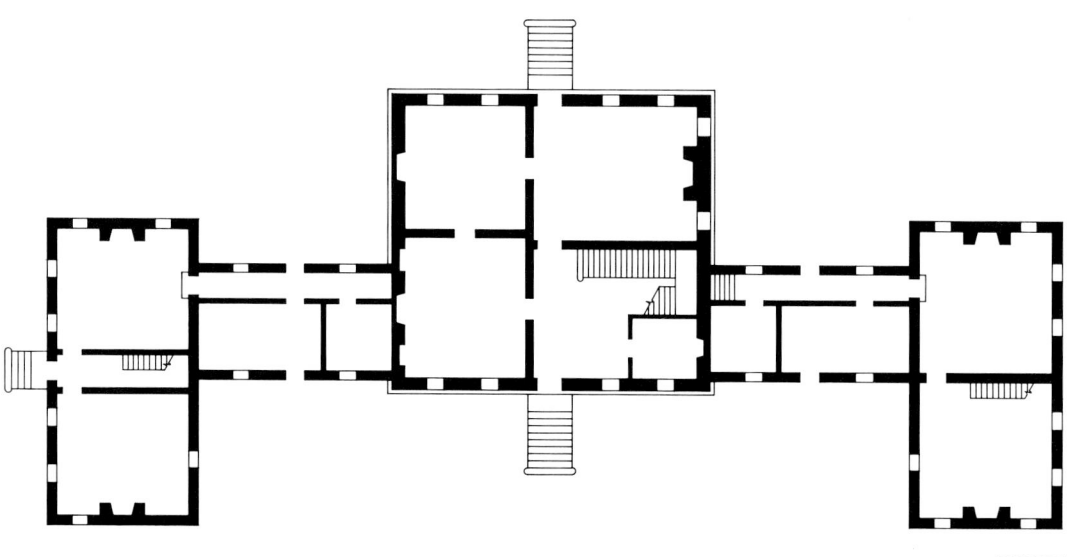

James Brice House, 42 East Street, Annapolis, 1767–1773. *Photograph from Maryland State Archives, Warren Collection of Annapolis Photographs*

Chimneypiece at James Brice House with its model, Plate LI of Abraham Swan's *The British Architect* (London, 1745). *Swan photograph from The New York Public Library*

Charles Carroll, "the Barrister," born at Annapolis in 1723, was a cousin of the more famous branch of the family that produced Charles Carroll of Carrollton, but the connection was so distant they could not figure out the relationship even in the 18th century. Sent to school in England at the age of ten, Charles (the Barrister) did not return to the colony until 1746 and was again sent to England to study law in 1751–55. In 1756, less than a year after his father's death, he began construction of a summer house at his plantation, Mount Clare, overlooking the Patapsco River near Baltimore, where he also owned ironworks, shipyards and mills.[35] Fitted out with glass, hinges, locks, nails and lead for the roof imported from England, this house and nearby kitchen were completed by early 1760. Carroll must have brought craftsmen from Annapolis, for many features of Mount Clare are found in Annapolis mansions of the period—walls laid in all-header bond, monumental pilasters and interior plaster molded to imitate wooden paneling.

After his marriage in 1763, Carroll began improving his house, ordering quantities of silk damask for curtains, leather-bottomed chairs and more silver and china for entertaining. In 1767–68 he enlarged the kitchen, built a new western wing, connecting this wing and the old kitchen to the house with hyphens; he also added a portico with a small chamber projecting above it lighted by a Venetian window. Though surviving records do not mention the name of a builder or designer, Carroll, ordering stone columns for the portico in July, 1767, enclosed a "Plan . . . for a Portico or Colonade" that delineated columns "of the Plain Doric order and the Proportions Exact" and an elevation "so plain that an Artist Can not mistake on Casting his Eye on the Plan."[36] Ingenious curvilinear gables provided headroom for a service stair leading from the one-story hyphens to the second story of the center block. After the Barrister's death in 1783, the widow Carroll "modernized" Mount Clare by adding a Diocletian or thermal window to the pediment of the southern front and installed new Adamesque chimneypieces in the parlor and dining room.[37] The wings and outbuildings were demolished in 1871, and the original window sashes were replaced with larger panes. In 1908 new wings and hyphens were added to the house, but without any attempt at historical accuracy. The Victorian window sashes were replaced about 1940. Mount Clare is open to the public.

The Barrister's cousin, Charles Carroll of Carrollton, was also born at Annapolis and studied in England in the 1760's. He was descended from the wealthier side of the family, with a grandfather who had come to Maryland from Ireland in 1688 and became an important colonial agent and immense landowner.[38] Doughoregan Manor, the family seat, was a

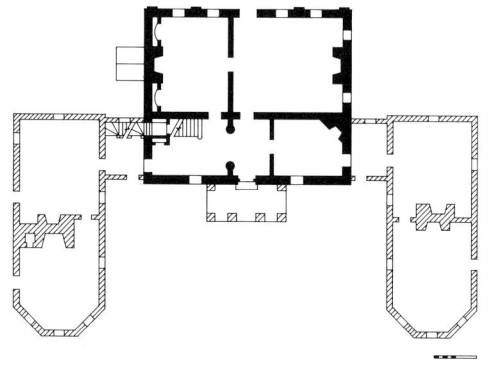

Mount Clare, Charles Carroll Mansion, Baltimore, 1756–1760, with the wings of 1767–68 that were demolished in 1871. This view appears as decoration on the back of a settee, 1800–1810. *Photograph from The Baltimore Museum of Art, Gift of Lydia Howard de Roth and Nancy H. De Ford Venable and Museum Purchase, BMA 1966.26.11*

Mount Clare, Charles Carroll Mansion, view of 1767–68 portico.

Mount Clare, Charles Carroll Mansion, view of stair from passage.

15,000-acre working plantation in Howard County. Despite the family's tremendous wealth, the 18th-century manor house was a relatively modest one-and-one-half-story brick gambrel building with a one-story brick kitchen and other outbuildings. During the Revolution, Carroll was a delegate to the Continental Congress and signed the Declaration of Independence. In the 1780's, with the decline of the Tidewater's importance, Charles Carroll of Carrollton made Doughoregan Manor his principal residence. Still, despite early additions, the house was not a grand edifice. After the death of Adams and Jefferson in 1826, Carroll became the last surviving signer of the Declaration of Independence, a living relic of the Revolutionary era. In 1827 Henry Gilpin visited the Signer. "A nice little old man . . . his hair very white & long, being tied with a ribbon behind," and his house, "an old one . . . the gradual growth of several generations . . . some one story, some two, so that although full of rooms, it is quite an insignificant place . . . their furniture a singular medley of old and modern fashions . . . fine new curtains of the gayest colours, sofas & chairs covered with glorious old cushions, so deep that you cannot sit but must really lie back in them."[39] Upon the death of Charles Carroll of Carrollton in 1832, his grandson, Charles Carroll of Doughoregan, added a second story to the central block and hyphens—to form a two-story façade three hundred feet long—and a rooftop balustrade and Grecian portico.

Doughoregan Manor, Carroll family mansion, Howard County, as it appeared in 1832 in a lithograph by Charles Hullmandel. *Maryland Historical Society*

Samuel Chase, an ambitious young lawyer who later became another signer of the Declaration of Independence, began construction of a massive three-story mansion in Annapolis in 1769. But two years later, in 1771, he was obliged to sell the incomplete building—only the basement, exterior walls, chimneys, cornice and floors were in place—to Edward Lloyd IV, a wealthy Talbot County planter who had been further enriched by a recent marriage to Elizabeth Tayloe, of the distinguished Richmond County, Virginia, family. It was probably Lloyd's father-in-law John Tayloe, who suggested the name of William Buckland to complete this shell of a mansion-to-be.[40]

William Buckland is the most well known of the English carver-builders who worked in Maryland.[41] Born in Oxfordshire in 1734, he was apprenticed at the age of seventeen to a London joiner named James Buckland, who may have been his uncle. In 1755, Buckland sailed to Virginia as an indentured servant to design and supervise construction of the interiors of Gunston Hall, home of a Virginia planter who lived in Fairfax County, ten miles south of Alexandria on the Potomac River. In 1761 Buckland and a team of skilled carvers who worked for him moved to Richmond County, where he received the patronage of the powerful Car-

William Buckland, portrait by Charles Willson Peale, 1789. *Yale University Art Gallery, Mabel Brady Garvan Collection*

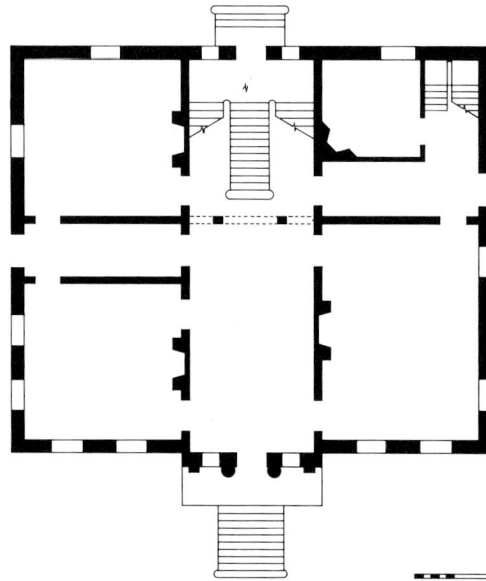

Plan of the Chase-Lloyd House, Annapolis.

Detail of the window shutters at Mathias Hammond House, Annapolis, by craftsmen associated with William Buckland.

ter family and worked on the interiors of Mount Airy, the Tayloe family's imposing Palladian mansion.

In the fall of 1771 Buckland and at least four assistants, John Randall, Samuel Bayley, Thomas Hall and John Callis, moved to Annapolis to complete the Chase-Lloyd House on Maryland Avenue. After November, 1772, while Buckland continued to supervise the decorative carving, additional work was undertaken by the London-trained stucco-workers John Rawlings and James Barnes and the "gentleman" William Noke, who had come to Maryland about 1769 to design and build Governor Robert Eden's house at Annapolis. The Chase-Lloyd House is open to the public.

In the spring of 1774 Buckland provided the plan of a five-part mansion with polygonal-fronted wings for Mathias Hammond, a rich young lawyer. Here Buckland introduced to Maryland the fashionable English concept of an elegantly appointed drawing room on the second story above a dining room of the same size on the first story. This arrangement allowed ladies to "withdraw" with greater privacy and style while the gentlemen lingered at table. The interiors of the Hammond House are relatively plain, reflecting the new taste for more austere neoclassicism. In November, while Hammond's house was under construction, Buckland was also working on a courthouse and prison in Caroline County. Suddenly, at the age of forty, Buckland died. An inventory of his possessions included five black workers, tools and instruments, supplies of lumber, brick, gold-leaf, mahogany and glue and architecture books by Isaac Ware, James Gibbs, Abraham Swan, Batty Langley and others.[42]

The Hammond House and Mount Clare may have inspired a similar design for Montpelier, Thomas Snowden's house in Prince George's County, ten miles south of present-day Laurel. Snowden was a planter and speculator who owned some nine thousand acres of land; his wife was the wealthy Ann Ridgely. Construction of the mansion, with its pedimented central block, may have begun as early as 1774, at the time of their marriage, but was probably not completed before 1783; the semioctagonal wings may have been added in the 1790's. Another wing with kitchen and servants rooms was added about 1916. Montpelier is open to the public.

In 1769 the colonial legislature appropriated funds for a new State House at Annapolis.[43] The design was provided by Joseph Horatio Anderson, an architect who later drafted house plans for Charles Carroll of Annapolis, the colonial agent John Morton Jordan, Daniel Dulaney the Younger, and the extensions at Whitehall for former Governor Horatio Sharpe. In 1770, writing to the authorities of Providence, Rhode Island,

Samuel Chase–Edward Lloyd IV House, 22 Maryland Avenue, Annapolis, 1769–1773.

Chase-Lloyd House, entrance hall.

Chase-Lloyd House, parlor ceiling.

Chase-Lloyd House, dining room window and doorcase.

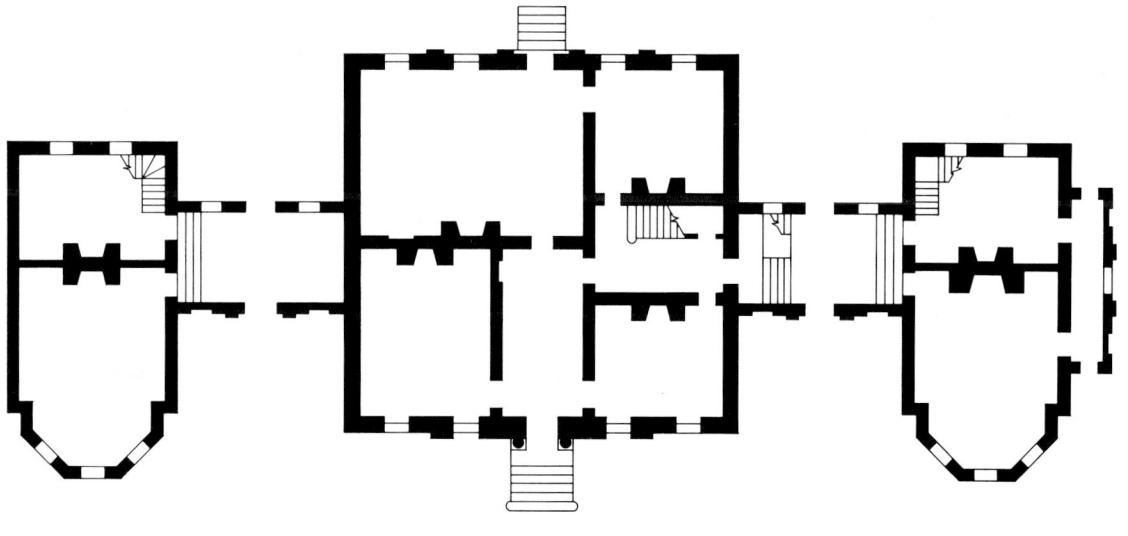

Mathias Hammond House, 19 Maryland Avenue, Annapolis, begun 1774. *Photograph by M. E. Warren*

Mathias Hammond House, dining room.

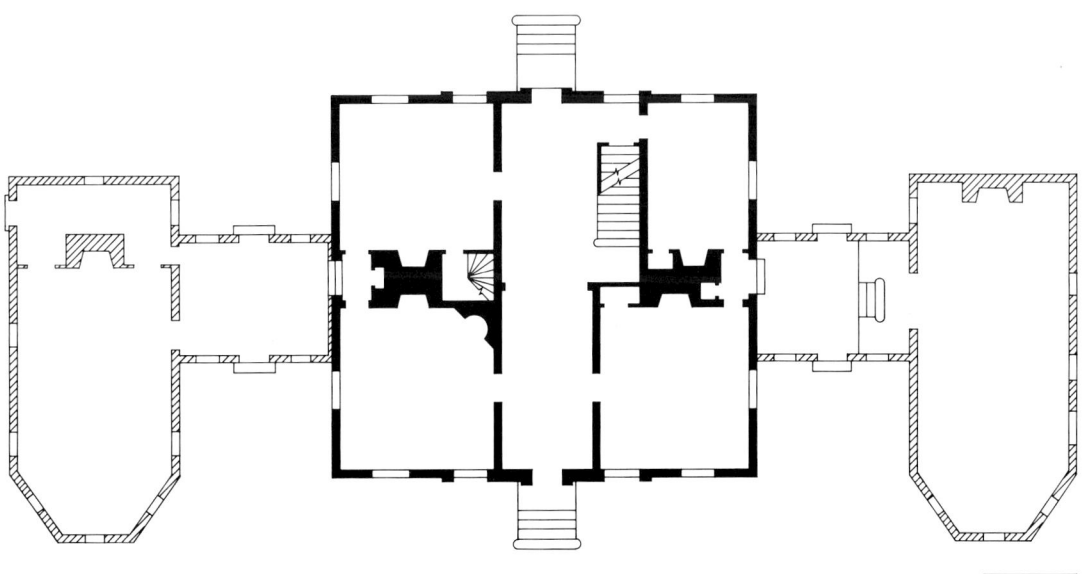

Montpelier, Thomas Snowden House, Laurel vicinity, c. 1774–83, wings added in the 1790's.

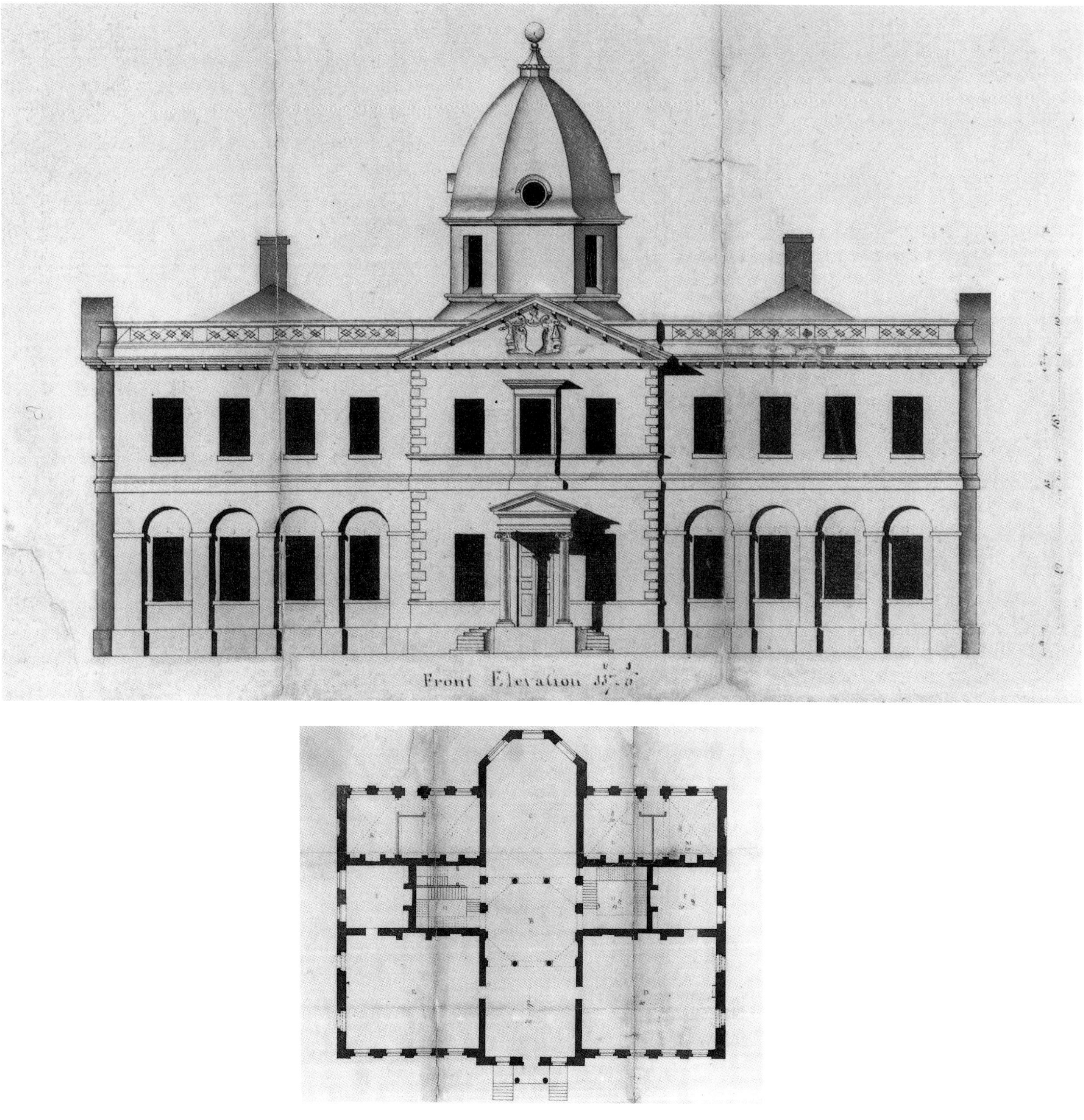

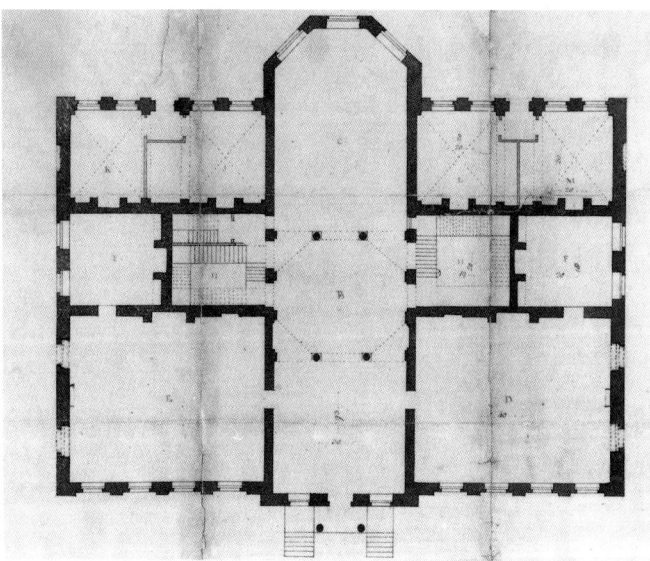

Elevation and plan of State House, Annapolis, by Joseph Horatio Anderson, 1769.
Johns Hopkins University Library

Anderson boastfully described himself as "Architect & Superintendent of the new State House at Annapolis, as well as several private edifices" with experience in "several Courts of Europe."[44] Unlike Buckland and other early "architects," Anderson seems to have been exclusively a designer and not a craftsman. Construction of the State House began in June, 1771, and continued for seven years under the direction of Charles Wallace, a local merchant who was a member of the building committee.[45] His friend Thomas Jennings rhapsodized poetically that Wallace "rears the Column and projects the Dome, And makes our Streets like those of ancient Rome / The Trav'ler views with pleas'd Surprise, Stupendous Fabricks reaching to the Skies/A grateful People shall preserve thy Fame, and rank with Jones and Wren thy honour'd name!"[46] The cornerstone of the State House was laid in late March, 1772, accompanied by "a cold collation, a few loyal and constitutional toasts and . . . three cheers." The roof was covered by the summer of 1774 but was blown off by a hurricane the next year, destroying the interiors of the upper rooms. In 1777, when the British fleet sailed into Chesapeake Bay, Wallace's workmen fled. Though not entirely finished, the legislative halls were in use by 1780.

In December, 1783, at a meeting of Congress held at the Maryland State House, General Washington resigned his commission and returned to the life of a country squire at Mount Vernon. In 1784 Congress, again meeting at the State House, ratified the Treaty of Paris, concluding the Revolutionary War. Construction of the incomplete State House was resumed in 1785, with a new roof and dome designed by Joseph Clark. In June, 1785, the carpenter Joshua Botts reported that he was "a going to take the Roof of[f] the State House and . . . a going to Raise it one story higher and the Dome to be Sixty foot hig[her] than the old one." Work, delayed by a lack of funds, was finally completed in the 1790's.[47] The present portico was added in 1882–83, and rear annexes were added in 1858–63, 1886–92 and 1902–06.

In the young Republic, Annapolis, though still the capital of Maryland, would become a sleepy provincial town of old-fashioned 18th-century buildings and the Eastern Shore an isolated backwater as the Tidewater's prosperity declined, while Baltimore and the interior would become new centers of commerce and culture, with an eager demand for new buildings and new styles of architecture.

Maryland State House, Annapolis, begun 1769, with the dome of 1785 and the portico of 1882–83. *Library of Congress*

II. *The Federal Era*

In May, 1782, only seven months after the British capitulation at Yorktown and sixteen months before the peace treaty at Paris would formally end the Revolution, George Washington contributed fifty guineas to a new college named in his honor at Chestertown, Maryland.[1] In 1780, William Smith, a Scottish-born priest and educator, had moved from Philadelphia to Chestertown, where he was appointed rector of a Kent County church and headmaster of the village academy. Under Smith's enthusiastic leadership, the academy was enlarged to become Washington College in 1782. Two years later the college announced ambitious plans to erect a "large and commodious building" for two hundred students.[2] The trustees' minutes described the building as four stories high, with a central block forty feet wide flanked by two wings, each sixty feet long, making the hall the largest building in Maryland in its time.[3] The College was designed by Joseph Rakestraw (c. 1735–1794), a prominent Philadelphia carpenter who would supply a weathervane for Washington's house at Mount Vernon in 1787, and by Nicholas Hicks, a mason from Philadelphia. The builder was Robert Allison, who was active in Philadelphia between 1770 and 1790 and subscribed to two copies of the Philadelphia edition of Abraham Swan's *The British Architect* in 1775. Allison brought his workers from Philadelphia, by boat to Kent County, Delaware, and then overland by wagon to Chestertown. Construction began in the spring of 1784, and the building was dedicated in June, 1788, although the interior was incomplete (and may have remained unfinished for many years). In 1796, a French traveler observed that the college was already "deplorably decayed" with walls collapsed in many places, no glass in any of the windows and no steps at the doors. The college hall burned in 1827, and the principal buildings now at Washington College were erected in 1844 and 1854 by Elija Reynolds, a Pennsylvania-born carpenter who lived in Cecil County.

One of the most interesting architectural personalities of the post-Revolutionary period was Joseph Clark (c. 1753–1799) of Annapolis.[4]

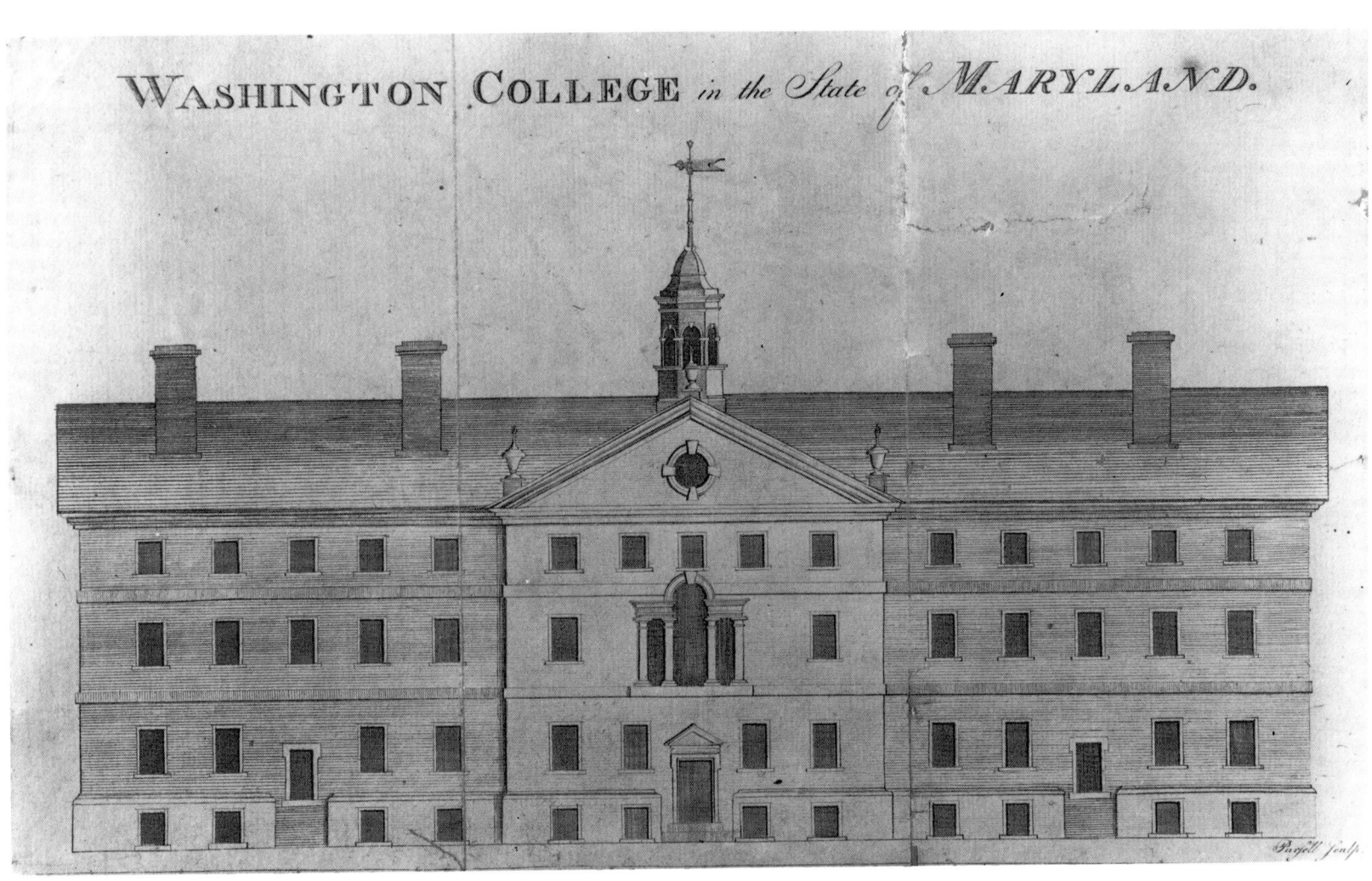

Washington College, design by Joseph Rakestraw and Nicholas Hicks, engraved by Henry Purcell of Philadelphia, 1784. *Maryland Historical Society*

Wye Hall, elevation and plan by Joseph Clark, c. 1790. *Maryland Historical Society*

The Annapolis lawyer Alexander Hanson recommended Clark to George Washington as "regularly bred to his profession in England."[5] In April, 1785, Clark described himself as an "Architect, Builder and Surveyor" who "composes designs, draws plans, elevations and sections of buildings of all kinds in civil architecture . . . makes calculations and estimates of the expense of the labour as well as the materials . . . directs workmen, and surveys the execution of the building."[6] In 1786 Clark began rebuilding the roof of the State House at Annapolis and prepared plans for the completion of Governor Bladen's mansion, which had been left as an unfinished shell for forty years. With new wings added, it would serve to house St. John's College. In 1792 Clark applied for the position of superintendent of public buildings in Washington, the new national city that, only months earlier, had been carved from chunks of Maryland and Virginia along the Potomac River. In September, 1793, Clark led the Masonic ceremonies at the laying of the cornerstone of the U.S. Capitol.[7] In 1794 Clark, boasting of thirty years' study and experience as an architect, announced plans to publish "Polymathy, or the American Builder," a pair of octavo volumes containing an anthology of writings on architecture with lists of materials, costs of labor, formulas for varnish, geometric tables, a dictionary of ancient and modern architectural terms and the orders of architecture, "viz. the Tuscan, Doric, Ionic, Corinthian, Composite, Chinese, Attic, Cargatic, Arabesque, Moresque, Grotesque, Saracenic, Rustic, Antique, Antiquo-Modern, Gothic."[8] There is no record that the books were ever published.

In the early 1790's, Clark designed a mansion for William Paca, the rich and ambitious lawyer who had been one of four Marylanders to sign the Declaration of Independence.[9] Deciding to retire from public life, Paca wanted to build a new mansion on a sprawling 1400-acre estate in Queen Anne's County, which he had inherited from his first wife. Joseph Clark's impressive elevation and plan for Wye Hall survives. With its semicircular Corinthian portico, overscaled bull's-eye window in the pediment, projecting center pavilion surmounted with a statue, Palladian windows set beneath a flattened arch and swags of carved wooden ornament, the wrought-iron lanterns atop the hyphens and two more statues on the pediment of each wing, Clark's drawing is a dreamlike idealization of English Georgian design. There is no record that the mansion was executed with all of these elegant details, but the 1798 tax inventory of William Paca's Wye Island listed "1 Dwelling House, main body 53 by 32, two Story, . . . 2 passages 12 by 20, one Story, . . . two wings, 25 by 34 each . . . 2 Venetain Windows," a description that parallels Clark's plan, but with shallower wings. The mansion burned in 1879. In 1795

Joseph Clark advertised for journeymen carpenters, "such as have a complete set of tools and are sober, judicious, able, willing . . . and have served a regular apprenticeship to their trade," offering them constant employment in Washington.[10]

Wye Hall's five-part plan—center block flanked by hyphens leading to symmetrical wings—became a special favorite of Maryland builders during the Federal era. Provincial builders were undoubtedly inspired by the temple-like Palladian mansions with wings illustrated in 18th-century English architecture books, but the influence of climate should not be overlooked. The five-part house was most popular in the upper South: northern Virginia, coastal Maryland and Kentucky, where many Virginians and Marylanders resettled. Hot in summer, these areas are cold in winter, especially along the storm-tossed shores of the Chesapeake Bay. Outbuildings, particularly kitchens, needed to be separated from the main house in summer, but it was convenient to have them linked to the house by a covered passage in winter. Significantly, at least half of Maryland's five-part houses were created by adding hyphens to connect formerly separate outbuildings to main houses.

The great five-part mansion of Hampton, outside present-day Towson to the north of Baltimore, was built in 1783–90 for Charles Ridgely, an extensive landowner whose fortunes had been substantially enhanced by inheritance from his father and brother in the early 1770's and by selling iron kettles, shot and cannons from the ironworks on his property during the Revolution.[11] Hampton is as notable for its old-fashioned Georgian style as for its tremendous scale; it was the largest house of its time in Maryland. With two-story porticoes and a giant cupola, both unusual for an 18th-century American house, the barnlike Hampton has the appearance of a pretentious colonial courthouse. Several carpenters were responsible for embellishing the mansion, among them Michael Shannon, William Fuller and others named Dotson, Smithson and Richardson.[12] Henry Carlisle installed "dentle Cornish, Winscot, Double Architrave," the chimneypiece and a fluted doorway with pilasters in the parlor. Jehu Howell, a master carpenter who supervised the work in general at Hampton, was paid for scrolls on the dormer windows, ten urns on the rooftop and porticoes, 2095 feet of modillion cornice, ten pediments for doorways and 2084 feet of Doric entablature.[13] Hampton was owned by the Ridgely family until 1948, when it was acquired by the National Park Service, which has preserved it for the public.

In early Maryland, as in 18th-century England, the large landowners were able to build great provincial power bases and displayed this power by building impressive country houses. Edward Lloyd IV was a rich and

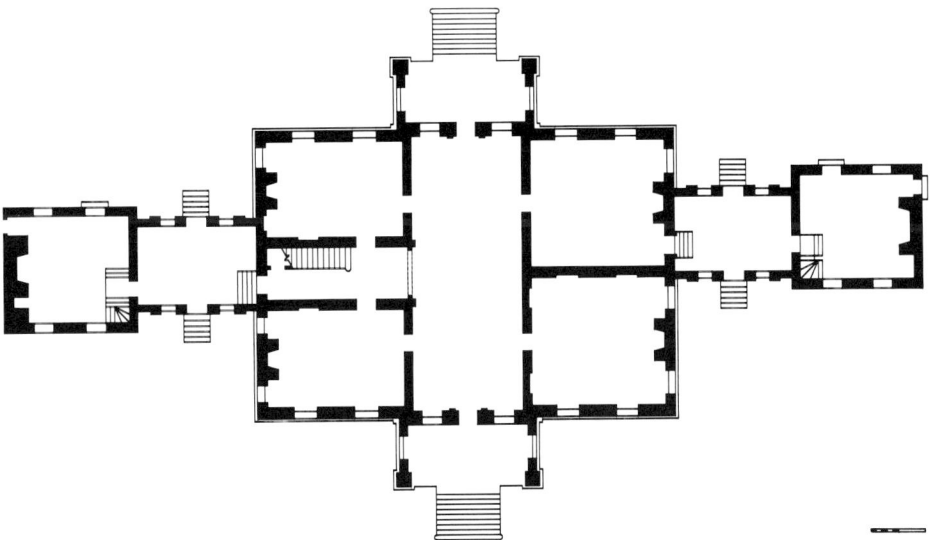

Hampton, Charles Ridgely House, Towson vicinity, 1783–90.

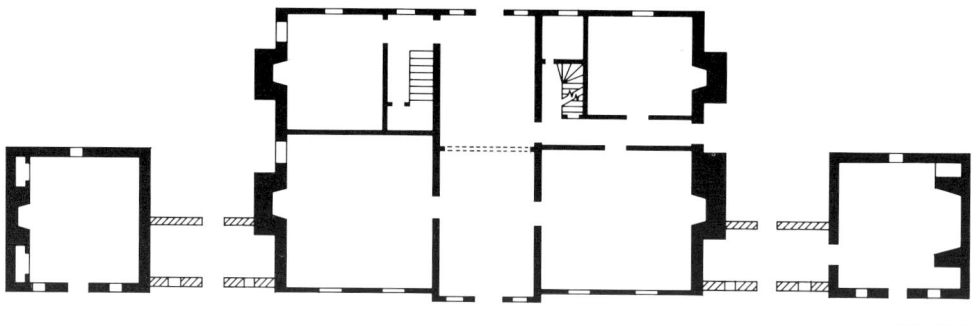

Rose Hill, Gustavus Brown House, Port Tobacco vicinity, c. 1783.

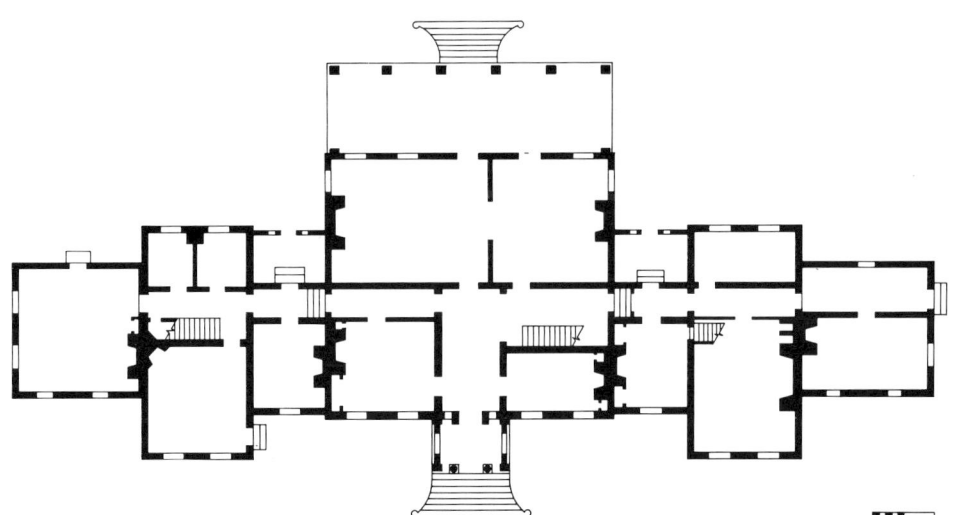

Wye House, Edward Lloyd IV House, Easton vicinity, c. 1780, wings and portico added in the 1790's.

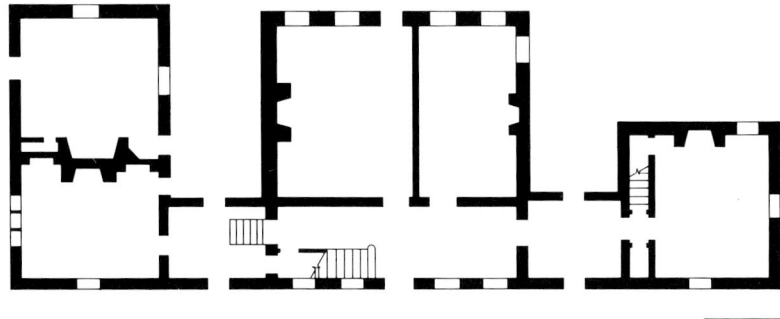

Kennersley, Richard Ireland Jones House, Centreville vicinity, c. 1786–98. *Photograph by Frances Benjamin Johnston, Private Collection*

powerful Talbot County landowner who became a colonial legislator during the Revolution and a state governor of the early Republic, as well as the builder of one of Maryland's most imposing mansions, Wye House, outside Easton. Built in the 1780's, it replaced an earlier house on the same site. Though the name of William Noke is mentioned in his ledgers, Lloyd may have been his own architect; for his library contained an unusually rich assortment of books by Palladio, Gibbs, Swan, Overton and other architectural writers.[14] The interiors of Wye, which lack paneling except on the chimneybreasts, reflect the transition from the heavy taste of the mid-Georgian period to the lighter Federal style. Additions to the far ends of the wings and the portico were made in the late 1790's, creating a façade 151 feet long. The roofs of the hyphens were raised in 1914.

The five-part house of Rose Hill, overlooking the river outside Port Tobacco, was built about 1783 for another country squire with powerful connections, Dr. Gustavus Brown, an Edinburgh-trained physician who attended President Washington during his final illness.[15] Despite its ungainly proportions, the house presents a noble southern front, with a pedimented frontispiece and projecting central pavilion, faced with flush boards. Though this is a frame house, the builder erected the end walls of brick, affording some safety against fire, which might spread from chimneys, without the expense of building a house entirely of brick.

The five-part mansion at Kennersley, outside Centreville, was built for Richard Ireland Jones some time between 1786, when he married Susannah Tilghman, a member of one of the most prominent Queen Anne County families, and 1798, when the mansion appears on a tax survey. The gable of the center block, like that at Wye House, faces forward to form a templelike pediment, a favorite architectural feature of the Federal period, especially in Maryland, Virginia and North Carolina. The brickmason took special care with details: the Flemish-bond walls, molded watertable and stringcourse. The wings and the hyphens, which, curiously, are not set behind the plane of the center block, were built at different times, though whether earlier or later is uncertain, as the documentation is not clear.

Another member of the Tilghman family, the planter Peregrine Tilghman, was the owner of Hope, another five-part house outside Easton. Built about 1805, Hope reflects the lighter, flatter, more attenuated taste of the Federal period. Though the house was remodeled in 1907, a faded photograph records the delicate dormers, Roman Doric portico, expansive semicircular fanlight and delightfully eccentric curvilinear-roofed passageways leading to frame offices, as well as the elegant proportions and brilliantly patterned Flemish-bond walls.

Hope, Peregrine Tilghman House, Easton vicinity, c. 1805, a mid-19th-century photograph. *Private Collection*

The five-part plan was so practical and so admired that as late as 1839 a horticulturist and builder named Robert Sinclair published his design for a five-part stone farm house he had built outside Baltimore nine years earlier. Little is known of Sinclair (1772–1853) except what can be gathered from his own statements in the October, 1839, issue of *The Cultivator*, that he had "in early life learned drawing and architecture" and had been "for several years engaged in the construction of buildings."[16]

Baltimore, founded in 1729 on the north branch of the Patapsco River, had become Maryland's largest town by the 1770's. For twenty-five years after the Revolution, while English and French competition for the lucrative Caribbean trade was disrupted by European wars, the merchants of Baltimore enjoyed "clear sailing" for their wheat, tobacco, flour, corn, lumber, shingles and bricks. By 1790, the city's population was 13,500, making it the fourth-largest city in America; by 1800, Baltimore was already larger than Boston; and by 1810, Baltimore was a bustling metropolis of 46,600 and 3500 houses; it was eager for new buildings and new styles of architecture.[17]

Until after the Civil War, there were few architects as we know the profession today. Typically, an individual or a committee would tell a master carpenter or mason to copy a sketch or an illustration from a book or to imitate another building in the neighborhood. Benjamin Latrobe, the English architect who was exceptional both in his professional training as well as his artistic gifts, complained that architecture in young America was left to gentlemen amateurs, who had a dilettantish knowledge of design from books but no practical experience, or to carpenter-builders, who knew their crafts but nothing of world architecture. Latrobe complained bitterly of both: the pretentious "vandals" of the merchant class and the clumsy craftsmen who plodded along in their old, boring habits. A sketchy plan, accompanied by a list of specifications, and a general promise that everything was to be done "in a workman-like manner" were all the early 19th-century builder generally gave his clients before commencing work.[18] In 1822 the Baltimore builder Matthew Campbell provided a client with a simple sketch for a new house, scribbled with a promise that it was to be "similar to Mr. Clark's in Hudson Street."

Though James Walker opened a school to teach "Architecture—viz. Drawings of Ground-Plans and Elevations of Buildings, with the different Orders and Proportions" in 1792[19] and J. J. Boudier offered "Lessons on Architectural Drawing" in 1795 in Baltimore,[20] permanent professional schools were not established in the United States until after the Civil War. Benjamin Latrobe sent his son John to West Point, because its lessons in civil engineering were the best academic training available at the time for

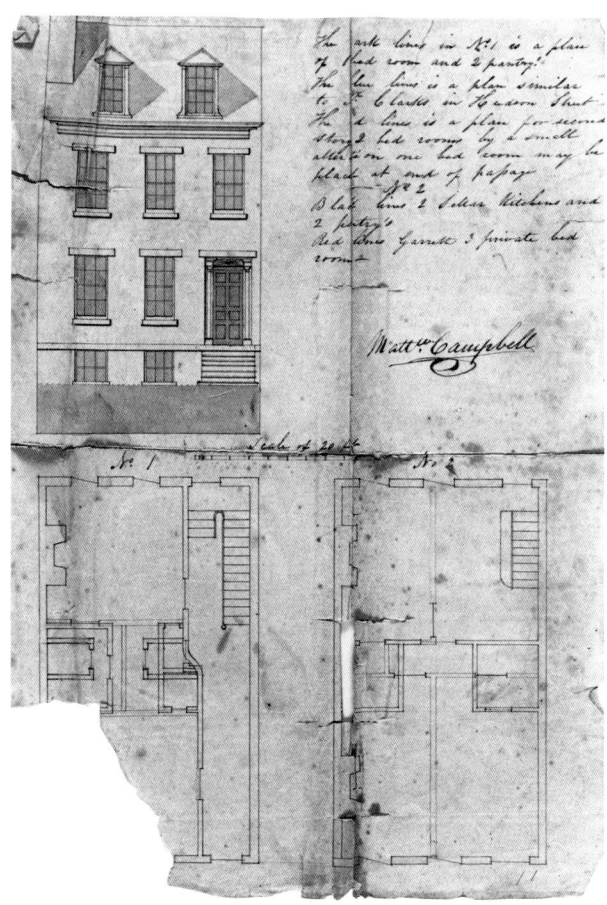

Plan and elevation for a Baltimore house by Matthew Campbell, c. 1820. *Maryland Historical Society*

a future architect. Without schools or the opportunity to travel in order to see the great buildings of the world, provincial builders had to rely on books picked up at a shop or library. Thus, in 1817 the builder Robert Cary Long, Sr., was praised because his great accomplishments, "unaided by early studies and travel in Europe," had been the result of "laborious research into the stores of antiquity, as exhibited in such works as are attainable and by incessant application."[21] In the same year, Judge William Cranch ruled that a bankrupt Maryland architect could not be obliged to sell his books to pay his creditors, opining, "The common house carpenter who keeps in his tool chest his *Builder's Assistant* or *Builder's Jewel* and refers to it for information every day, would think it hard to separate them from his chisels and plane."[22]

Architecture books were available in early 19th-century Baltimore, though apparently not in large quantity. In 1783 the bookseller John McClure offered a variety of books containing designs and instructions for carpenters, painters, cabinetmakers, carvers, smiths and other craftsmen.[23] Three years later, Spotswood and Clarke sold Thomas and Batty Langley's *The Builder's Jewel* (London, 1741).[24] In 1787 Hugh Barkley advertised Abraham Swan's *The British Architect* (London, 1745) and *Town and Country Builder's Assistant*.[25] In 1794 J. R. Rice offered *The British Architect, The Practical Builder or Workman's General Assistant* and *The Country Builder's Assistant*.[26] In 1795 Ambrose Clark and James Keddie sold Nicholson and Pain's "*Carpenter*," Pain's *Practical Builder*, copies of *Builder's Jewel*, John Crunden's *Convenient and Ornamental Designs* (London, 1767) and John Miller's *Country Gentleman's Architect* (London, 1787).[27] Most of these works reflected the taste of mid-18th-century England and contributed to the conservative style of architecture in Maryland during the early Federal period. The design of a chimneypiece at the c. 1785 house of the Chestertown lawyer Peregrine Letherbury, 107 Water Street, was copied from an illustration in William Salmon's *Palladio Londinensis*, first published in 1734 but so popular it appeared in at least eight editions. The steeple of Baltimore's German Reformed Church, Second Street, was copied by the builder George Rohrback in 1803–04 from designs in James Gibbs's *Book of Architecture*, published in 1728. Inevitably, experienced architectural talent also came from abroad.[28] Many "redemptioners," indentured craftsmen who traded periods of service for passage to America, were "sold" at the Baltimore docks in the 1780's.

One of the earliest identified builders was Leonard Harbaugh (1749–1822), a mason and inventor of agricultural machinery. The son of German parents in Pennsylvania, Harbaugh moved to Baltimore in 1755. In

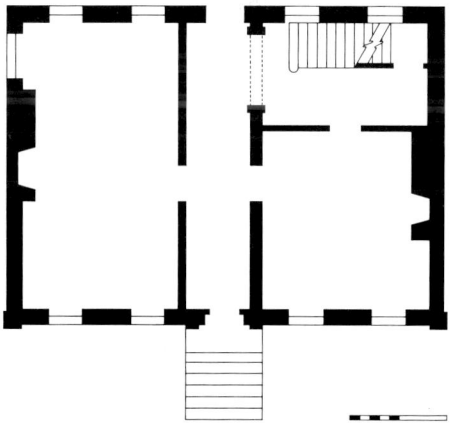

Peregrine Letherbury House, 107 Water Street, Chestertown, c. 1785.

86

Chimneypiece at Peregrine Letherbury House and its model, Plate I from William Salmon's *Palladio Londinensis* (London, 1762). *Salmon illustration from the John Carter Brown Library, Brown University*

The steeple of the German Reformed Church, Baltimore, with its model, Plate 29 from James Gibbs's *A Book of Architecture* (London, 1728). *Nineteenth-century photograph of the Church from the Maryland Historical Society; Gibbs illustration from The New York Public Library*

1786 he added a masonry arch under the 1768 brick Baltimore Courthouse when the hill on which it stood was undercut to make way for an extension of Calvert Street to the north. This architectural curiosity survived until about 1812. Harbaugh was the builder of Ivy Neck, built in 1787 for James Cheston about ten miles below Annapolis on the Rhode River. James Hogan, a house carpenter, came to Baltimore from Dublin in 1784 with George McCutchan and other Irish workmen, offering to "draw plans, elevations and estimates for any building" and "supervise them."[29]

Jacob Small, Sr. (1746–1794), was the builder and, probably, the designer of the German Evangelical Reformed Church on Conway Street in 1784–85. Now known as the Otterbein Church, this is the last surviving 18th-century church in Baltimore. Small built a bridge, with a then remarkable ninety-foot span, over Jones Falls in 1786. In 1792 he submitted three designs in the competition for the Capitol at Washington. Additional designs for the public buildings of Washington were submitted by two other Maryland builders: Philip Hart, an obscure carpenter from Taneytown, and James Diamond, an Irish-born builder of Somerset County. Their drawings are now at the Maryland Historical Society.[30]

Michael Diffenderffer (1744–1809) designed the Episcopal Church at East Baltimore and North Front streets in 1785. Six years later, in 1791, John and James Hannan, architects and builders, offered to draw plans, prepare estimates, superintend buildings and construct geometrical staircases, groin arches and fancy windows.[31] In 1791, the carpenter John Dalrymple (c. 1757–1817) and the Massachusetts-born bricklayer James Mosher (1760–1845) built First Presbyterian Church at Fayette and North streets. After towers were added to the Church in 1795, it was generally regarded as the most impressive building of early Baltimore; the church was demolished in 1859. Jacob Wall, Sr. (1768–1823), and his brother George (c. 1767–1822), who shared lodgings on Lexington Street, built the Light Street Meeting House, a two-story brick structure with a front-facing gable, in 1796. In that same year, Ludwig Herring (1762–1817), a builder from Lancaster, Pennsylvania, erected the German Reformed Church on Second Street, but, as we have already noted, its prominent steeple was added in 1803–04 by George Rohrback; the German Reformed Church was demolished in 1866. Rohrback, with the carpenter John Mackenheimmer, built the German Lutheran Church on North Gay Street in 1808, and he was the first superintendent of construction at Benjamin Latrobe's Catholic Cathedral in 1806–11.

The Irish-born carpenter George Milliman (1773–1850), described by John H. B. Latrobe as "a self-instructed architect but a man of taste and

First Presbyterian Church, Baltimore, 1791, towers added 1795, a 19th-century sketch. *Maryland Historical Society*

Courthouse, Baltimore, 1806–09, before its demolition in 1895. *Maryland Historical Society*

Second Presbyterian Church, Baltimore, 1802–05, detail from Thomas H. Poppleton's 1823 map of Baltimore. *Maryland Historical Society*

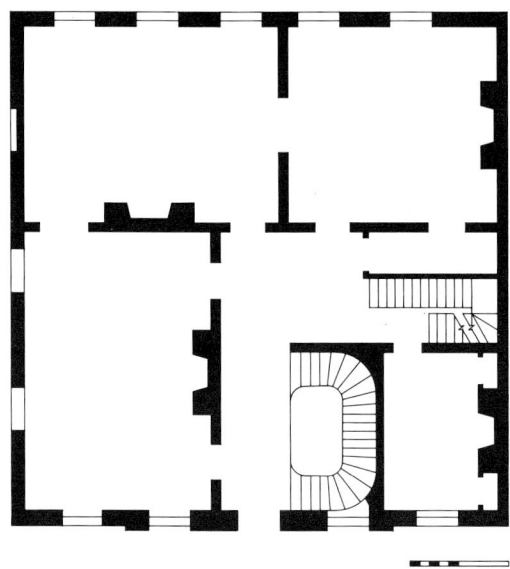

Plan of Carroll Mansion.

judgment," designed and supervised the carpentry of the 1806–09 Courthouse on Monument Square.[32] Milliman also built the Second Presbyterian Church on East Baltimore Street in 1802–05 and later became superintendent of city streets and pumps. The work at the Courthouse was supervised by the bricklayer James Mosher. With Jacob Small, Jr. (1772–1851), Mosher built two "spacious houses" on North Calvert Street for the merchant James Buchanan in 1799. The stonework of the Courthouse was supervised by William Steuart (1780–1839), the Baltimore-born son of a Scottish stonemason.[33] Steuart supplied stone for the U.S. Capitol in 1804–05 and for Latrobe's Baltimore Exchange in 1816. Milliman, Mosher and Steuart collaborated on several important buildings, including a hospital for the insane completed in 1812, and continued in the building business until the early 1830's. The Courthouse was awkwardly sited on a narrow lot perched upon a steep hillside, which prevented the building from facing the square, but its street façades were enriched with slightly projecting pavilions, tall, slender Ionic pilasters of white marble and semicircular relieving arches over the first-story windows. The Courthouse was demolished in 1895.

Several French builders, fleeing to a former Catholic colony from the turbulent aftermath of the French Revolution and slave uprisings in the Caribbean Islands, came to Baltimore in the 1790's. Many other French builders flocked to the former Catholic colony of Louisiana. We have already noted that in October, 1795, J. J. Boudier, a copperplate engraver from Paris, offered to give lessons in architectural drawing and prepare elevations, sections and plans of buildings and superintend their erection.[34] Soon thereafter, about 1800, Augustin Chevalier, a sculptor and designer who described himself as "a pupil of Monsieur Monot and formerly of the French Academy of Paris," was in Baltimore drawing plans for gardens, making sculptures of wood and plaster to decorate ceilings, cornices and façades—"everything in the newest and most approved taste of Paris." Chevalier executed the relief carving on the pediment of Robert Cary Long, Sr.'s 1807 Union Bank and on the front of a house for the merchant Samuel Smith on Water Street; he designed and decorated with carving two houses nearby for two other merchants, John Hollins and Cumberland Dugan, in 1813–14; he assisted Robert Cary Long, Sr., with the design of the Law Institute on South Street and carved embellishments for its façade in 1824; he designed and executed the gates leading into the country estate of the iron merchant Joseph Patterson and the statue of Flora, goddess of flowers and fertility, in his garden.[35]

The house now known as the Carroll Mansion, 800 East Lombard Street, is one of the last surviving houses of a rich early 19th-century

Carroll Mansion, 800 East Lombard Street, Baltimore, 1804–12.

Carroll Mansion, view of stair from second story.

Baltimore merchant.[36] The history of the building is far more complicated than its name would suggest. In fact, it never belonged to anyone named Carroll. Built about 1804 for Robert Lawson, enlarged for the merchant Henry Wilson in 1808, further enlarged about 1812 for another merchant, Christopher Deshon, a refugee from the slave uprisings on Santo Domingo, the house was sold in 1818 to the English-born Richard Caton, whose father-in-law Charles Carroll of Carrollton used it as his winter home. The fabric of the building is also something of an architectural puzzle, for the enlargements and alterations various owners made to the small house that is part of the southwest corner of the present structure have been obscured by an overzealous restoration in 1965. The most impressive feature of the Carroll Mansion is its façade: the graceful proportions, slightly projecting center pavilion, white marble belt course between the first- and second-story windows and recessed panels between the second- and third-story windows. The portico is a restoration, and a doorway that formerly led into the ground-story counting rooms has been replaced with a window. Carroll Mansion is open to the public.

We have already observed how American builders were dependent on British commerce and culture after the Revolution, despite the protestations of national independence that culminated in the War of 1812. In the last third of the 18th century, inspired by excavations at Pompeii and Herculanaeum, which revealed the everyday life of the ancients, English architects began to reinterpret Classical architecture. Instead of generalized, monumental forms derived from ancient public buildings during the Renaissance, designers could now imitate Roman domestic architecture and interior decoration. This neoclassical style took its name from the Scottish-born architect and interior designer Robert Adam, who once described himself as "antique-mad." In place of Palladianism's cool, impersonal, solemn, splendid grandeur, Adam's neoclassicism was cheerful, personal, vivacious, intimate. Rooms that had earlier been uniformly rectangular were now given a variety of shapes, with vaults, niches, screens of columns and rounded ends. Circular motifs were favored, including intricate fanlight entrances, round-headed windows set under relieving arches, and cascading spiral stairs. Intricate patterns of carved decoration in plaster and wood swirled across the surfaces of doors, window frames and mantels. Adam's fame reached its peak in England in the 1770's, but the style associated with his name did not cross the Atlantic until after the Revolution. Adam died in 1792, but his influence continued to dominate the American architectural scene for thirty more years. It took time for tastemakers to write and publish the books that would transmit the new look to America where it came to be called the Federal style.

In the 1790's, Baltimore newspapers were crowded with advertisements for India nankeens, Barbados rum, Muscavado sugar, Marseilles quiltings, Holland beer, Irish linens, Spanish cigars, Leghorn hats—and for architectural supplies and services that reflected the acceptance of the new Federal style. A 1797 advertisement offered "a parcel of the much admired composition ornaments for chimney pieces, door caps, frontispieces, pillaisters, rich flower festoons, wheat festoons, neat small flowers, vine and ivey."[37] In 1801 Thomas Leaman, who had come to Baltimore from London by way of Philadelphia, offered his skills as a "composition ornament Maker."[38] Wallpapers were sold with "festoon borders"[39] or "mock Pannelling to imitate Wainscot."[40] With an ingenuity not without its ironies, painters offered to paint walls "in Imitation of Paper-Hangings"[41] and to simulate marble of various kinds in vivid shades of blue, green and pink.[42]

Many architectural books, also reflecting current as well as conservative British taste, were available at the Library Company of Baltimore, a private gentlemen's library organized in 1796.[43] Its collections included Leoni's edition of Palladio's *Four Books of Architecture* (London, 1715–16), William Pain's *British Palladio* (London, 1786), James Paine's *Plans, Elevations and Sections of Noblemen's and Gentlemen's Houses* (London, 1767), Charles Middleton's *Picturesque and Architectural Views for Cottages, Farm Houses and Country Villas* (London, 1793), Pain's *Carpenter's and Joiner's Repository* (London, 1778), John Soane's *(Designs in Architecture* (London, 1778), Robert and James Adam's *Works in Architecture* (London, 1778–86), Antoine Desgodetz's *Edifices Antiques de Rome* (Paris, 1779), William Chambers's *Treatise on Civil Architecture* (London, 1759), Francis Price's *British Carpenter* (London, 1753), James Stuart and Nicholas Revett's *Antiquities of Athens* (London, begun 1762), Robert Mitchell's *Plans and Views in Perspective* (London, 1801), George Richardson's *Series of Designs for Country Seats or Villas* (London, 1795), John Soane's *Sketches in Architecture* (London, 1798), Bernard Belidor's *Architecture Hydraulique* (Paris, 1737–53), Richard Elsam's *Essay in Rural Architecture* (London, 1803), Peter Nicholson's *Principles of Architecture* (London, 1795–98), James Peacock's *Ichnographic Distributions for Small Villas* (London, 1785), Pain's *Builder's Pocket Treasure or Palladio Delineated* (London, 1763), James Malton's *Essay on British Cottage Architecture* (London, 1804) and Thomas Warton's *Essays on Gothic* (London, 1800).

Not all members of the upper and merchant classes were amateur architects, let alone good ones (indeed, the number and skill of American amateurs have probably been overestimated), but these volumes do re-

Belvidere, John Eager Howard House, Baltimore, 1786–94, seen before its demolition in 1876.
The Peale Museum, Baltimore City Life Museums

flect a sincere enthusiasm for architecture among the shareholders of the Library Company. Its members included Robert Gilmor, George Grundy, John Eager Howard, Samuel Smith, Thoroughgood Smith, Charles Carroll, Jr., and Nicholas Rogers—all of whom built villas on the hillsides to the north and west of Baltimore, in an effort to escape the yellow fever that visited the harbor each summer.[44] Views of some of these houses were made by Francis Guy, an English-born silk dyer and sometime oilcloth maker, painter and dentist, who came to Baltimore about 1798.[45] Visitors to these country houses were delighted by "strawberry parties," with berries, cream, ices, pineapples and champagne, accompanied by music and dancing.[46]

Some of these houses were old-fashioned and conservative, especially the earlier ones. Belvidere was built in 1786–94 for John Eager Howard, a tremendously wealthy landowner and hero of the Revolution, who declined President Washington's invitation to become Secretary of War. Belvidere was a country house of the traditional 18th-century type, with a projecting pedimented pavilion and flanking wings. Its furnishings were sold only three weeks after Howard's death in 1827. At that time, the dining room contained a mahogany sideboard, bookcase, table with claw feet, breakfast table with claw feet, twelve chairs, three window seats, prints, red moreen curtains and painted floorcloth; the drawing room contained yellow moreen curtains, fifteen yellow and gilt cane-bottom arm chairs with cushions, three window seats, a pier table, a tea table and a Brussels carpet; the bow-fronted room on the garden side contained twelve blue chairs with cane bottoms, two matching sofas, a pair of card tables, and three sets of blue and white window curtains.[47] Belvidere was demolished in 1876.

Nearby stood Bolton, the home of George Grundy, an English-born merchant who had come to Baltimore by way of Philadelphia. Built in 1786–94, Bolton was another hip-roofed two-story mansion with a projecting center pavilion and bow-fronted room on the garden side. The basement was occupied by the kitchen, scullery and servants' rooms; the first story contained a round-ended or oval saloon, 24 by 30 feet, flanked by a drawing room and dining room, each 18 by 22 feet; the second story contained six chambers and storerooms for china and glass. Bolton was demolished in the late 1890's.

Oakley, built for Levi Pierce about 1795–1800, and Willow Brook, built for the merchant Thoroughgood Smith about 1796, were Palladian houses similar to the smaller farm houses illustrated in the books of Robert Morris and William Halfpenny, English popularizers of Palladian design for less ambitious builders.[48] Each of these buildings was com-

Bolton, George Grundy House, Baltimore, 1786–94, front and rear views painted by Francis Guy, 1800–1810. *Enoch Pratt Free Library, Maryland Historical Society*

Top: Oakley, Levi Pierce House, Baltimore, 1795–1800. Middle: Willow Brook, Thoroughgood Smith House, Baltimore, c. 1796. Bottom: Beech Hill, Robert Gilmor House, Baltimore, c. 1795, views that were painted on the backs of furniture by Francis Guy 1800–1810. *The Baltimore Museum of Art, Gift of Lydia Howard de Roth and Nancy De Ford Venable and Museum Purchase, BMA 1966.26.9, BMA 1966.26.6, BMA 1966.26.5*

Willow Brook, Thoroughgood Smith House, ceiling of oval room. *The Baltimore Museum of Art, Gift of the City of Baltimore, installation and renovation made possible by contributors to the Willow Brook Fund*

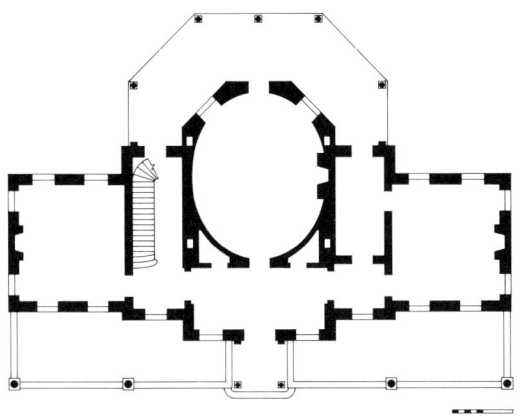

Plan of Willow Brook, Thoroughgood Smith House.

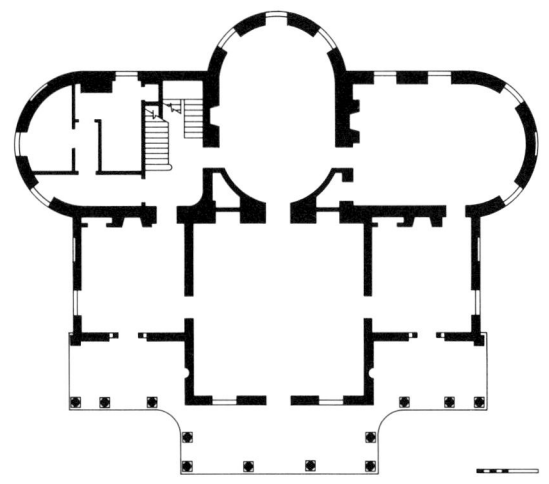

Plan of Montebello, Samuel Smith House, as executed.

posed of a two-story central block, its gable facing forward to form a templelike pediment, flanked by one-story wings. The greatest advantages of this form were that it afforded grandeur on a small scale and extra ventilation and natural light in each of the principal rooms. Oakley, demolished about 1880, was embellished with round-headed windows with keystones. Willow Brook, demolished in 1965, featured an oval room projecting into the garden front. This room, with its splendid Adamesque plasterwork, is preserved at the Baltimore Museum of Art.

A few of the country villas around Baltimore were more daring in design, probably reflecting the architectural enthusiasm of their owners. The house at Beech Hill, built in the 1790's for Robert Gilmor, a Scottish-born merchant, appears in a view by Francis Guy that shows a center block connected to flanking dependencies by long porches and passageways embellished with Chinese latticework and Gothic arches. Gilmor's son, Robert, Jr., wrote that Beech Hill was "a cottage sort of house with a one-story-&-half, basement and Portico but afterwards added wings, connected with the Portico by Arcades."[49] Beech Hill was demolished in the third quarter of the 19th century.

Montebello, 1796–99, was the summer home of the Baltimore banker and ironmaster Samuel Smith.[50] The creator of its most unusual plan—a two-story block with round ends and a large projecting one-story, skylighted room for entertaining—may have been the landscape designer William Birch. Birch laid out the gardens at Riversdale mansion and was described in 1802 as "an architect who is at the same time an artist."[51] Birch drew a perspective view of Montebello for a published book of country seats. More intriguing is his surviving plan for the first story of Montebello. Several differences between this drawing and the house as built suggest that Birch may have prepared the plan as architect prior to construction.[52] Montebello was demolished in 1909.

Only one of Baltimore's suburban villas has survived: Homewood, built in 1801–03 for the twenty-five-year-old Charles Carroll, Jr., the extravagant son of Charles Carroll of Carrollton, one of the richest men in America, who gave the land, house and an allowance to his son at the time of his marriage to Harriett Chew of Philadelphia.[53] In January, 1801, the son sent the plan of the house to his father, who approved it in February; in March, the first payments were made to the carpenters Robert and William Edwards and the bricklayer Michael Keplinger. After two years of construction, accompanied by mutterings of complaint from the elder Carroll, who was paying the ever-escalating bills, Homewood was complete enough for bride and groom to move there. Charles, Jr., must have suffered from the exaggerated expectations of his energetic and rigor-

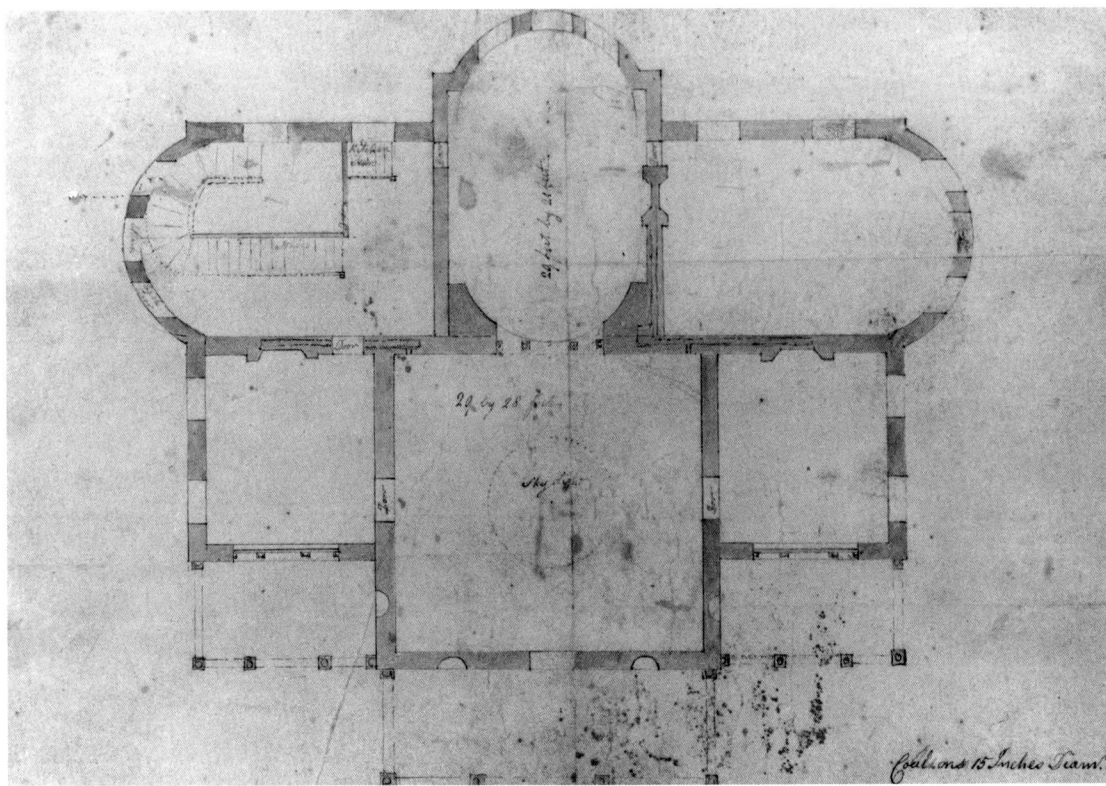

Perspective view and plan of Montebello, Samuel Smith House, Baltimore, by William Birch, c. 1796. *The Baltimore Museum of Art, presented in honor of Calman J. Zamoiski, Jr., BMA 1980.165.1, BMA 1980.165.2*

100

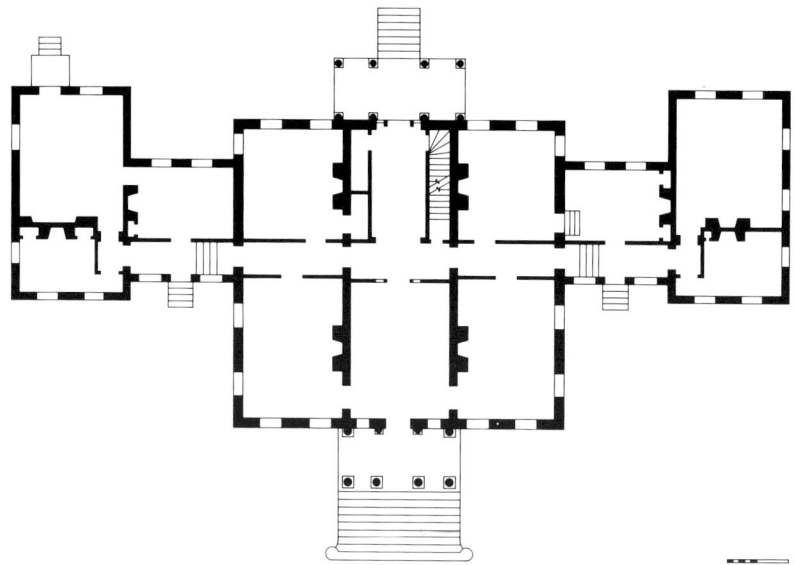

Homewood, Charles Carroll, Jr., House, 3400 North Charles Street, Baltimore, 1801–03.

Homewood, Charles Carroll, Jr., House, front passage.

Homewood, Charles Carroll, Jr., House, lateral passage.

ously self-disciplined father, who continued to take daily horseback rides and cold baths till near the end of his life at the age of ninety-five. When the Philadelphia lawyer Henry Gilpin visited Homewood in September, 1827, he found Charles, Jr., lying languorously on a sofa, miserable despite his wealth because he had no profession to occupy his time.[54] Soon, the idle and purposeless Charles lapsed into alcoholism and hypochondria, and life at Homewood was not happy. The house is rather academic, with the five-part plan typical of Federal Maryland, enriched with unusually refined plasterwork and all magnificently restored by the Johns Hopkins University in 1984–87. Homewood is open to the public.

Probably the greatest of Maryland's gentleman architects was Nicholas Rogers (1753–1822), a native-born mill owner and flour merchant.[55] Wealthy, prominent and well-traveled, Rogers became a principal architectural arbiter of Baltimore during the first two decades of the 19th century. He designed his summer house, Druid Hill, 1796–1798, ornamenting it with a Roman Doric portico, pilasters, denticulated cornice and rooftop balustrade. Rogers may have provided a design for Greenwood, the country seat of his brother Philip. In 1795 Rogers designed the Assembly Rooms at a corner of Holliday and Fayette streets. This two-story brick building with pedimented frontispiece, central pediment, engaged columns, windows set under relieving arches and a rooftop balustrade, contained rooms for the Library Company and public gatherings. The Baltimore County Jail, with polygonal battlemented wings, was also designed by Rogers, a member of the building committee, in 1799.[56] Druid Hill was drastically remodeled in Italianate style in 1862 by John H. B. Latrobe; the Assembly Rooms burned in 1873; the Jail was demolished in 1859.

The Assembly Rooms of 1795–97 and Jail of 1799–1802 were built by Robert Cary Long, Sr. (1770–1833), a Maryland-born house carpenter active in Baltimore for thirty-five years and the father of another important Maryland architect. It is believed that Long, Sr., designed Robert Oliver's house on South Gay Street, built in 1805–07 for an Irish merchant who had come to Baltimore in the early 1780's. It was one of the largest mansions of Baltimore with a ballroom, greenhouse and aviary. An inventory of the furnishings included a large secretary and bookcase, hair-seat sofas and rocking chairs, statuary, three looking glasses, two girandoles, two crimson damask sofas and fifteen matching crimson damask-covered armchairs, two pier tables with marble tops, one round center table with a marble top, crimson damask window curtains, and six dining and breakfast tables with claw feet.[57] Long may have added the new Roman Doric portico about 1825 to the side elevation of Green Mount, Oliver's old country house on the York road.

Druid Hill, Nicholas Rogers House, Baltimore, 1796–1798, painting by Frances Guy, c. 1800. *Maryland Historical Society*

Assembly Rooms, Baltimore, 1795–97, details from Warner and Hanna's 1801 map of Baltimore. *Maryland Historical Society*

Robert Oliver House, Baltimore, 1805–07. *Elevation by Michael Trostel*

Rose Hill, Thomas Owen Williams House, Williamsport vicinity, c. 1808.

Rose Hill, Thomas Owen Williams House, stair.

Union Bank, Baltimore, 1807, a 19th-century photograph. *Maryland Historical Society*

In 1807 Long designed the Union Bank, at the corner of Fayette and North Charles streets in Baltimore, and built it with the assistance of veteran builders William Steuart and James Mosher, who also constructed Robert Oliver's house.[58] Pedimental sculpture on the Bank depicted Neptune and Ceres, emblems of maritime commerce and the harvest. The design of this sixty-eight-foot-square building appears to have been adapted from an unimpeachable source, an illustration in John Soane's *Sketches in Architecture* (London, 1798), which Long borrowed twice from the Library Company in 1807–08.[59] But Nicholas Rogers condescendingly derided it as "wonderfully full of deformity, a sort of *oyster* in Architecture!"[60] The Union Bank was demolished in 1931.

Long's Medical College, Green and Lombard streets, was completed by James Mosher and Thomas Towson in 1812.[61] The building was named for John B. Davidge, a surgeon from Annapolis who was one of the founders of the institution in 1807. Long got his idea for the two stacked auditoriums, dome and skylight from 18th-century French books. The Medical College is open to the public at limited times.

With William Steuart and James Mosher, Long built the Holliday Street Theater in 1812–13. A contemporary source says the design was provided by an obscure "Mr. Robins," a scenery painter who worked for the resident theatrical company, though other contemporaries credit Long.[62] In any case, the architect, Long or Robins, made an ambitious effort with the theater. A rusticated ground story forms a podium for six monumental Doric pilasters that support an entablature complete with triglyphs and metopes. Spectators could enjoy three tiers of boxes, a dome, gas lights and "all the complicated fixtures and machinery of scenic display." In September, 1814, "The Star-Spangled Banner," written by a Frederick County–born lawyer named Francis Scott Key, was first performed in public at the Holliday Street Theater. Rebuilt after a fire in 1873, the theater was demolished in 1917.

In 1813–14 Long designed and built the Baltimore Museum at 225 Holliday Street for Rembrandt Peale, the son of the artist Charles Willson Peale; the younger Peale moved to Baltimore in 1814.[63] The Museum was to be "an elegant Rendez-vous for taste, curiosity and leisure," part science, part art and part entertainment, displaying pictures, statues, stuffed birds, beasts and the skeleton of a giant mastodon (which the elder Peale had unearthed in New York State), plus live Indians and dead Egyptian mummies. Though it was the first building in America designed expressly as a public gallery, the Baltimore Museum looked like a big house with a recessed portico and pilasters. As this building illustrates, except for churches, the concept of public architecture different from domestic ar-

Green Mount, Robert Oliver's country house outside Baltimore, a 19th-century painting. *Maryland Historical Society*

Holliday Street Theater, Baltimore, 1812–13, from John H. B. Latrobe's *Picture of Baltimore* (Baltimore, 1832). *Maryland Historical Society*

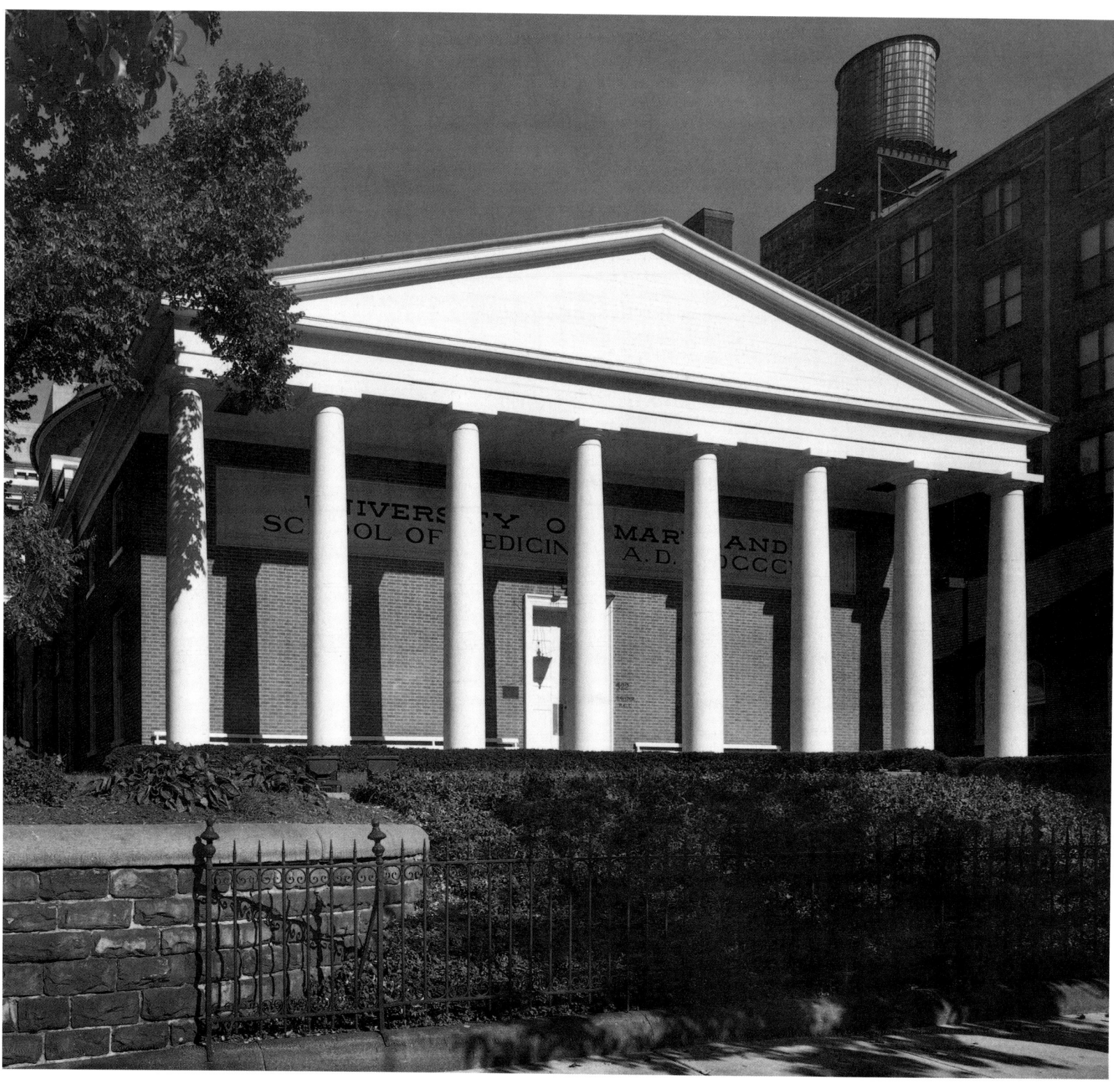

This page and opposite: Interior and exterior views of Medical College, corner Green and Lombard streets, Baltimore, 1811–12.

Design for a Temple of Divine Worship by Nicholas Rogers, 1814. *Maryland Historical Society*

chitecture had not yet evolved in America. Unfortunately, the Museum's opening coincided with the British invasion of Washington and their attack on Baltimore in 1814, and the Museum soon failed. Remodeled by William F. Small in the Grecian style in 1830, when it was converted into a city hall, the Museum's original façade was vaguely recreated in the 1930's. Today the building is a city museum.

In early 1814 the amateur architect Nicholas Rogers sent the Rev. James Kemp a design for the new St. Paul's Church, which was to be built on Charles Street in Baltimore. The Episcopalians were eager to outshine the Presbyterians and Catholics, who were worshiping proudly in splendid buildings. Rogers's pretentious elevation for a "Temple of Divine Worship" presents a projecting entrance encrusted with Ionic pilasters and festoons of carved stone or stucco, with a rooftop balustrade and statues of saints, serving as the base for a four-stage steeple bearing rustication, urns, a clock, oval windows, a slender dome and a figure of St. Paul. Rogers feared that his drawing would soon be "murdered and mangled" by Robert Cary Long, whom he disparaged as a builder of "so many curious & comical things." Long, Rogers said, would "pass [the drawing] off for his own . . . a favorite trick of the Architects."[64] Though he may have been inspired by Rogers's idea of an enormous steeple over the front of the church, Long created an original and pioneering Grecian design for St. Paul's in 1814–17. A portico with paired Doric columns and a triglyph-and-metope frieze was surmounted by a 126-foot, three-stage steeple with superimposed orders, Ionic and Corinthian. Inside, the barrel-vaulted nave was surrounded by twenty-four scagliola Greek Doric columns, supporting galleries draped with red damask on three sides and forming a screen in front of an apsidal chancel on the fourth side.[65] St. Paul's Church burned in 1854.

Robert Cary Long was also the builder of a curious house on Bank Lane near St. Paul Street about 1816. This was the home of William Gwynn, an Irish-born newspaper editor, wit, amiable eccentric and misogynistic bachelor. Gwynn called his house The Tusculum and claimed to have designed this pastiche of Classical columns, entablature and balustrade himself, though he credited Long as builder. Gwynn described The Tusculum as "a little palace, resembling in appearance those delicate, princely pastels and castles . . . of the bird-cage order . . . the architecture composite . . . composed of all the prettiness displayed in the Classical school."[66] A less enthusiastic contemporary described it as a "pretentious little house, all portico and stucco."[67] Only a single photograph of the rear façade is known. For many years, The Tusculum was meeting place of the Delphinian Club, whose nine members were devoted to the arts,

Peale's Museum, Baltimore, 1813–14, detail from Thomas H. Poppleton's 1823 map of the city. *Maryland Historical Society*

St. Paul's Episcopal Church, Baltimore, 1814–17, from John H. B. Latrobe's *Picture of Baltimore* (Baltimore, 1832). *Maryland Historical Society*

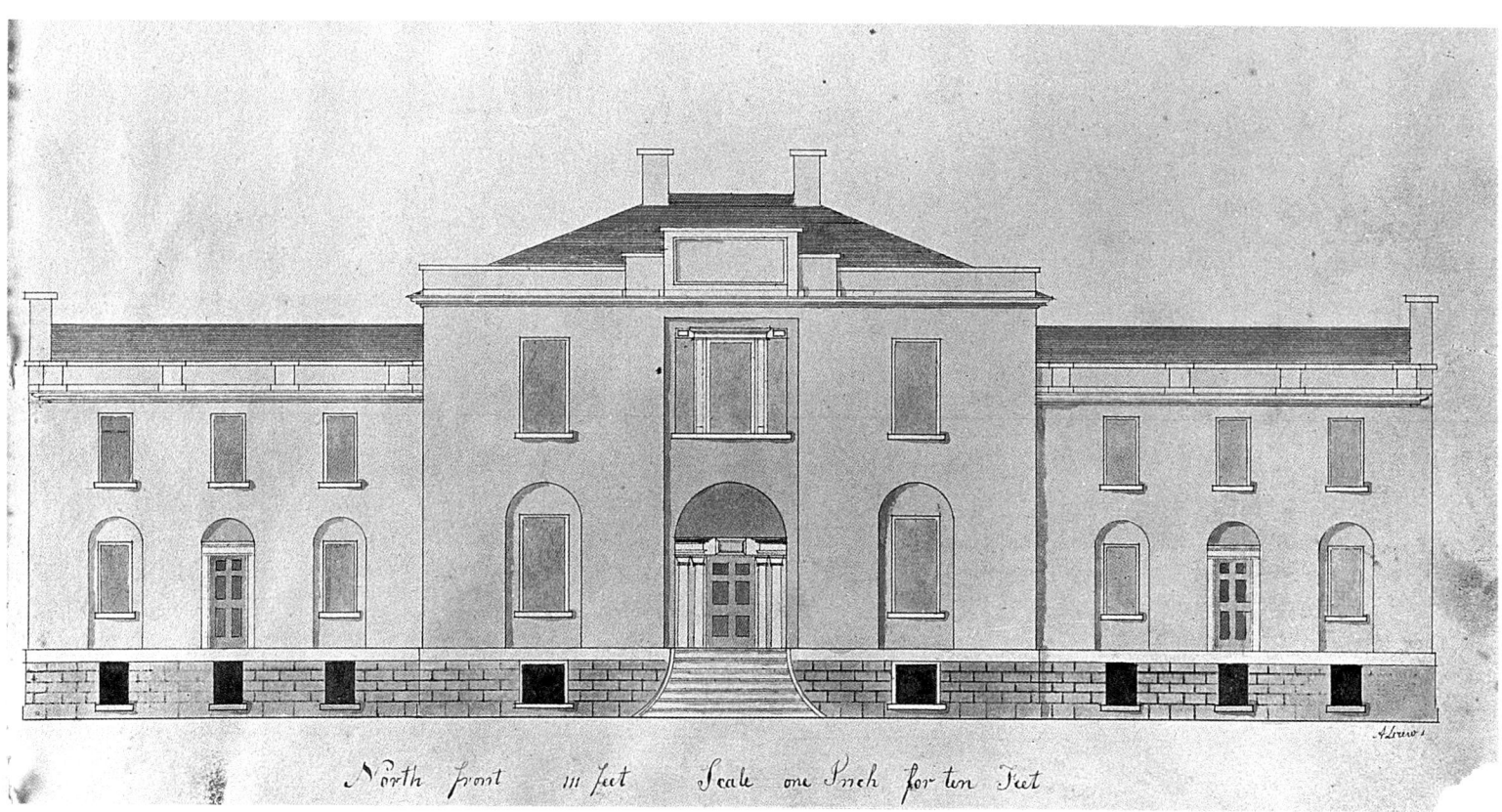
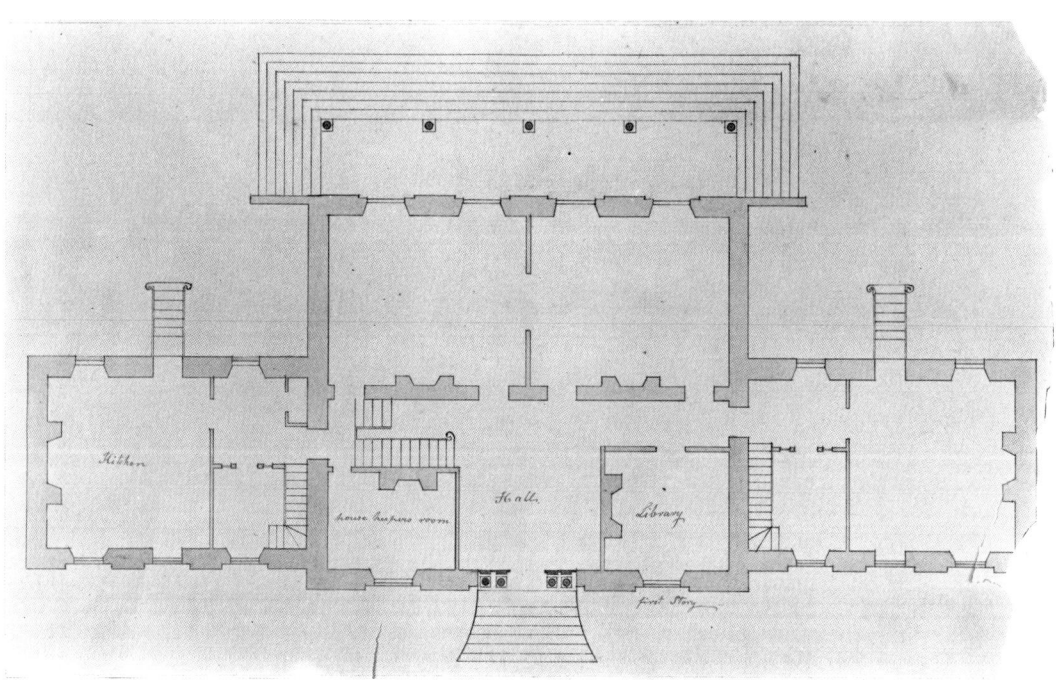

Oakland, Charles Sterett Ridgely House, Ellicott City vicinity, elevation and plan by Abraham Lerew, 1810. *Maryland Historical Society*

each adopting one of the nine ancient muses as his "consort" and each assessing fifty cents per meeting for champagne. The Tusculum was demolished in 1891.

In 1817 Robert Cary Long submitted a design for the proposed Baltimore Library Company, but it was not built. In 1824 he and Augustine Chevalier designed the Law Institute on South Street for Professor David Hoffman. The appearance of this building, the first university law school in America, is unknown. We can only hope that more can be uncovered about the later works of Robert Cary Long, Sr., since he remained active until the early 1830's.

One surviving album of drawings gives us a unique glimpse of the work of Abraham Lerew, a house carpenter active in Baltimore between 1796 and his death in 1817.[68] In 1810 Lerew made "various designs . . . in different Styles" for Charles Sterett Ridgely's house at Oakland, some five miles south of Ellicott City. The principal front presents several refined flourishes: a recessed central bay, first-story windows set under shallow relieving arches and a dignified rooftop parapet. Construction began in July, 1810, and was finished in September, 1811. The house was restored for adaptive use in 1988–89.

Benjamin Henry Latrobe (1763–1820) worked in Maryland, on and off, for nineteen years. Born in Yorkshire, the son of an Irish-born Moravian minister and an American mother, Latrobe possessed amazing artistic gifts enhanced by firsthand knowledge of current English architectural fashion and professional training. He studied engineering in London and worked for the architect Samuel Pepys Cockerell before sailing to Norfolk, Virginia, in 1796. After three disappointing years in Richmond, Latrobe moved to Philadelphia, at the time the cultural capital of the youthful United States. In 1803, President Jefferson appointed him surveyor of public buildings at Washington.

Latrobe's career was as vertiginous as it was brilliant. Frustrated by professional opportunities often too modest for his tremendous talents, Latrobe moved frequently, in search of challenging work and elusive prosperity, living at Philadelphia until 1807, Washington in 1807–12, Pittsburgh in 1813–15, again in Washington (where he supervised the reconstruction of public buildings after the British invasion during the War of 1812) in 1815–18, Baltimore in 1818–19 and New Orleans in 1819–20. Latrobe constantly struggled to establish the profession of architecture in America. He ridiculed the pretentious merchants of Baltimore, calling them "the mushrooms of fortune."[69] Of their taste, he wrote: "I believe anything that can be said of the vandalism of the Baltimoreans in the arts, provided it is exceedingly absurd and ridiculous."[70]

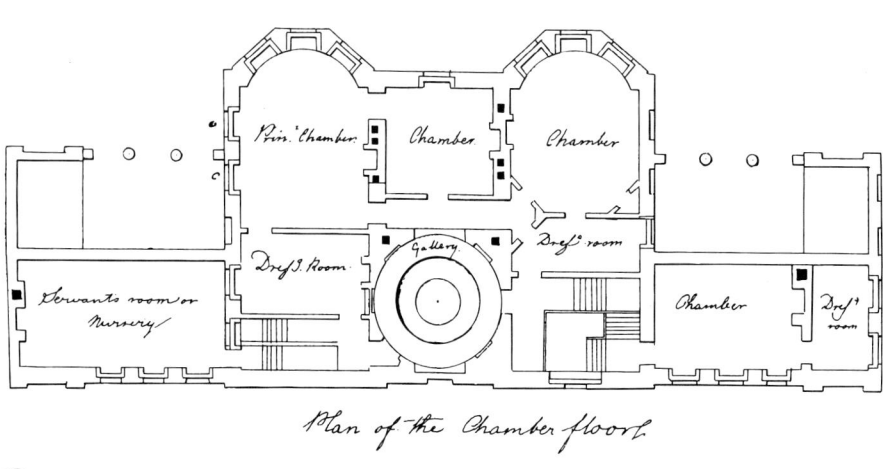

Elevations and first-story plan drawn for Henri Joseph Stier by Benjamin H. Latrobe, 1801. These have been redrawn from photographs of lost originals.

Latrobe, an amateur poet, playwright, musician and wit, struggled to defend his dignity among the merchants and planters of Maryland who looked down on architects. "As an Engineer and Architect, I am placed by the Mercantile and agricultural professions far beneath them, on the score of my being held to be a Surveyor and Mechanic."[71] Reduced to bankruptcy in late 1817, Latrobe moved to New Orleans in 1819. In a moment of profound discouragement, he wrote to his friend Maximilian Godefroy in Baltimore: "It is a great misfortune to be born and educated a *Gentleman,* at least on this side of the Atlantic."[72]

Latrobe's first documented work in Maryland was a design that was never built. In early 1801 the architect, then in Philadelphia, prepared a preliminary plan and elevation for a mansion for Henri Joseph Stier, a Belgian aristocrat who had fled to Philadelphia from the French Revolution in 1794.[73] Having decided to build a house near Bladensburg, at present-day Riverdale, Stier wrote to his son Charles in November, 1800: "We are still debating the house plan. . . . I find . . . a square building . . . less attractive than a house designed with wings. . . . We have now opted for wings, so please proceed with the plan as rapidly as possible and have it drawn up by Latrobe." In February, 1801, though brickmaking had begun, there were still no drawings from Latrobe. "I see already," Stier complained, "that Latrobe is an architect who will not suit us. . . . I imagine he is one of those men who do not finish their work. We must write him again that we cannot wait any longer." Soon, Latrobe delivered his designs. But it was too late. In March, 1801, Stier had hired William Lovering as his architect and Robert Goin Lanphier as his builder. Stier took Latrobe's belated plans back to Belgium, where they were recently discovered in a family collection.[74] Latrobe kept copies, which he later adapted for a house that was built at Richmond, Virginia, in 1804.

William Lovering, an English-born architect in Washington, built William Thornton's Octagon House in the capital and the Prince George's County Courthouse (demolished 1881) at Upper Marlboro; Robert Goin Lanphier (1765–1856) of Alexandria, Virginia, had been trained by his Irish father and worked at Washington's Mount Vernon in the 1770's. Stier proved to be a demanding client, and one hard to please. He found Lovering's first designs "rather ingenious but complicated & with unattractive façades." In the late spring, Stier complained of Lovering: "Two days ago he brought me some monstrous plans for the *grand salle* & the *salle des milieu,* and since for a couple of the windows in the wings. . . . It is so massive that the cornice looks sufficient for the roof of a large building!" In October, Stier wrote: "My head is spinning . . . with mistakes and with hurrying the work along, but finally the building is up to

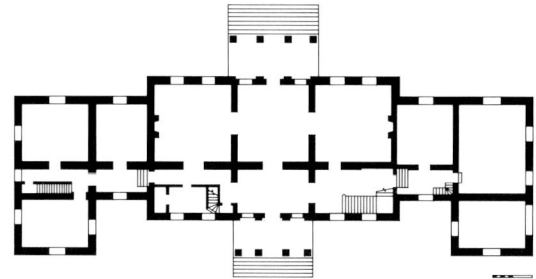

Riversdale, Stier family house, Riverdale, 1801–02. *Photograph from Library of Congress*

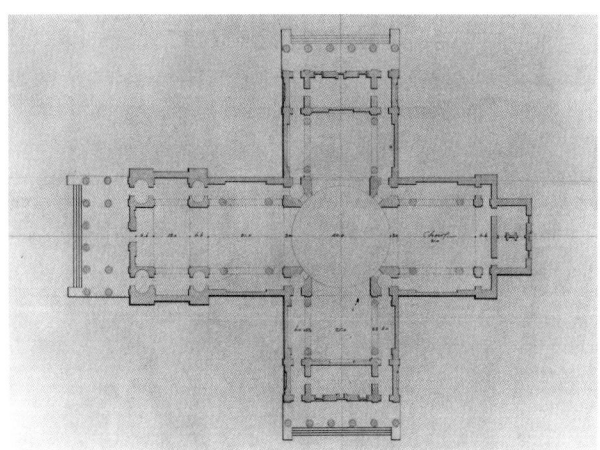

roof level and only awaits the carpenter to be covered." Madame Stier lamented: "Lovering is the biggest blockhead I have ever seen—he makes everything askew. Lanphier doesn't have enough presence of mind for so many workers." In the winter of 1802, there were more grievances from Madame Stier about Lovering, who "does nothing or does stupid things," and Lanphier, who was "a stupid fellow . . . extremely expensive and wasteful of wood." The family was able to move into the east wing in late summer of 1802. Somewhat confusingly, though it stands in the town of Riverdale, the mansion is called Riversdale. At this writing, the house is undergoing restoration; when this work is completed, the mansion will be open to the public.

In 1804 Latrobe was employed as engineer for the Chesapeake and Delaware Canal, which was to connect the Chesapeake and Delaware bays across the Delaware-Maryland peninsula. Among Latrobe's assistants were two young men who would be important in the next generation of professionally trained architects in America, William Strickland and Robert Mills. Within a year, Latrobe had supervised construction of the first five-and-one-half miles of canal, but work then ceased and was not completed until 1829. Meanwhile, Latrobe purchased a sixty-acre farm near Elkton, Maryland, which served as summer house and headquarters for the canal project. He also began visiting Baltimore in search of good stone for the U.S. Capitol and enrolled his son Henry in school at Baltimore.

In April, 1804, having been asked to comment on plans that had been submitted by another, unidentified architect for a new Roman Catholic Cathedral at Baltimore, Latrobe offered his services without charge except for out-of-pocket expenses. A year later, in April, 1805, he dispatched two designs to Archbishop John Carroll: a Gothic plan he preferred for its religious symbolism, and a Classical design that was less expensive. After the authorities expressed their approbation for the Classical submission, the architect submitted five more designs during the next three years. A third submission in July, 1805, reduced the height of the dome, widened the aisles and added an apse to the second—Roman—design. A fourth submission of December, 1805–January, 1806, further widened the building and aisles. A fifth design, in February, 1806, lengthened the building and removed the porticoes at the ends of the transepts. A sixth submission, in May, 1807, reduced the height of the Cathedral, eliminated demilune windows in the upper façade and clerestory and enlarged the western portico. A seventh set of revisions of February–March, 1808, provided a larger dome and removed four pillars from the nave. These were adopted by the authorities in October. A magnificent sectional view of this seventh design was sent to Archbishop Carroll in March, 1808.

This page and opposite, bottom: Elevations and plan for Baltimore Cathedral, the first design, by Benjamin H. Latrobe, 1804. *Archives of the Catholic Archdiocese of Baltimore*

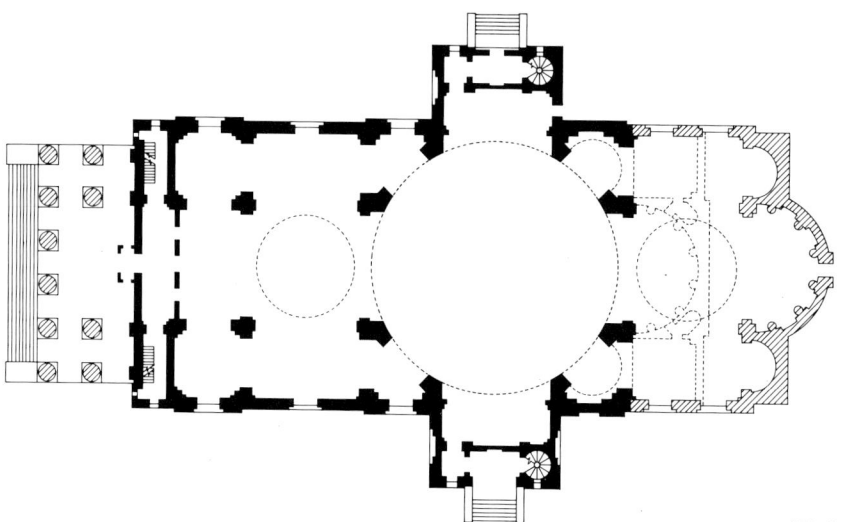

Baltimore Cathedral, perspective view by Benjamin H. Latrobe, with a plan showing additions to the Latrobe building. *Drawing from Maryland Historical Society*

Baltimore Cathedral, Cathedral Street, 1804–21, portico and domes 1862–63.
Enoch Pratt Free Library, Baltimore

Sectional view of the Baltimore Cathedral by Benjamin H. Latrobe, 1808. *Archives of the Catholic Archdiocese of Baltimore*

Baltimore Cathedral, interior view from rear.

Some of these revisions, and several threats of resignation, were the result of controversies between Latrobe and the builders, John Hillen and George Rohrback. When Latrobe heard they wanted to thicken the walls and add extra columns—partly because they had misread a sectional view of the foundations *upside down*—the architect complained to the Archbishop: "Who can think of a Cathedral and keep thick walls out of his head? . . . Having for three weeks devoted part of every day to the consideration . . . of the parts of those Walls, of all their stress and perpendicular action of the lateral pressure upon them, and of their weight and solidarity, I would rather take six inches *from* their thickness than *add* six inches!"[75] When Latrobe, on a visit to Baltimore, discovered that Hillen and Rohrback had scratched changes on his drawings, the architect exclaimed: "It is impossible for me to look at my altered and mutilated drawings and at the impractical absurdities that are scrawled over them without indignation! . . . A disgrace to vandalism!"[76]

In Washington, early in 1811, Giovanni Andrei and three assistants were carving stone capitals and columns for the Cathedral. But the trustees, having already exhausted their funds, called a halt to the work. The War of 1812 caused further delay, and the columns were stored in a log shed until construction resumed in 1817 under the direction of a new Archbishop and a new builder, John Hayden. The Cathedral was finally dedicated in 1821, a year after Latrobe had died. The north tower was built in 1837 by John F. Connolly. A cast-iron fence around the Cathedral grounds, replacing a line of wooden hitching posts, was designed by Robert Cary Long, Jr., in 1840. The foundations of the portico were built in 1841; the portico and incongruous onion-shaped domes were added by John Whitelaw in 1862–63.[77] The building was lengthened in 1879 and again in 1890.

Latrobe's Cathedral was one of the largest buildings of its time in America. The architect's skills as engineer and designer created a work of austere grandeur, at once strong and graceful, its bold geometry facilitated by sophisticated engineering and vast springing vaults, but free of superfluous ornament, which was reduced to finely chiseled lines on plain surfaces. The glory of the Cathedral is Latrobe's low central dome, sixty feet wide; actually, it is an ingenious double dome, an inner construction of brick and stone covered by an outer wooden shell, with a ten-foot gap between them, allowing indirect light—what the French called *lumière mystérieuse*—to filter softly into the interior.

Latrobe was not entirely alone in his struggles against the "vandals" of Baltimore. His friend, the French *émigré* Maximilian Godefroy, was also eager to raise architecture to a respected profession in America and also

Commercial and Farmers Bank, Baltimore, 1812–13, from John H. B. Latrobe's *Picture of Baltimore* (Baltimore, 1832). *Maryland Historical Society*

sensitive to slights inflicted upon his own dignity.[78] Godefroy (1765–c.1840) was born in Paris and studied civil engineering in the French army. In the aftermath of the French Revolution, he was arrested in 1803 for suspicious activities, imprisoned for nineteen months and then sent into exile in 1805. Coming to Baltimore by way of New York, Godefroy was hired to teach drawing at St. Mary's College, for which he designed a Gothic-style chapel in 1806 (see pages 166–172). In 1809, while continuing to teach at the college, Godefroy offered public classes in "Planning & Architecture, landscape & human figure, & fortification."[79] He and Latrobe remained close until 1815–16, when they attempted to collaborate on a Commercial Exchange, a building so ambitious it destroyed their friendship.

One of Latrobe and Godefroy's achievements—a major contribution to American architecture—was a simple but revolutionary idea: to create public architecture that was entirely different from domestic architecture. The Talbot County Courthouse at Easton, built by Cornelius West in 1793–94, looked like a Palladian country house with a cupola. Robert Cary Long, Sr.'s Union Bank of 1807 was based on a house design from an English book, and his Museum of 1813–14 looked like a town house with a big front door. But Godefroy's Commercial and Farmers Bank, built at Howard and Redwood streets in Baltimore in 1812–13, could not have been mistaken for a house. The entrance, placed daringly at the building's corner, was a gigantic apse, with a coffered half-dome flanked by sculptural figures of Mercury and Ceres, emblems of commerce and agriculture. Carved by Giuseppe Franzoni and Giovanni Andrei, this entrance was an adaptation of details for a triumphal arch Godefroy had designed to honor George Washington.

Another of Godefroy's commanding public buildings in Baltimore, the Masonic Hall on St. Paul Street, has a complicated history that begs several possibly unanswerable questions. The Hall was designed about 1812, and construction began about 1813 but was halted about 1814. By the time work resumed, in 1818–19, the original design, known through a previously published engraving, had been raised an additional story and also lengthened to accommodate city courts. Some scholars have conjectured that these changes were made by William F. Small, a young architect who was son of the Masonic Hall's builder, Jacob Small, Jr. However, the treatment of the principal façade is so unified and so French, with its powerful screen of Greek Doric columns leading into a barrel-vaulted recessed portico—and so different from William F. Small's documented works—I believe that Godefroy completed the revisions to the façade before leaving Baltimore and that Small may have added only

Masonic Hall, Baltimore, Maximilian Godefroy's original design in an 1817 engraving. *Maryland Historical Society*

Masonic Hall, Baltimore, as completed, detail from Thomas H. Poppleton's 1823 map. *Maryland Historical Society*

Masonic Hall, Baltimore, 1813–19, a 19th-century photograph. *Maryland Historical Society*

the rear extension of the building, which is more in his style. The Masonic Hall was demolished in 1895.

Another French *émigré* who came to Baltimore in the early nineteenth century was Joseph Jacques Ramée (1764–1842), who left France in 1793 and, after spending several years in Hamburg and Copenhagen, came to New York City in 1812. Two or three years later, Ramée arrived in Baltimore, where he designed a house and gardens at Calverton, the country seat of Dennis Smith on the western outskirts of the city.[80] This mansion featured a two-story portico with an arched ceiling leading to an apsidal entrance. The first and second stories each contained pairs of circular rooms, twenty-six feet in diameter, that projected as segmental bays from the side walls.[81] According to a plan Ramée published in France a few years later, the mansion may have been flanked by covered passageways leading to octagonal offices. The Calverton mansion was converted into an orphanage in 1823 and burned in 1873. Ramée sailed to Belgium in 1816 and, after a sojourn there, returned to France in 1823.

In the summer of 1815, Ramée was one of several architects, including the builder Jacob Small, Jr., and Latrobe's pupils William Strickland and Robert Mills, who submitted designs for a Commercial Exchange in Baltimore.[82] A few months later, this commission was given to Latrobe and Godefroy. Latrobe, busy in Washington, joined forces with Godefroy because he believed that a local architect would help win the competition and could supervise construction on site. Intended to occupy the entire city block bounded by Water, Gay, Second and Exchange streets, the Exchange, if completed, would have been the largest building in America at the time except for the U.S. Capitol. But Godefroy quarreled with Latrobe and withdrew from the project after a few months, cursing his former friend.[83] Latrobe later summarized his view of Godefroy's pique: "At last an opportunity offers to him to found a name upon the Design and construction of the largest Edifice in one of the most important cities in America. His most intimate friend, however, steps in and, under pretence of assisting, robs him of . . . the immortality to be acquired in building the Exchange."[84] Latrobe later stated that the general plan of the building was his own and that Godefroy had designed only the south front.

For the Exchange, Latrobe projected an immense H-shaped building with a domed exchange in the center and four wings containing custom house, post office, branch of the Bank of the United States, warehouses and offices. The Baltimore Exchange opened in June, 1820.[85] A visitor ascended twelve steps and passed beneath an apsidal entrance, through a screen of Ionic columns, into a central rotunda, which was surrounded by balconies bearing cast-iron Greek honeysuckle ornaments and which

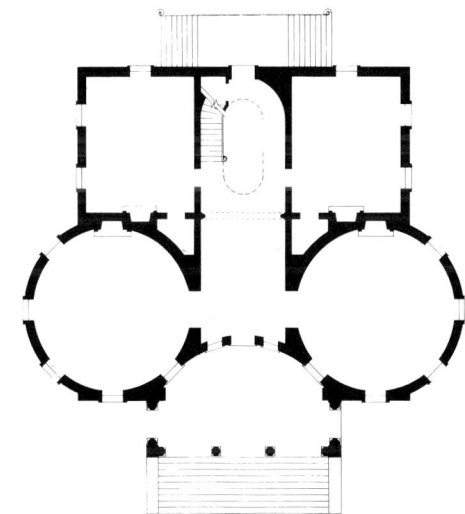

Calverton, Dennis Smith House, Baltimore, 1815, detail from a 19th-century engraving. *Engraving from Maryland Historical Society, plan by Michael Trostel and Peter Pearre*

This page and opposite: Studies for the Baltimore Exchange by Benjamin H. Latrobe, 1815. *Maryland Historical Society*

127

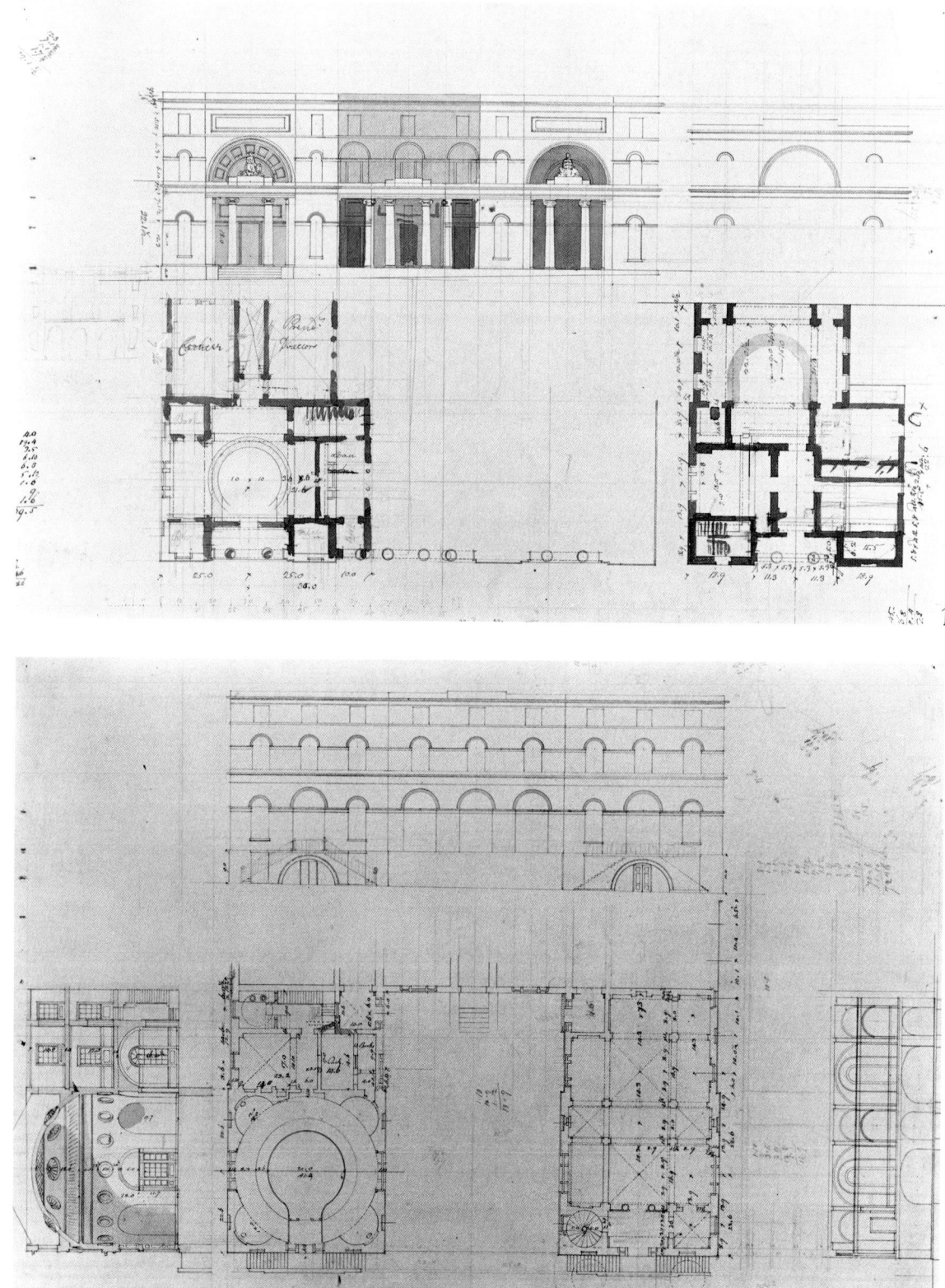

Studies of wings for the Baltimore Exchange by Benjamin H. Latrobe, 1815. *Maryland Historical Society*

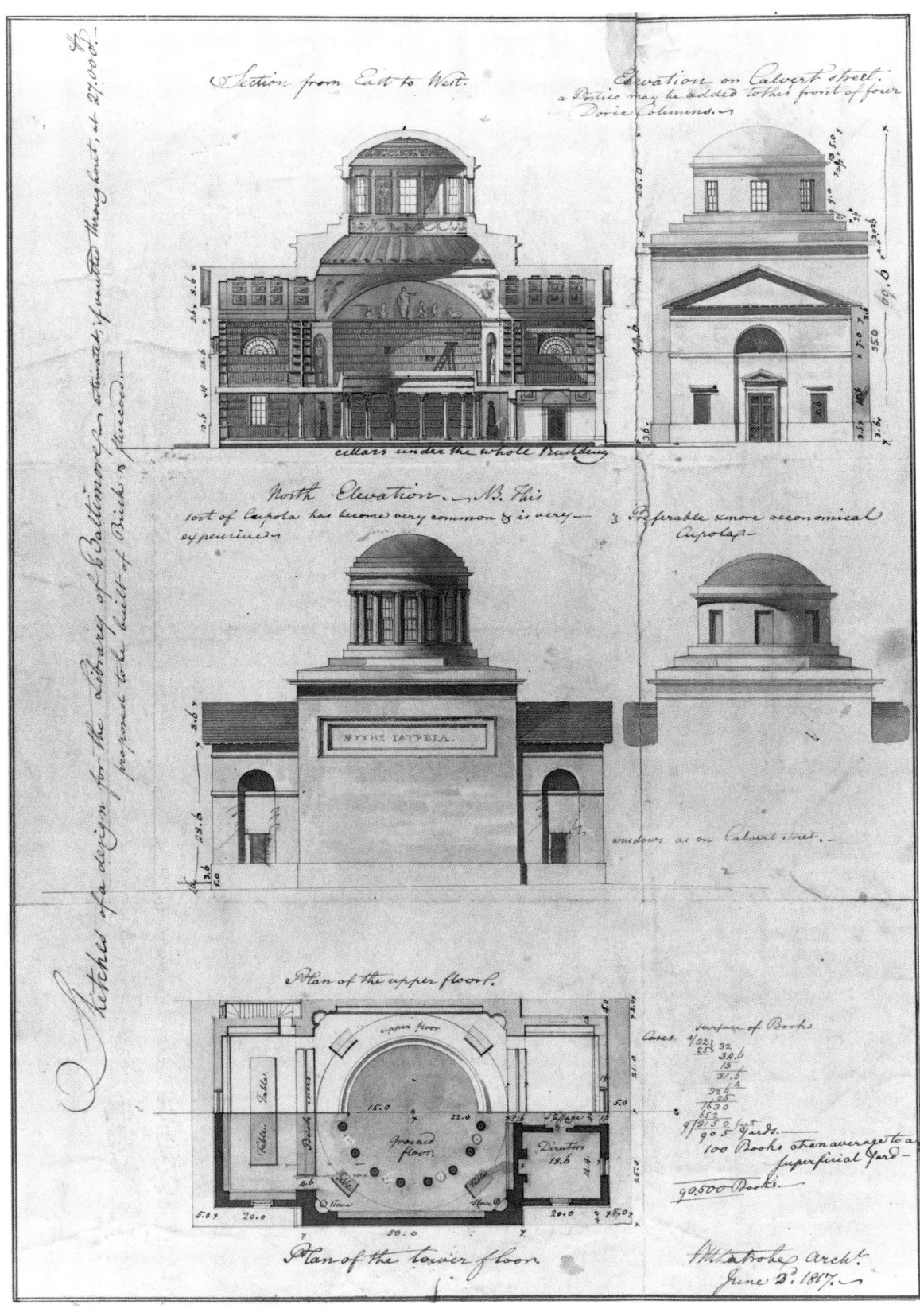

Sketches of a design for the Library of Baltimore by Benjamin H. Latrobe, 1817.
Maryland Historical Society

Courthouse, Hagerstown, 1818–22, a 19th-century drawing. *Washington County Historical Society*

rose to a dome 115 feet high. Beneath the exchange hall were twenty offices for brokers, attorneys and merchants; flanking it were rooms for reading and refreshment. The principal builders were the carpenter Jacob Small, Jr., the stonecutter William Steuart and the bricklayer Thomas Henning. The western wings were not erected until 1871—and then they were only one story high. The Exchange was demolished in 1904.

In March, 1817, Latrobe sent drawings for a new Washington County Courthouse at Hagerstown to Samuel Ringgold, a local planter who was a commissioner for the new building.[86] Ringgold, who was also a congressman, had asked the architect to produce a design similar in style to that of St. John's Episcopal Church, by Latrobe two years earlier, which Ringgold had admired in Washington, D.C. The Courthouse was built by Thomas Harbine in 1818–20 and burned in 1871.

Latrobe's other great Baltimore friend, the lawyer Robert Goodloe Harper, who was married to the younger daughter of Charles Carroll of Carrollton and thus an influential patron, offered Latrobe the commission to design a new hall for the Library Company of Baltimore in May, 1817. The dimensions of the Library, 50 by 90 feet, were determined by the site, the southeast corner of Calvert and Lexington streets.[87] Harper further specified that the Library was to be a one-story stuccoed brick structure with a dome, containing offices for the librarian and directors and a large room for books, "with a very light gallery all round to communicate with the upper shelves and suitable accommodations below for readings, writing, &c. . . . perhaps . . . circular or Elliptical." In June, 1817, Latrobe presented two designs—one Classical, which survives, and one Gothic, which has been lost. Submissions were also received from Robert Cary Long, Sr., and Robert Mills. Funds could not be raised, however, and the Library was never built.

In April, 1817, Latrobe made preliminary sketches for a Unitarian Church in Baltimore but withdrew when he heard that Godefroy was also offering drawings for the project. Godefroy's design, erected at the corner of Charles and West Franklin streets in 1817–18, was simple but sophisticated: a cube surmounted by a dome—an uncompromised expression of the architect's French neoclassicism. Attempting to create a new public architecture in an era of rapid social change, French designers in the late 18th century had stripped Roman architecture of unnecessary ornament and reduced it to pure geometric forms: the sphere, the pyramid and the cube. The visitor entered the Church through a recessed, arcaded Tuscan portico with a pedimental sculpture of the Angel of Truth. The interior was another study in abstract geometry: an eighty-foot-high dome, painted to imitate coffering, resting on four great semicircular

Perspective view of the Unitarian Church, Baltimore, by Maximilian Godefroy, 1817. *First Unitarian Church; photograph from The Peale Museum, Baltimore*

Sectional view of the interior of the Unitarian Church, Baltimore, by Maximilian Godefroy, 1817. *First Unitarian Church; photograph from The Peale Museum, Baltimore*

arches. When the interior was remodeled in 1893, the dome was covered with a barrel vault, but the original dome can still be found above the modern ceiling.

In November, 1817, Latrobe, busy rebuilding the capital after the British invasion, quarreled with Samuel Lane, commissioner of public buildings at Washington, resigned as architect of the U.S. Capitol and moved to Baltimore in January, 1818. Reduced to bankruptcy and hoping to recoup his fortunes by building a public waterworks, Latrobe moved to New Orleans in 1819, where he died of yellow fever the next year. Meanwhile, Godefroy sailed to England in 1819 and, afterward, returned to France, where he served as architect of the city of Rennes and Department of Mayenne. Godefroy died about 1840.

Despite his disappointments, Latrobe did succeed in the most important of his aspirations: laying the foundations of professional architecture in America. One of his pupils, Robert Mills, later claimed to be the first professionally trained, native-born architect in America. Born in Charleston, South Carolina, in 1781, the son of a tailor, Mills may have learned the rudiments of the profession from his older brother Thomas, who had returned from a trip to England with a copy of William Halfpenny's *Modern Builder's Assistant* and who advertised as a teacher of architectural drawing and construction in 1795. In 1800, at the age of nineteen, Mills moved to Washington to work for James Hoban, the Irish architect who was building the U.S. Capitol. There Mills met Thomas Jefferson, a lover of the fine arts and architecture, who encouraged the young Carolinian's studies by hiring him to make drawings of Monticello, offering him the use of his library and writing letters of introduction for him to other architects. In 1803 Mills began working for Latrobe, making surveys for the Chesapeake and Delaware Canal; though Mills set up an office of his own at Philadelphia in 1808, he continued to work for Latrobe, off and on, until about 1815. Perhaps Mills's personality and taste were too serious, for his designs were sometimes plodding and lacked a sufficient measure of imagination. Latrobe once commended Mills's modesty, but later he accused his former student of cribbing his designs and said the modesty was entirely justified. "Mills is a wretched designer," Latrobe wrote in 1814. "He came to me too late to acquire principles of taste. He is a copyist and fit for nothing else."[88]

Latrobe's criticism may have been too severe, but Mills's career was certainly propelled by his bourgeois claims of patriotism, piety and professionalism. In April, 1815, he moved to Baltimore to supervise construction of a Washington Monument he had designed for that city in 1813–14. This 165-foot Doric column, surmounted by a statue of Wash-

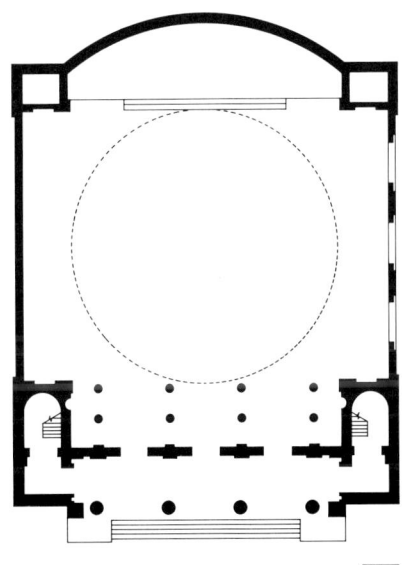

Unitarian Church, Charles and West Franklin streets, Baltimore, 1817–18. *Photograph from The Peale Museum, Baltimore*

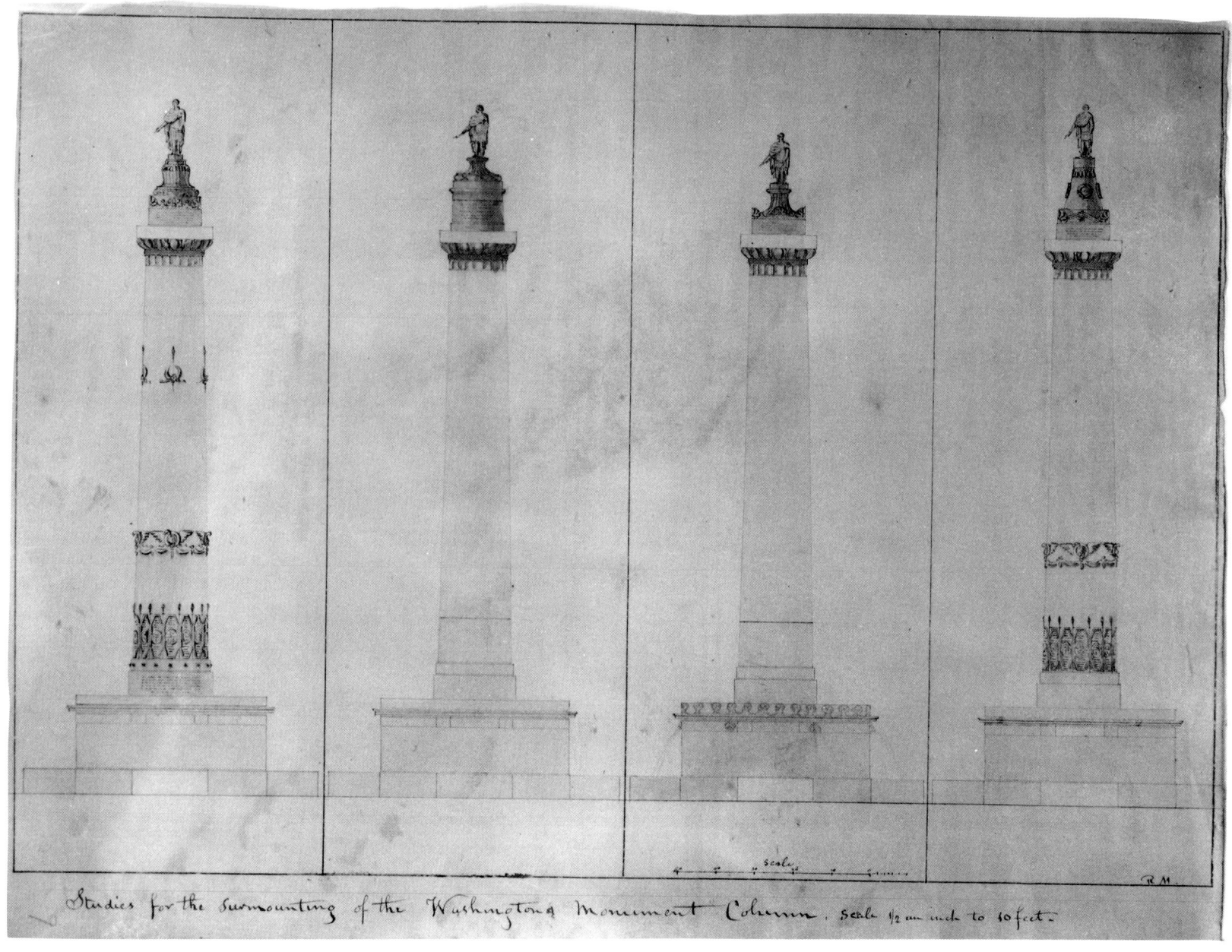

Studies for the Washington Monument, Baltimore, by Robert Mills, c. 1815.
Maryland Historical Society

ington, would not be completed until 1829. Mills's diary for 1816 gives us some idea of the variety of his activities: a house for J. Williams and a design for the Exchange in January; the First Baptist Church, a design sketch for Mr. Cox, the Bank of Baltimore, a store for the bookseller Fielding Lucas in February–March; a school and an office front door for W. B. Freeman in July; a house for the merchant Thorndike Chase, a front door for Mr. Winchester and a country house for another merchant, Benjamin Sterret, in November; a house for Colonel Buchanan in December.[89] This detailed chronology suggests how little historians really know about the vast variety of activities of the architects they survey.

The First Baptist Church, built at the corner of Lombard and Sharp streets in Baltimore, comprised a circular auditorium, shallow projecting rectangular entrance and an Ionic portico. A big round room served the needs of eloquent, soul-stirring preachers in a democratic age by placing them near the flock rather than in a distant chancel. This was Mills's fifth domed church, preceded by the Circular Congregational Church, Charleston, 1804–06, the Samson Street Baptist Church, Philadelphia, 1811–12, the First Unitarian Church, Philadelphia, 1812–13, and the Monumental Church, Richmond, 1812–17. (Of these, only the Monumental Church survives.) Mills's drawings for the First Baptist Church were made in February, 1816, advertisements for builders were published in March, digging of foundations began in April, detailed drawings occupied the architect sporadically throughout the year—those for the dome were not made until February, 1817—and the Church was dedicated in March, 1818. It was demolished in 1878.

In December, 1816, Mills completed the design for a block of twelve, three-story brick houses, Waterloo Row, on North Calvert Street, on land owned by the Baltimore Water Company, which employed him as chief engineer. The use of repetitive arches, three-part windows and a stringcourse running as an extension of the second-story window sills recall Franklin Row, designed by Mills at Philadelphia in 1809. The simple and practical plan of each house consisted of two rooms and a side hall with a rear projection for service rooms. Completed in 1819, Waterloo Row was demolished in 1967. A passage and two parlors assembled from parts of the Row are exhibited at the Baltimore Museum of Art.

In July, 1817, Robert Mills dispatched drawings of a house for the Potts family, cousins of Mills's wife, at Frederick, Maryland. The Potts house was built by a family of local builders, Andrew McCleery (1777–1853), his brother Henry and son Robert. Robert designed an impressive Exchange, which was to be built at Frederick in 1815, with a sixty-foot-high rotunda surrounded by eight large columns.[90] The McCleerys also

One house in Waterloo Row, Baltimore, 1816–19, before its demolition in 1867. *Library of Congress*

First Baptist Church, Baltimore, 1816–18, before its demolition in 1878. *Maryland Historical Society*

built All Saints Episcopal Church, with a façade enriched by two Palladian windows, semicircular relieving arches on the first story, Doric pilasters on the second story and a large lunette window in the front-facing gable. This building now serves as a parish hall for All Saints Church.

In July, 1817, Mills submitted a design for the Library Company of Baltimore that was to be built at the corner of Monument Square. Mills described his plan to John Hoffman, a Baltimore merchant who was a member of the building committee: "The Library occupies the Rotunda in the Center which rises above the main walls of the building and is crowned with a Dome. To furnish wall space for the book shelves, all the windows may be kept above the cases. . . . The communication with the galleries is made easy by small stair cases in the angles. The access to the principal floor from the street is public & commodious by stair cases right & left from an open Colonnade fronting on Church St. Adjoining the Library to the West is the Reading Room 47×20. . . . East of the Library are three Rooms appropriated to objects connected with natural history, botany, minerology, painting, &c. besides providing the requisite apartments for the offices of the institution. An open Court is left to the South of the Rotunda for light & air & other conveniences."[91] The Library was never built, but Mills's plans for the first and second stories have survived.

Mills provided designs for two other public buildings in Baltimore. St. John's Episcopal Church, Liberty Street, was built in 1817 and burned in 1904. The House of Industry, a residential training school for the city's unemployed, to be built on the east side of the Jones Falls, was designed in 1818.[92] In December, 1820, Mills returned to Charleston and worked in South Carolina, principally on courthouses, until 1829, when he returned to Baltimore. After a year, Mills moved to Washington, designing several custom houses for the Treasury Department. Appointed Architect of Public Buildings by President Jackson in 1836, Mills designed and supervised construction of several important buildings, including his most famous work, the Washington Monument, 1845–52. Retiring from office in 1851, Mills died in 1855.

In December, 1817, when Benjamin Latrobe declared bankruptcy, he sent his pupil, twenty-one-year-old William F. Small, to save the personal possessions that would not have to be sold to satisfy his creditors. William F. Small (1798–1832) was the grandson of Jacob Small, Sr., builder of the 1784–85 Otterbein Church, and son of another Baltimore builder, Jacob Small, Jr., one of the contractors of the Baltimore Exchange. William began working for Latrobe at Washington in March, 1817, moved to Baltimore with Latrobe in early 1818 and continued to

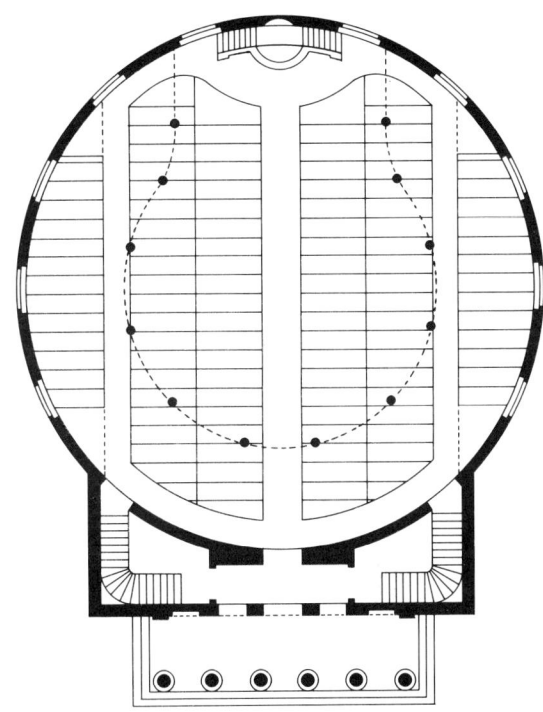

Plan of First Baptist Church.

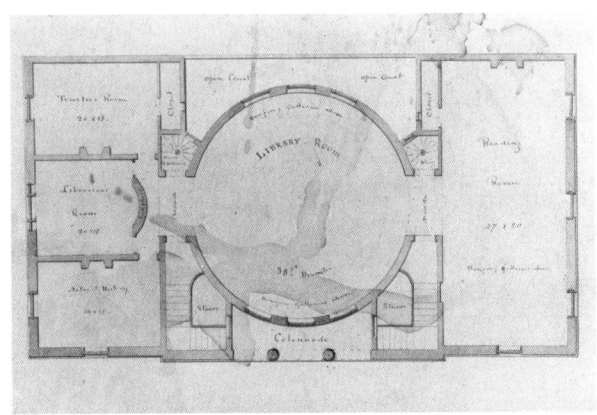

A proposed plan for the Library Company of Baltimore, by Robert Mills, 1817. *Maryland Historical Society*

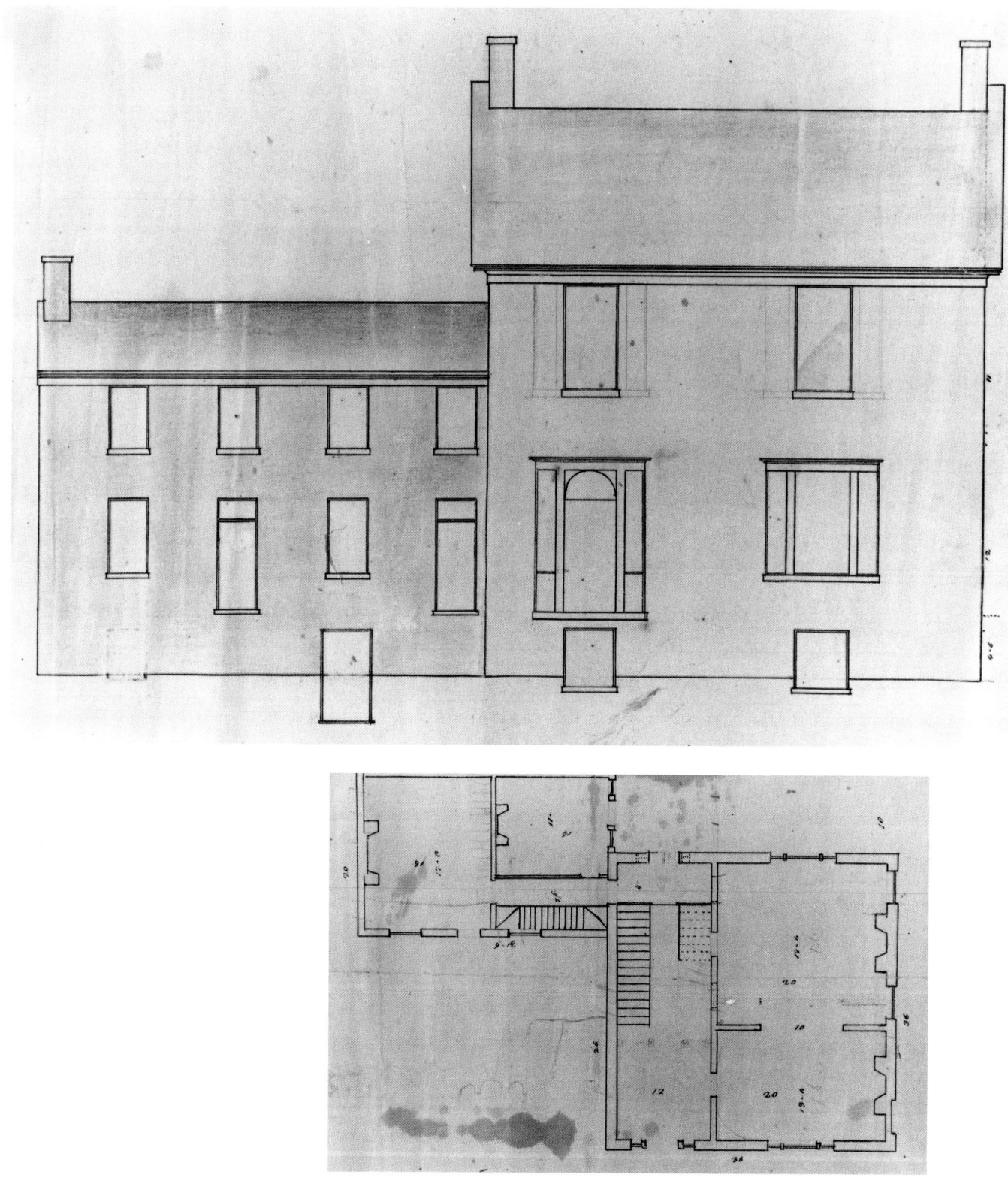

Elevation and plan of Potts family house, Frederick, 1817, by Robert Mills. *The Winterthur Library, Joseph Downs Collection of Manuscripts and Printed Ephemera, 82x363.7, 82x363.4*

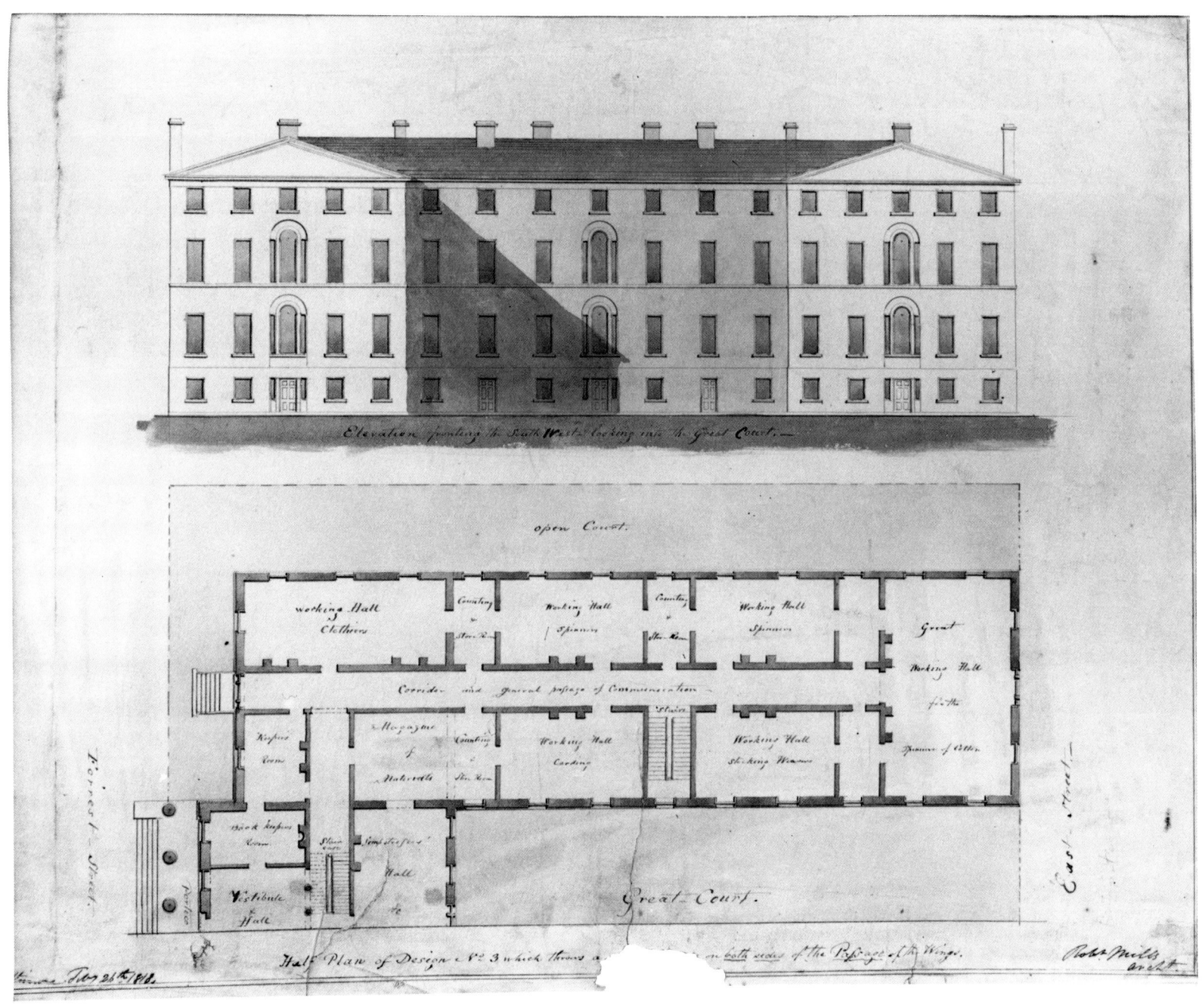

"Half Plan of Design No. 3" for the Baltimore House of Industry, by Robert Mills, 1818. *The Historical Society of Pennsylvania*

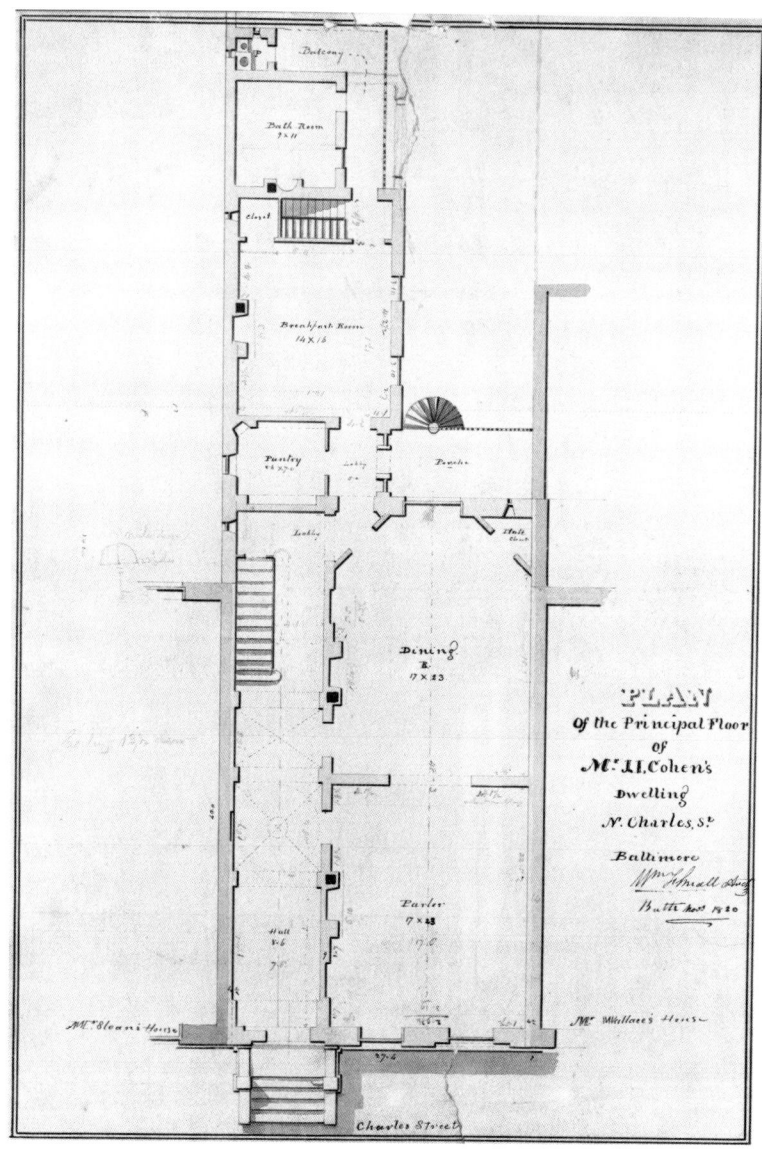

Elevation and first-story plan of Joshua Cohen House, Baltimore, by William F. Small, 1826. *Maryland Historical Society*

work at the Cathedral and Exchange after Latrobe moved to New Orleans in 1819.[93] Small later made drawings for an office of the Bank of the United States and for a hotel intended for wings of the Exchange. By 1824, when he designed a gigantic triumphal arch to welcome Lafayette to Baltimore, William Small was already well established as "a young citizen of fine talent."[94]

Three of Small's public buildings in Baltimore, the 1824–26 Athenaeum, built at a corner of St. Paul and Lexington streets for a subscription library, the 1825–26 City Hotel on Monument Street and the 1826–30 Seamen's Bethel on Fell's Point, typify the architect's style of work.[95] These buildings feature a general simplification of details, walls broken into slightly projecting and receding planes, frequent use of three-part windows set beneath shallow relieving arches, and plaster panels set into the walls between the first- and second-story windows. The Athenaeum burned in 1835, the City Hotel was remodeled in 1856 and demolished in 1889, and the Seamen's Bethel has also been demolished. Similar features appear in houses on North Charles Street by Small: two houses for the banker brothers Benjamin and Joshua Cohen, 1827–28 and 1830–34,[96] and the Catholic Archbishop's Residence, 1829. Benjamin Cohen's house has been demolished; the Joshua Cohen House was remodeled in the 1930's; and a third story, bay windows and wings were added to the Archbishop's Residence in 1865–66.

Other works designed by William Small include unexecuted 1828 plans for a warehouse for the Baltimore Exchange, two houses for Dr. Ashton Alexander on Monument Square in the same year, the 1829–30 Maryland Penitentiary, a five-story structure with 320 cells,[97] the 1831 St. Mary's County Courthouse at Leonardtown[98] (burned about 1910), an 1831 design for St. Mary's College outside Ellicott City (the building finally completed in 1848 may not have been Small's design) and an unexecuted 1833 design for a hotel in the Baltimore Exchange. Small's final works of the early 1830's venture into the Greek Revival.

Seamen's Bethel, Baltimore, watercolor by John H. B. Latrobe. *Enoch Pratt Free Library, Baltimore, Maryland Historical Society*

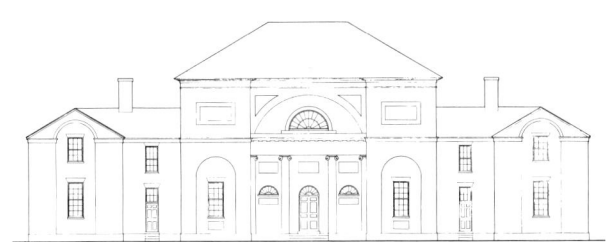

St. Mary's Courthouse, Leonardtown, 1831. *Elevation by Michael Trostel and Peter Pearre*

III. *The Greek Revival*

St. Andrews Church, Baltimore, c. 1840, a 19th-century view. *Maryland Historical Society*

Despite its association with the young nation's democratic ideals and with the great white columns of the Old South, the Greek Revival was neither particularly American nor particularly Southern. The road from Athens to Baltimore traveled by way of Paris, Berlin, London, Philadelphia and New York. It was an English publication, James Stuart and Nicholas Revett's *Antiquities of Athens,* the first three volumes of which appeared in 1762–94, that became the architectural bible for 19th-century Anglo-American builders because it illustrated the principal ancient monuments that became icons of the Grecian style: the 5th-century Ionic Temple on the Ilissus, the 4th-century Corinthian Monument of Lysicrates and the 1st-century Tower of the Winds. The English-born Benjamin Latrobe, who worked in Baltimore intermittently between 1805 and 1820, described himself as "a bigoted Greek." The little spring house he designed for Oaklands, the country estate of his friend, the lawyer Robert Goodloe Harper, was described by a contemporary in 1827 as "taken from the little temple on the Ilissus given by Stuart." Robert Cary Long, Jr.'s 1839 design for a new Baltimore city hall featured a tall tower supporting a circular temple copied from the Monument of Lysicrates—"that choice relic of Grecian antiquity"—and porticoes copied from the Tower of the Winds.[1] At least two copies of Stuart and Revett's great work were available in Baltimore, one at the Baltimore Library Company and another in the extensive personal library of the amateur architect William Howard.

The Greek Revival swept across the Western world at the end of the 18th century, as far east as St. Petersburg in Russia and as far west as Philadelphia in young America, but it did not really catch hold until 1820, and it enjoyed greatest popularity in the 1830's and 1840's. In addition to the little temple Latrobe designed for Robert Harper, other early efforts at Grecian architecture in Maryland included a preliminary design for Baltimore's Washington Monument by Maximilian Godefroy, a Doric temple in the form of a rotunda; Robert Mills's 1814 design for the Washington Monument, a gigantic Doric column, correctly Greek in its

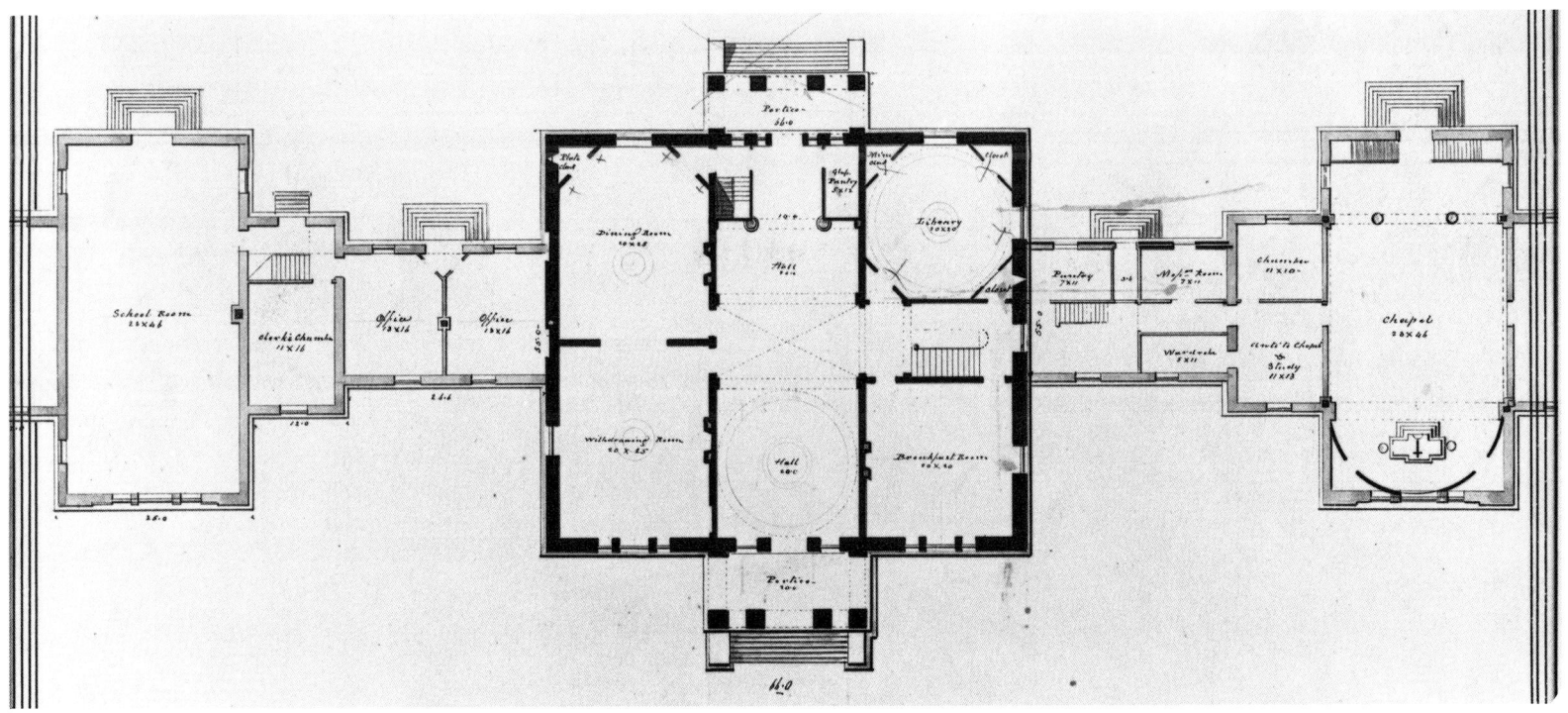

Elevation and plan of Folly Quarter, John McTavish House, Howard County, by William F. Small, 1831. *Maryland Historical Society*

Folly Quarter, John McTavish House, Howard County, 1831–32.

robust proportions—though unfluted; Robert Cary Long, Sr.'s St. Paul's Church of 1817, with its Greek Doric portico and interior Greek Doric columns; and the interior of the 1831 Odd Fellows Hall, Baltimore, designed by John F. Hose.[2]

William F. Small, who had worked for Latrobe for three years in Washington and Baltimore during 1818–20 before establishing his own office, experimented with Greek designs in the last few years of his career, before his death at the age of thirty-four in June, 1832. Drawings have survived for the house Small designed in November, 1831, for Folly Quarter, the plantation home of Emily Caton, granddaughter of Charles Carroll of Carrollton, and her husband, John McTavish, a twenty-eight-year-old Scottish-born merchant who came to Maryland by way of Canada. Small's drawings present a two-story house with a tall gable roof, lantern and projecting center pavilion. In the elevation drawing, the one-story Greek portico—similar to one Small added in 1830 to Rembrandt Peale's Museum when it was converted into Baltimore's city hall—seems no more important than the three-part windows and less important than the large Palladian windows in flanking wings, both favored by Federal-era builders. As completed in 1832, the house at Folly Quarter seems more strongly Greek than Small's drawings. The wings and hyphens, which would have created a five-part plan so typical of the Federal era, were never erected (the drawings indicate they were intended to be additions). The builder eliminated the graceful arches over the first-story windows and replaced them with severe rectangular panels between the first and second-story windows. The choice of local Patapsco granite for the building material, and the elevated site, which diminishes the visibility of the gable roof, further emphasize the heavy monumentality of the mansion. Folly Quarter is now owned by a Catholic order.

In 1829 Baltimore established its first public schools, and in the early 1830's William Small was employed to design the first school buildings. Small's father was then mayor of the city, and Joshua Cohen, for whom Small designed a house in 1830, was secretary of the school building committee. Small was the documented designer of Male School Number Three, Aisquith Street, which opened for three hundred students in 1831, and Male School Number One, Green and Fayette streets, which opened for four hundred students in 1832.[3] Both of these were templelike buildings with long gable roofs extending to form Doric porticoes and one large classroom for the entire school on the main floor. Small may also have provided the design for yet another Male and Female School, Broad and Bank streets, which opened in 1834, two years after the architect's death.

Male School Number Three, Baltimore, 1831, and Male School Number One, Baltimore, 1832, from John H. B. Latrobe's *Picture of Baltimore* (Baltimore, 1832). *Maryland Historical Society*

Though these public schools have been destroyed, a more interesting academic hall designed by Small, in association with the amateur architect William Howard, survives—and gloriously so, for it is one of the most academically correct Greek Revival buildings of Maryland. The McKim Free School was built at 1120 East Baltimore Street in 1832–33 for a family of Quaker merchants who wished to educate poor children.[4] William Howard (1793–1834) was a physician and skilled amateur architect who also practiced as a civil engineer.[5] He had the means to indulge his tastes for foreign travel—he scaled Mont Blanc in Switzerland in 1819 and privately published a book describing that adventure—and to accumulate a large library. Indeed, his was the largest recorded collection of architecture books in Maryland and reflects the extraordinary erudition of its owner.[6] The collection, well representing the highways and byways of Western architectural writing, included Peter Nicholson's *Principles of Architecture, Mechanical Exercises,* and *Practical Builder* (London, 1795–98, 1812, and 1823–25), Jean N. L. Durand's *Précis des Leçons d'Architecture* (Paris, 1802–05), Johann Karl Krafft's *Recueil d'Architecture Civile* (Paris, 1812), the Society of the Dilettanti's *Antiquities of Ionia* (London, 1797–1821), George Richardson's *The New Vitruvius Britannicus* (London, 1802–08), Colin Campbell's *Vitruvius Britannicus* (London, 1715–71), Asher Benjamin's *Practical House Carpenter* (Boston, 1830), Minard Lafever's *Modern Builder's Guide* (New York, 1833), Roland Fréart de Chambray's *Parallèle de l'Architecture* (Paris, 1650), James Stuart and Nicholas Revett's *Antiquities of Athens* (London, 1762–1830), Robert Wood's *Ruins of Balbec* (London, 1757), Robert Chambers's *Treatise on the Decorative Part of Civil Architecture* (London, 1725), John Loudon's *Encyclopedia of Cottage, Farm and Villa Architecture* (London, 1833), John Britton and Augustus Pugin's *Illustrations of Public Buildings in London* (London, 1825–28), John Cruden's *Convenient and Ornamental Architecture* (London, 1767), an edition of Vitruvius, the first-century B.C. Roman architect, and volumes of "[John] Smeaton on Civil Engineering," "Architecture and Antiquities," "Architectural Miscellanies," an "Engineer's *Vade Mecum*" and French "*Traités.*"

William Howard seems to have been responsible for dragging William Small beyond the old-fashioned Federal taste, which epitomized most of his works, for two other Baltimore buildings with prostyle Greek porticoes are also attributed to their collaboration—the First English Lutheran Church, Lexington Street, 1825–26 (burned 1873), and William Howard's own mansion, North Charles and Franklin streets, 1828–29 (demolished 1910).

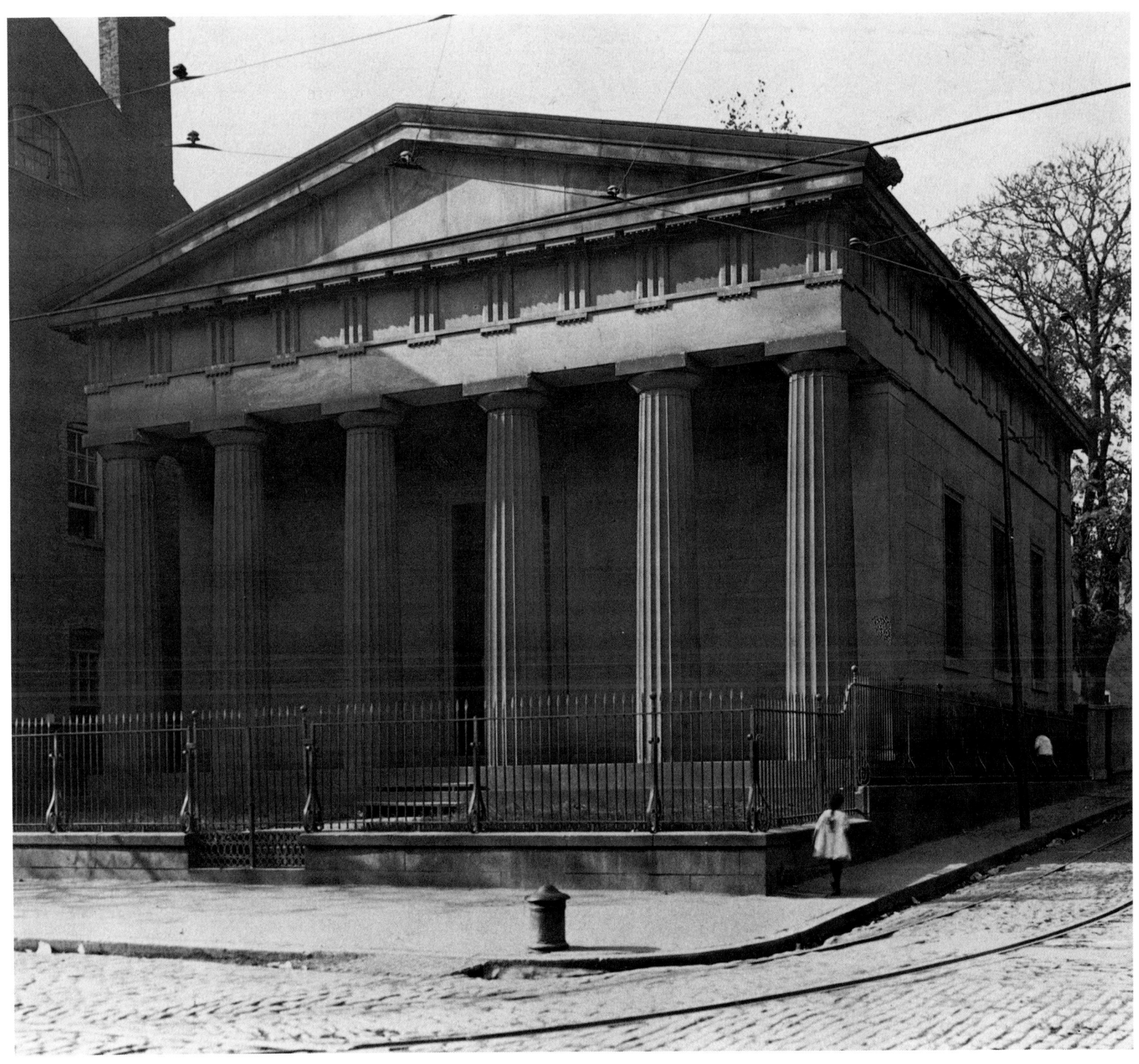

McKim Free School, 1120 East Baltimore Street, Baltimore, 1832–33, a 19th-century photograph. *Maryland Historical Society*

Design for a Baltimore storefront by Alexander J. Davis, 1833. *Avery Architecture and Fine Arts Library, Columbia University*

In January, 1833, Alexander Jackson Davis and Ithiel Town, leaving their partner James Dakin in charge of their New York office, came to Baltimore, where they planned to open a new office to serve clients in Baltimore and nearby Washington while supervising construction of a Gothic mansion on an estate north of town (see pages 172–175).[7] Born in New York in 1803, Davis, the son of a religious publisher, worked as a printer and studied architectural drawing before becoming the partner of Ithiel Town, the Connecticut-born bridge builder and Greek Revival architect, in 1829, when Davis was only twenty-six. The Town and Davis partnership lasted until 1835 and was resumed briefly in 1842–43. Upon his arrival in Baltimore in 1833, Davis hired two "very pleasant" rooms in the Athenaeum, arranged to board next door with Mrs. Frances Messersmith[8] and placed advertisements in the local newspapers: "Ithiel Town and Alex J. Davis, of the firm of Town, Davis & Dakin, Architects, Clinton Hall, New York, have taken rooms in the upper part of the Baltimore Athenaeum and intend such a division of their time between the cities of New York, Baltimore and Washington, as may best accommodate their professional business in each city."[9] In an era of booming railroad construction, it was not surprising that the architects mentioned in particular their special skill and experience as bridge engineers.

Davis designed an eye-catching folly—a small Doric "Temple of Ceres" honoring the ancient goddess of the harvest—for Robert Gilmor's country estate, Glen Ellen, north of Baltimore. The architect also made studies of a mansion for Gilmor's uncle, a Baltimore art collector also named Robert Gilmor. It was to be a stuccoed mansion with an elevated basement serving as podium for a monumental Corinthian portico.[10] The plan features a domed stair and a circular library. Davis also sketched a three-story hotel, which was to be built in one wing of Latrobe's incomplete Exchange, a "new front" for Fielding Lucas's bookstore on Baltimore Street and a façade—"plain, with a large single door"—for a bank.[11]

In April, Davis journeyed to Annapolis, at the request of the principal of St. John's College, Hector Humphries, to inspect the site for a new hall that was to be built at the College.[12] After operating for some thirty years, St. John's was still struggling, with only seventy students, five teachers and one substantial building.[13] Like many Yankee schoolteachers who came to the South, the Yale-educated Humphries, who had come to Maryland from Connecticut in 1831, was eager to improve the cultural landscape beyond the Mason-Dixon Line. After conferring with the trustees, Davis prepared the design for a new College hall on April 23: a two-story, temple-like building with a recessed Ionic portico and antae, or

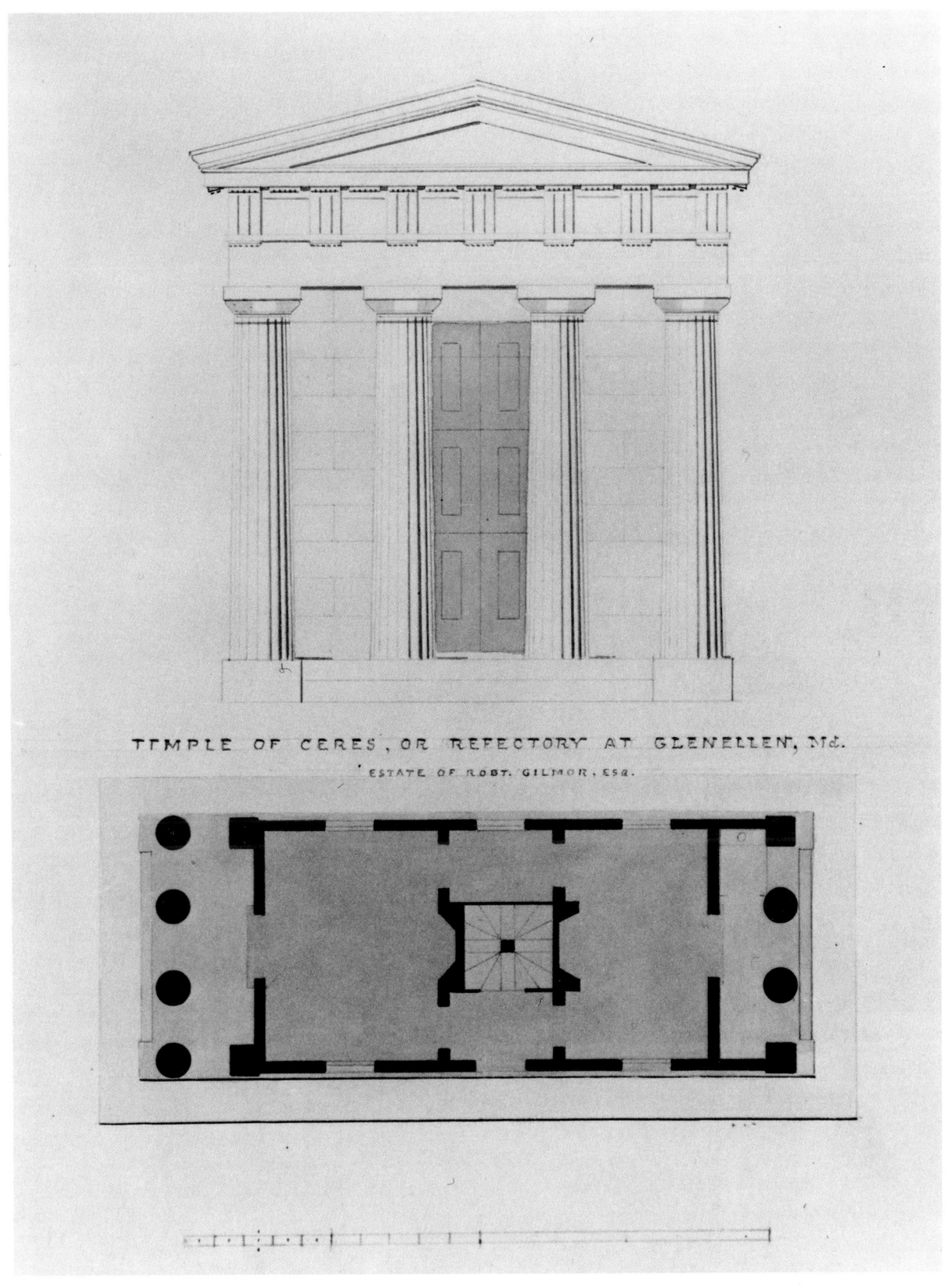

Temple of Ceres, design for a folly at Robert Gilmor's Glen Ellen, by Alexander J. Davis, 1833. *Avery Architecture and Fine Arts Library, Columbia University*

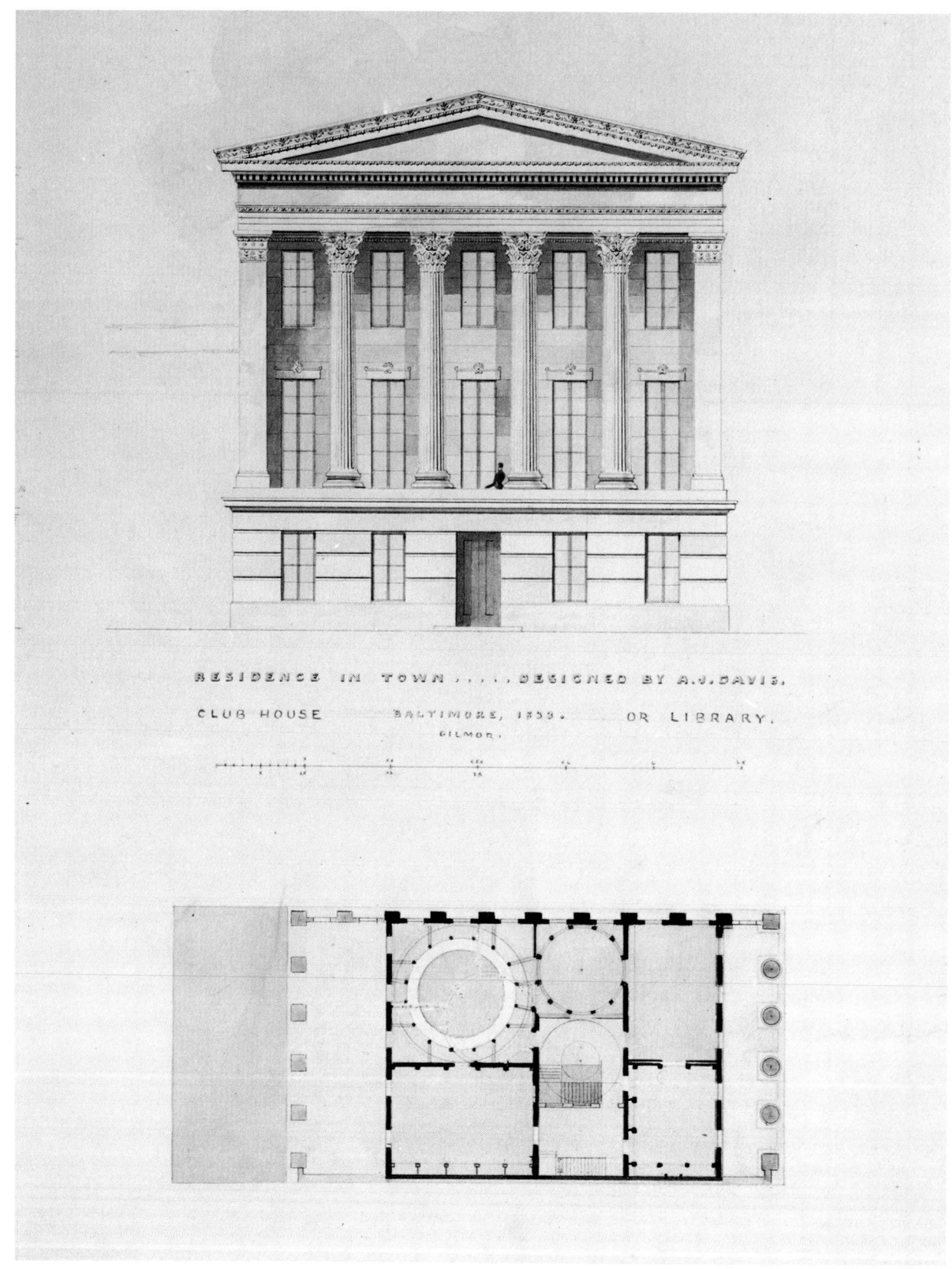

Design for a town house, Baltimore, for Robert Gilmor, by Alexander J. Davis, 1833. The architect later proposed redeveloping this design for a club or library. *The Metropolitan Museum of Art, Harris Brisbane Dick Fund, 1924. [24.66.1406(32)]*

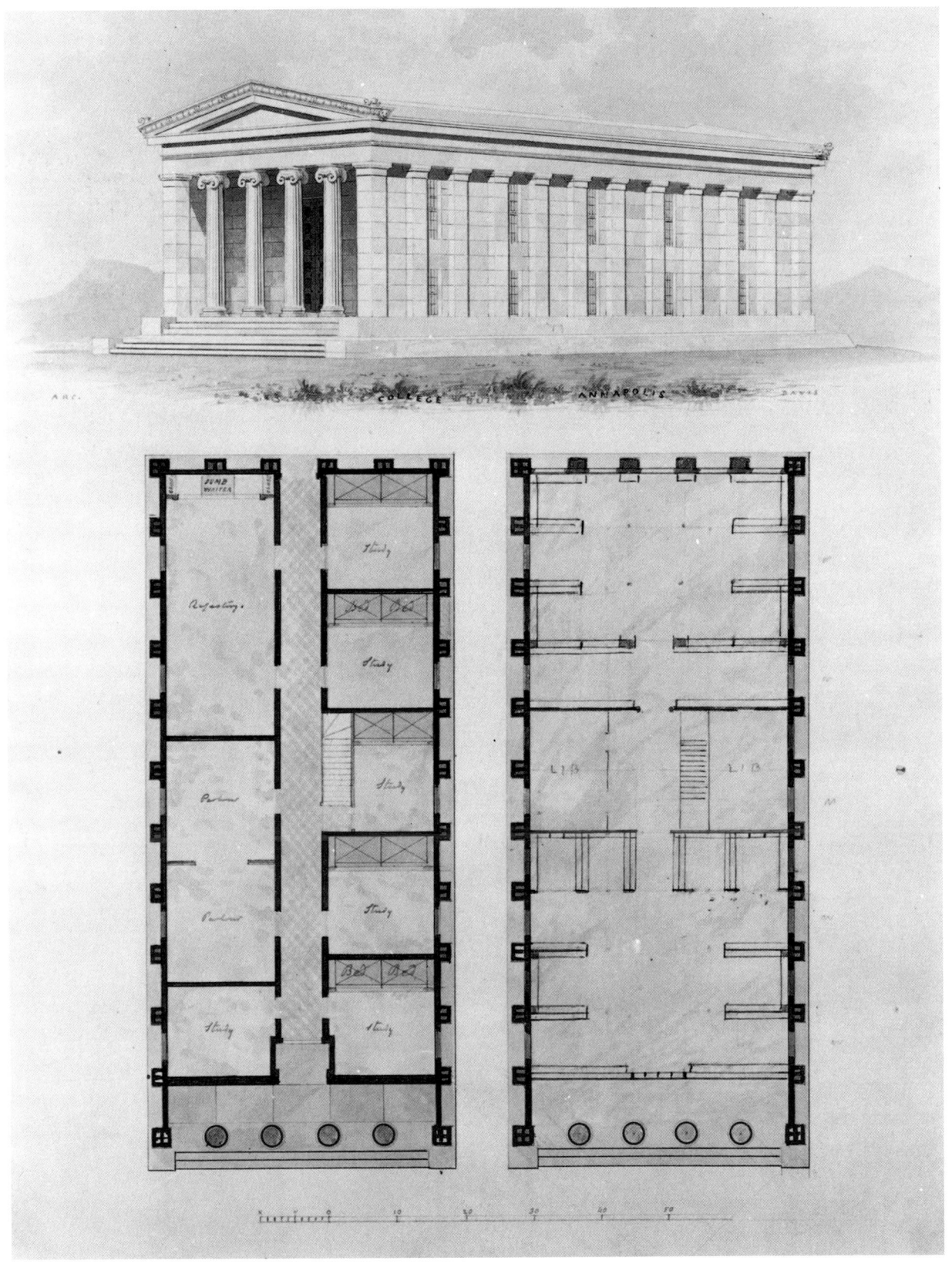

Design for a new hall at St. John's College, Annapolis, by Alexander J. Davis, 1833. *The Metropolitan Museum of Art, Harris Brisbane Dick Fund, 1924.* (24.66.1132)

square pillars, along the side and rear walls. The first story would provide two parlors, dining room and several study-bedrooms for faculty members; the second story would provide two library rooms divided by offices for the librarian. On May 11, the building committee approved this design, and three days later advertisements in Baltimore newspapers began inviting builders to inspect the "Drawings and minute specification of the plan . . . prepared by Messrs. Town and Davis."[14] But Humphries feared that local builders might not be able to do the design justice or that the costs would be too great.[15] The latter probably proved to be true, and a financial panic in 1834 must have stunned the cautious trustees. Davis, discouraged by the slack building business in Baltimore, closed his office and returned to New York in late May, 1833.

It was not until two years later, in 1835, that St. John's College finally began construction of its new hall—and then the trustees discarded Davis's design in favor of a new one by another architect, Robert Cary Long, Jr. (1810–1849), the son of the veteran Baltimore builder Robert Cary Long, Sr., with whom he shared an office at the corner of Fayette and St. Paul streets between at least July, 1832, and his father's retirement at the end of 1833.[16] Long, Jr., may have received some of his first training in the New York office of Martin Thompson, an early partner of Ithiel Town and designer of two Manhattan landmarks, the 1822–23 Second Bank of the United States and the 1827 Merchants Exchange. Another reason that Alexander Davis closed his Baltimore office may have been his realization that he and Town were facing strong competition from Long, Jr., who combined unusual intellectual ambition and a knack for both Classical and Romantic designs with New York training and the further advantage of family reputation and excellent local social connections.

Though he may have helped his father on other projects without credit, Long, Jr.'s earliest documented work was the Patapsco Female Institute, a two-story T-shaped building with a Doric portico, now in ruins, on top of a hill overlooking Ellicott City, west of Baltimore.[17] The town was named for the family of Pennsylvania mill owners who came to the Patapsco Valley of Maryland in the 1760's.[18] In February and April, 1834, Long, Jr., advertised for stone masons and carpenters to build the Institute, a school for girls sponsored principally by the Ellicott and Dorsey families of Howard County.[19] Local granite for the walls was supplied by a twenty-three-year-old stonemason named Charles Timanus. While the Institute was under construction in Ellicott City, Long, Jr., was also erecting a new three-story commercial building at the corner of St. Paul and Lexington streets in Baltimore, site of the Athenaeum that had burned in

Patapsco Female Institute, Ellicott City, 1834, detail from Simon J. Martinet's 1860 map of Howard County. *Maryland Historical Society*

1835, and improvements to the old Assembly Rooms built by his father some thirty-five years earlier.[20]

In February, 1835, the Baltimore Courthouse, another building of the Federal era, was damaged by fire, and the authorities appointed a committee to repair the Courthouse and build a new fireproof Record Office, which was to contain courtrooms, clerk's office and record storage.[21] Long, Jr., submitted at least two designs for the new building, but the cautious authorities passed over an exciting Egyptian design (see pages 176–177) in favor of an academic Grecian alternative that Long had also prepared. The young architect may not have enjoyed the unlimited confidence of the building committee, for at the end of March, 1835, Solomon Etting, the retired merchant who was its chairman, wrote to Robert Mills in Washington and William Strickland in Philadelphia, asking them to comment on the fireproof vaulting proposed by Long. Mills sent a description of his own fireproof Public Record Office in Charleston, with two drawings of it, and offered to prepare a new design for the front of the Record Office in Baltimore.[22] Strickland sent a drawing of suggestions for vaulting in the orphans' court. In mid-April, Long, Jr., was sent to Philadelphia to confer with Strickland, whom he described as "an old friend of my father," and with John Haviland and Thomas U. Walter, who showed him the arched stonework of Girard College.[23] Long, Jr., later prepared revisions "to meet Mr. Strickland's recommendations," and T. U. Walter was eventually paid $50 for unspecified services.[24] In December, 1835, advertisements solicited builders' bids, and the cornerstone was laid at Lexington and St. Paul streets in January.[25] Granite for the walls was supplied by Charles Timanus, contractor for the stonework at the Patapsco Female Institute. The Record Office was completed in 1840 and demolished in 1895.[26]

The civic authorities must have been impressed by their architect's skill and diligence, for in the fall of 1839 the commissioners adopted Long, Jr.'s design for a new City Hall, a mammoth L-shaped building that was to be built on a block between Hanover and Camden streets. Four Corinthian porticoes were to be based on the Tower of the Winds, and a 185-foot-tall tower would feature a town clock, observation gallery and circular temple modeled on "that choice relic of Grecian antiquity, the Choragic Monument of Lysicrates."[27] The ground story would be used as a public market, with fountains for washing down the floors at the end of each day; the upper stories would contain a grand central rotunda, thirty feet in diameter and forty-two feet high, flanked by a "town hall," 163 feet long, on one side and by an armory and drill room for the city's military companies on the other side. Long, Jr.'s drawings for this Greek be-

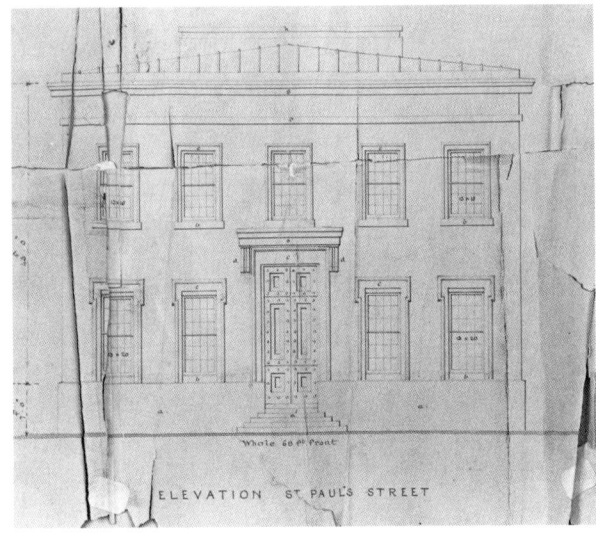

Design for the Record Office, Baltimore, by Robert C. Long, Jr., 1835. *Baltimore City Archives*

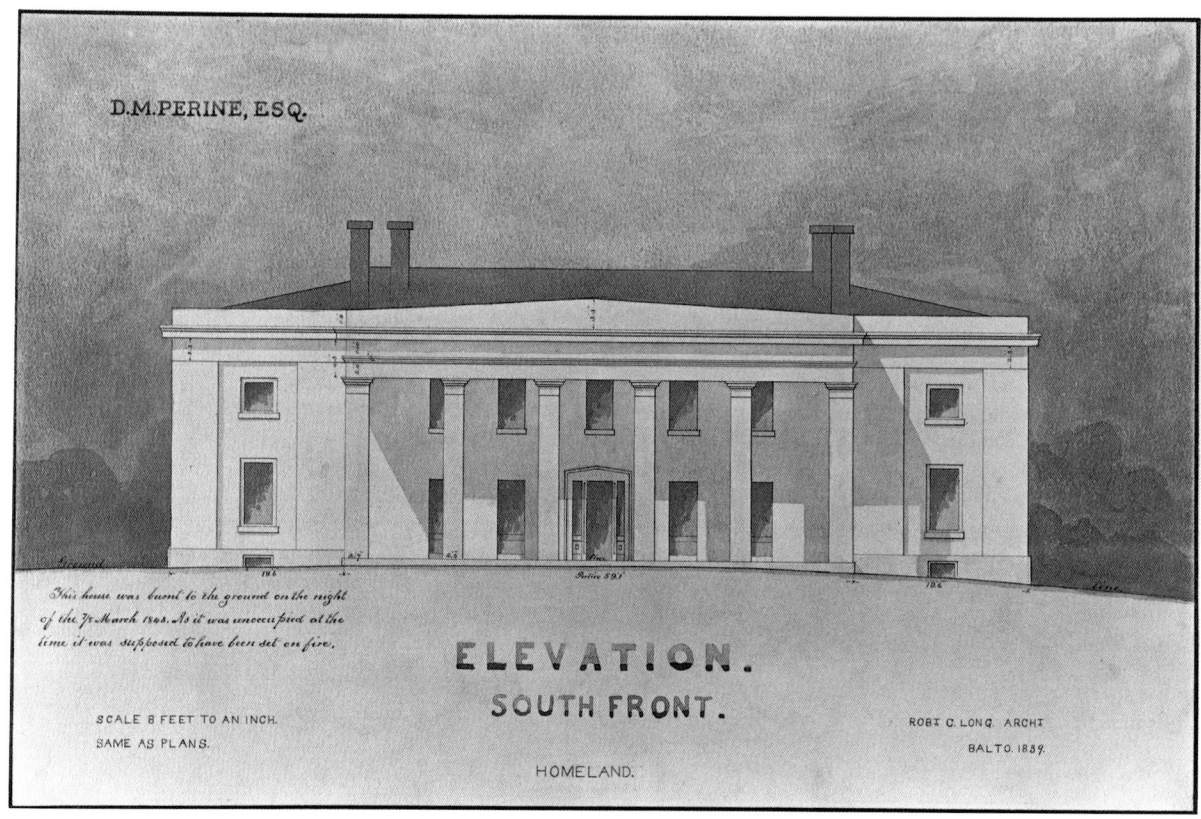
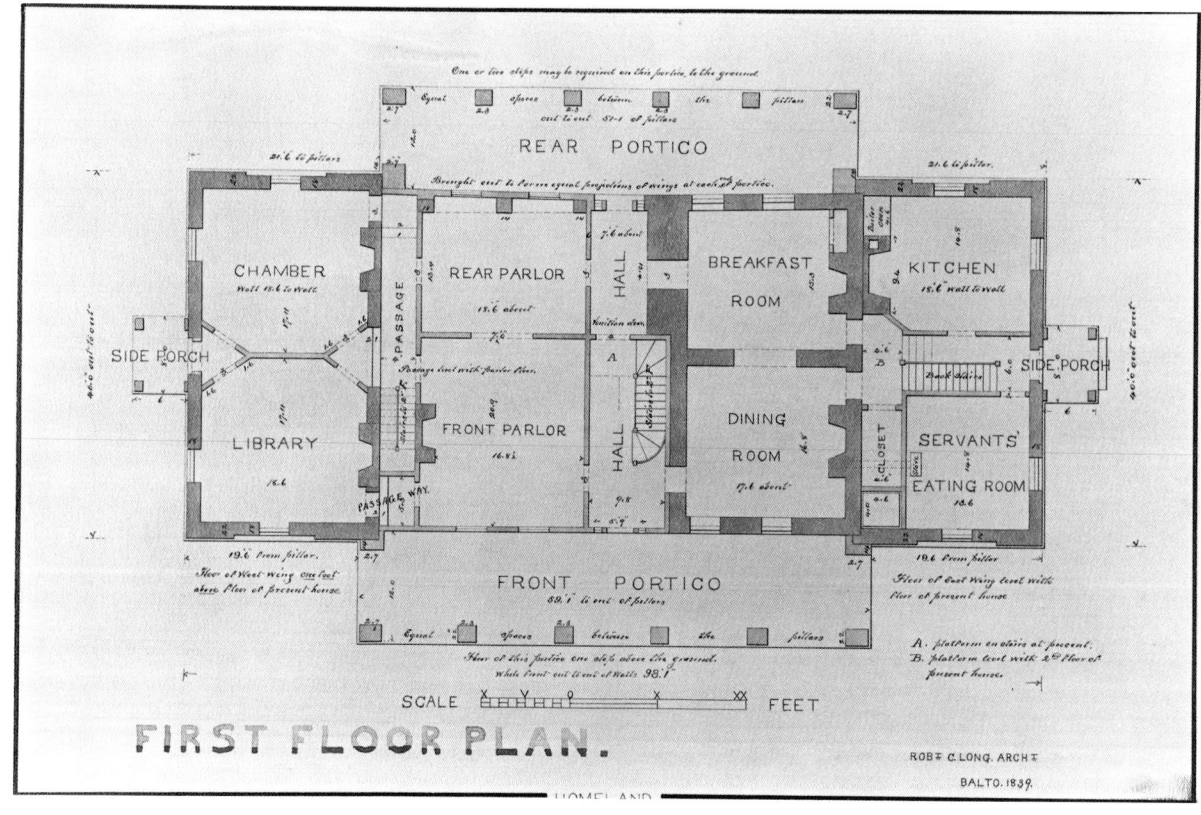

Design for enlarging Homeland, David M. Perrine House, Baltimore vicinity, by Robert C. Long, Jr., 1839. *Maryland Historical Society*

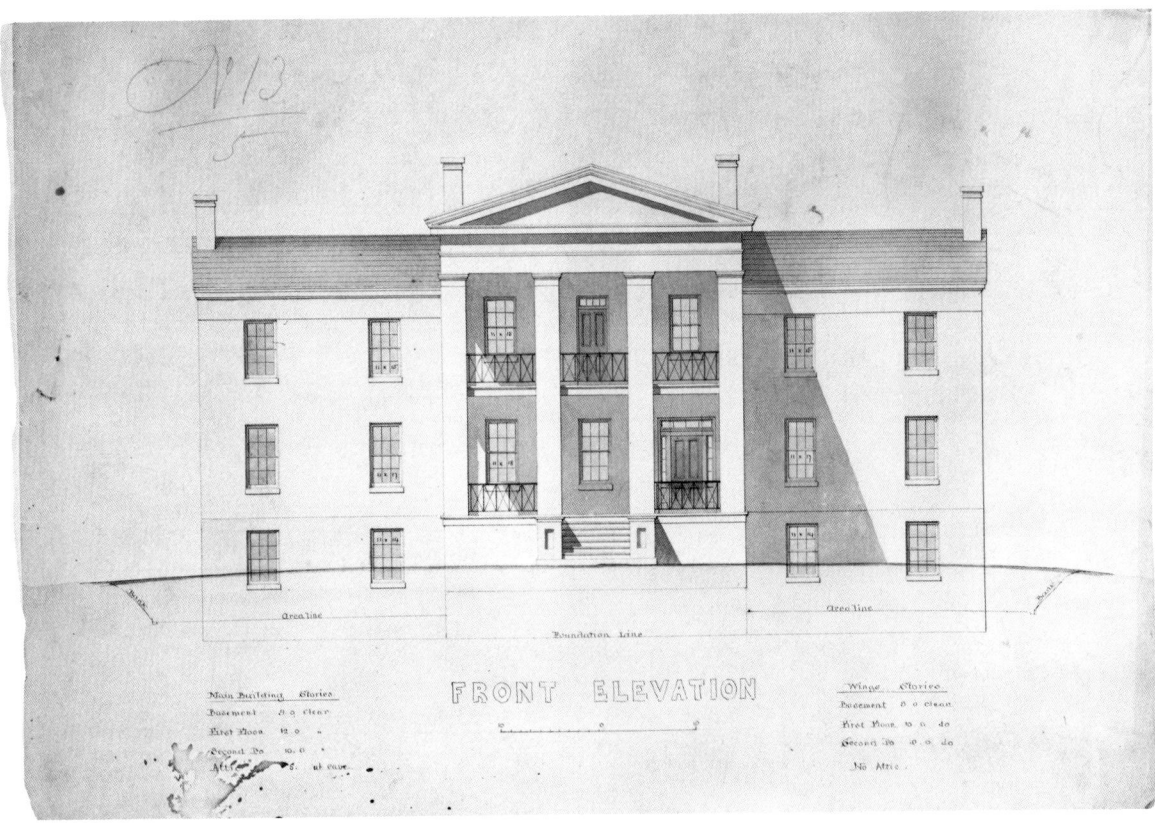

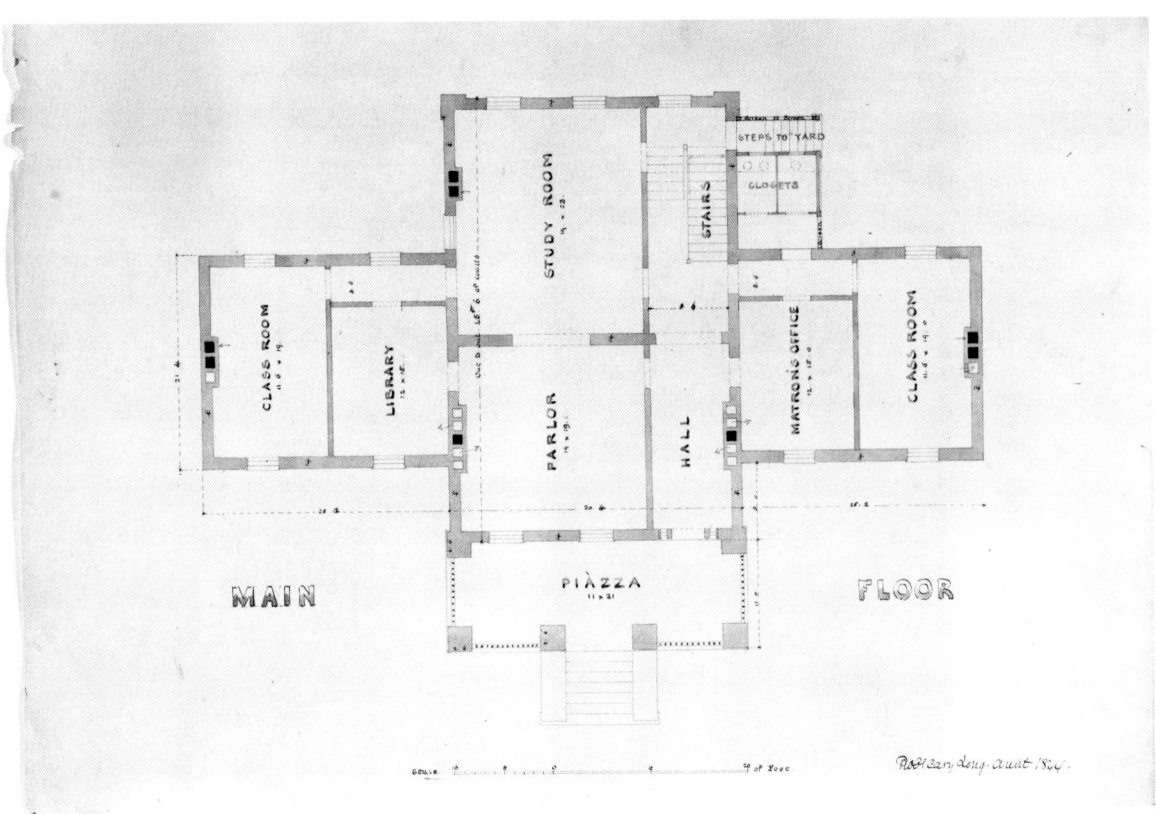

Design for an unidentified school by Robert C. Long, Jr., 1844. *The Winterthur Library, Joseph Downs Collection of Manuscripts and Printed Ephemera, 68x198.53a/b*

Lloyd Street Synagogue, 11 Lloyd Street, Baltimore, 1841–45.

hemoth were displayed at Thomas Palmer's looking-glass and fancy hardware store on Baltimore Street in November, 1839. The newspapers predicted confidently its speedy erection, but this magnificent edifice was, in fact, never built, probably because of the erratic economic conditions.

In 1839 Long, Jr., enlarged and remodeled the house of David M. Perine, an independently wealthy county official, at Homeland in the northern suburbs of Baltimore. To an older dwelling, consisting of two rooms and side hall, shown in one ink color, Long, Jr., added new servants' rooms, kitchen, chamber, library and service stair, shown in a second ink color. The old house and enlargements were given a unified appearance by adding a colossal Doric portico. When Homeland burned in March, 1843, Long, Jr., was again employed to remodel the house. This time he salvaged surviving walls of the end rooms, which had been added four years earlier, and rebuilt the center rooms, which must have been completely destroyed in the fire. This "third" Homeland was demolished in 1924.

Other Long, Jr., projects of the 1840's in Baltimore include the Lloyd Street Synagogue, 11 Lloyd Street, 1841–45 (enlarged 1860),[28] and St. Peter's Roman Catholic Church, Poppleton and Hollins streets, 1842–44, with similar Greek Doric porticoes;[29] remodeling St. John's Methodist Church, Liberty Street, a new brick front added to a church of 1815–20;[30] and 1843 Union Engine House, Balderston Street, a fire house featuring an 80-foot-tall steeple with twelve columns enriched with carvings of griffins and other animals;[31] additions to the Park Avenue mansion of Jerome N. Bonaparte in 1846;[32] and an 1848 brownstone residence for Samuel W. Smith, also on Park Avenue.[33]

Long, Jr., was also active outside of Baltimore and outside of Maryland. An 1844 design for a girls' school is unidentified, but it is similar to St. Mary's Female Seminary at St. Mary's City, completed by the builder Thomas Evans in October, 1845. (St. Mary's Seminary burned in 1924.) In Virginia, Long, Jr., designed the School for the Deaf and the Blind at Staunton in 1839; its commanding Doric portico, flanked by long wings and porches, overlooks the valley below the school. In 1847, also in Virginia, he designed Kinloch, the Essex County residence of the planter-lawyer Richard Baylor. In Pennsylvania, Long, Jr., produced a mansion at Altoona for Elias Baker, a Lancaster County ironmaster, in 1844. (Long's essays in Romantic design are surveyed on pages 175–186.)

An old friend of Robert Cary Long, Sr., William Strickland was the designer of Baltimore's Christ Church, built on the southwest corner of Gay and Fayette streets in 1835–36. Strickland was hired in the fall of 1834, when three members of the building committee had gone to Phila-

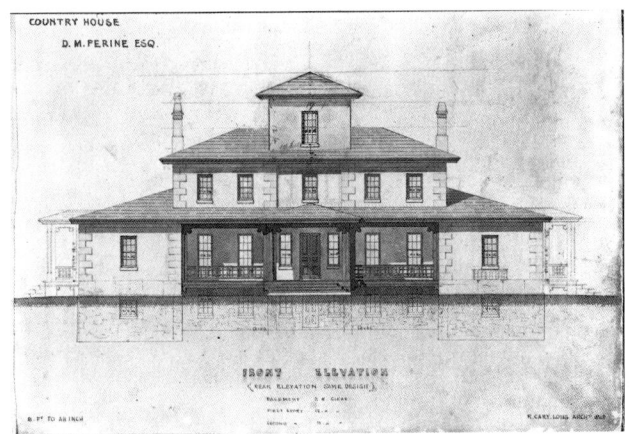
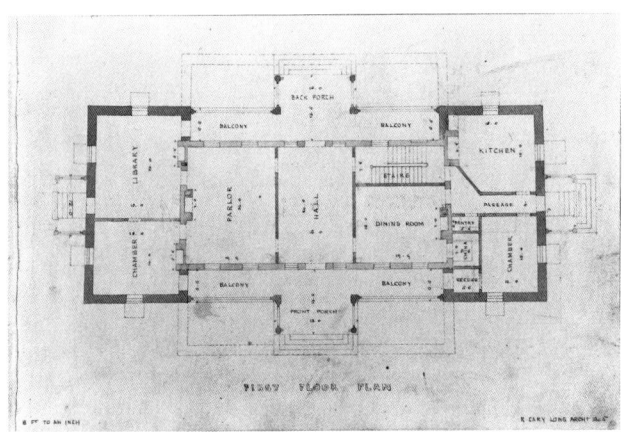

Design for rebuilding Homeland, David M. Perrine House, Baltimore vicinity, by Robert C. Long, Jr., 1845. *Maryland Historical Society*

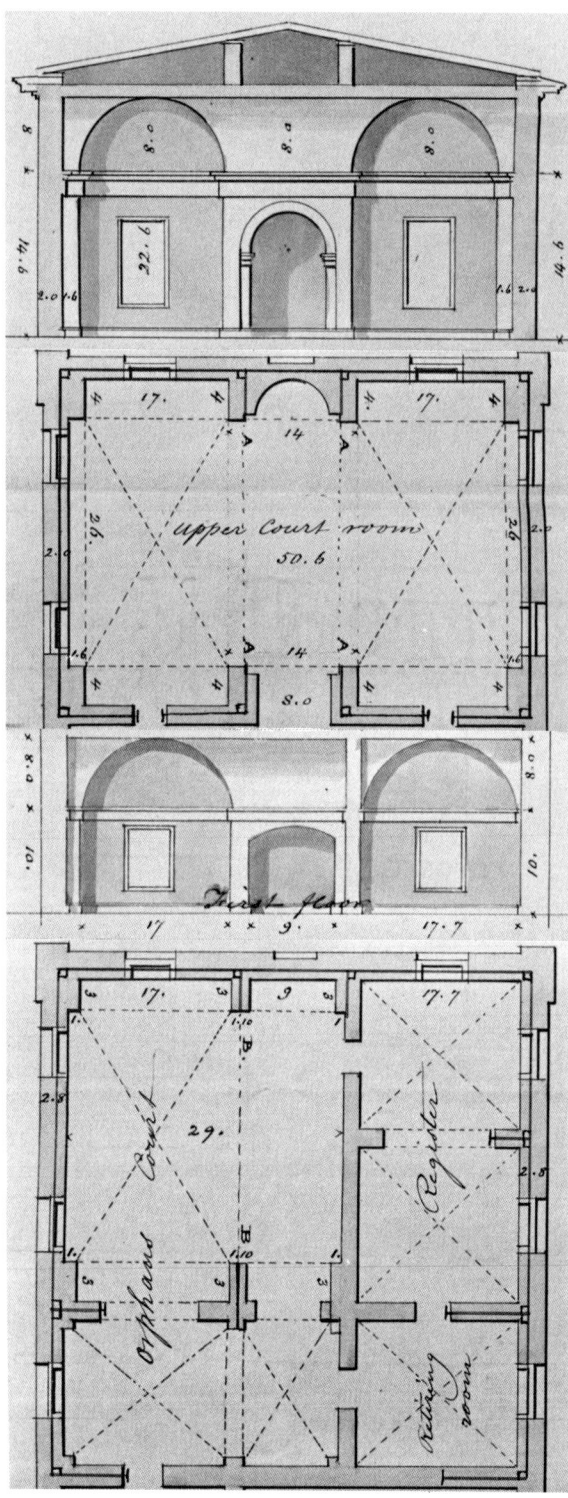

William Strickland's 1835 suggestions for revising Robert C. Long, Jr.'s design for the Public Record Office. *Baltimore City Archives*

delphia to inspect model churches and obtain drawings from Strickland.[34] Born in New Jersey, Strickland (1788–1854) had been introduced to Latrobe by his father, a carpenter working on the Bank of Pennsylvania, the first important example of Grecian architecture in America, and then studied for three years with Latrobe. In 1816 Strickland had exhibited a design for the Baltimore Exchange—prepared for the competition won by Latrobe and Godefroy—at the Pennsylvania Academy of Fine Arts, Philadelphia.[35] One of Strickland's early plans for Christ Church, retained by the architect, proposed an exuberant rotunda entrance fronted by a narrow portico and flanked by stairs and tiled terraces. The interior featured a semicircular apse framed by four monumental Corinthian columns. Christ Church, later used as the Church of the Messiah, burned in 1904.

We have already seen that Strickland advised the commissioners of the new Record Office in Baltimore about construction of cooper roofs and stone vaulting in 1837. In the same year, Strickland also designed the Allegheny County Courthouse at Cumberland, a two-story stuccoed brick building that was completed in 1841 and burned in 1893. In 1840–44 a Strickland design was also used to build Christ Church in Easton, though this Gothic design was simply adapted by the rector, the Rev. Henry M. Mason, from Strickland drawings that had already been used to build a church at Salem, New Jersey, in 1836–38. In 1845 Strickland moved from Philadelphia to Nashville, Tennessee, to supervise construction of his masterwork, the Tennessee State Capitol.

Before professional schools were established in America following the Civil War, books were the greatest teachers of architecture, explaining solutions to technical problems and spreading a knowledge of sophisticated design. John Haviland's *The Builder's Assistant*, published at Philadelphia in 1818, was the first American book to include Greek details; a copy was purchased by a carpenter named John Creamer at the sale of a bankrupt Baltimore bookseller, Joseph Robinson, in December, 1840.[36] The conservative Massachusetts housewright Asher Benjamin did not include Greek details in his books until the sixth edition of *The American Builder's Companion* in 1827; but three years later, in his *Practical House Carpenter*, Benjamin observed: "Since my last publication, the Roman School of architecture has been entirely changed for the Grecian." Other books available in Baltimore in the 1830's included the second edition of Haviland's *Builder's Assistant*,[37] Peter Nicholson's *Carpenter's New Guide* (London, 1792), Martin's *Carpenter & Joiner's Instructor*,[38] Robert Bindley's *Compendium of Civil Architecture*[39] and Minard Lafever's *Modern Builder's Guide* (New York, 1833).[40]

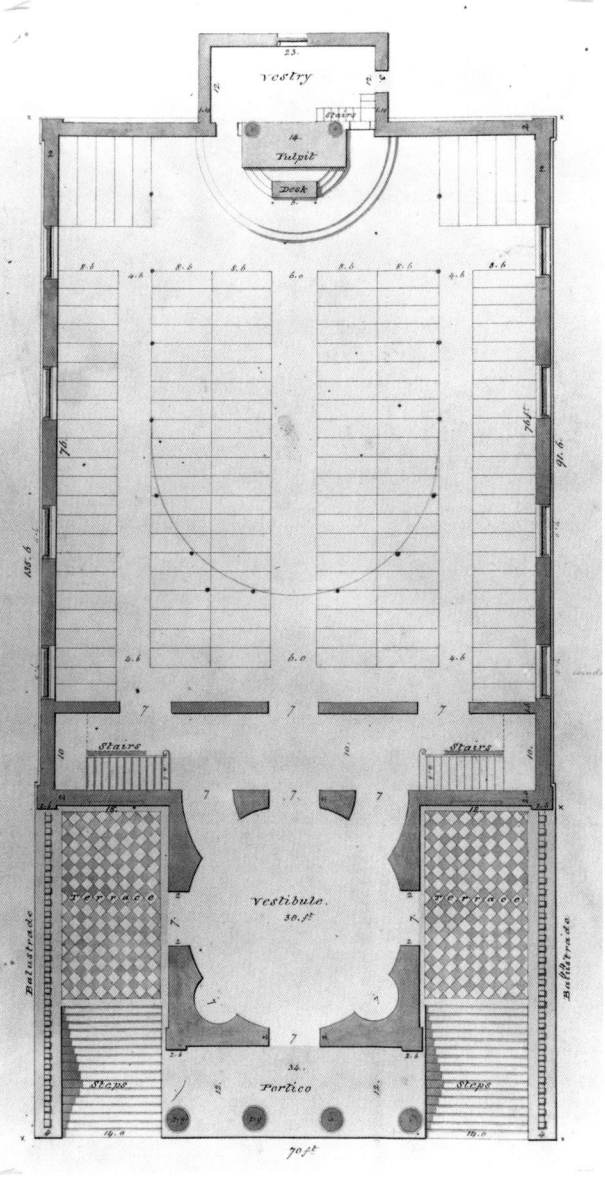

Christ Church, Baltimore, 1840–44, a 19th-century photograph and an alternate Strickland design for its plan. *Photograph from Maryland Historical Society, drawing from Tennessee State Archives*

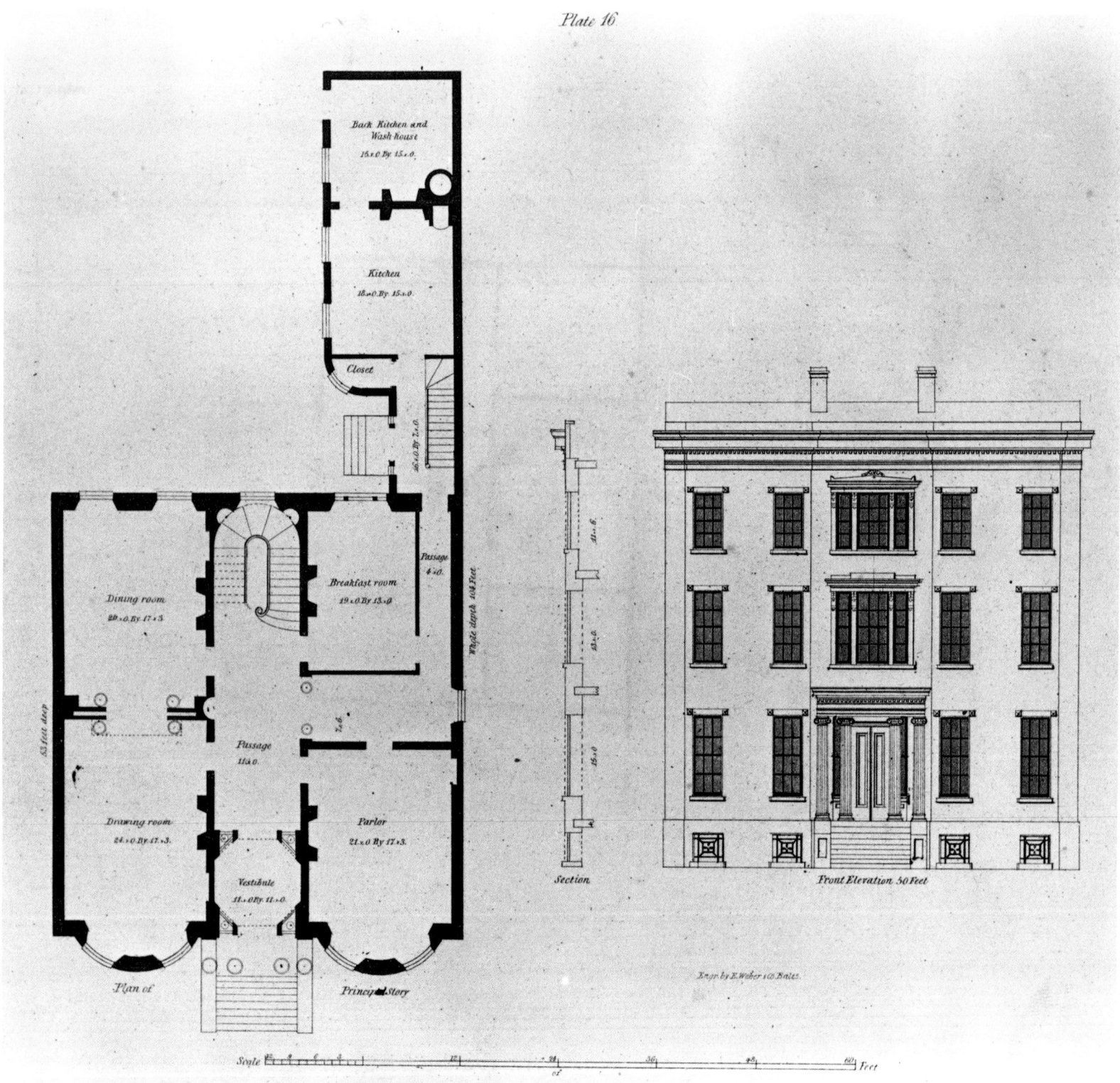

A town house design from James Hall's *A Series of Select and Original Modern Designs for Dwelling Houses* (Baltimore, 1840), one of the few architecture books published in the South. *Maryland Historical Society*

Most of these books had been published in the cities of England and New England, another example of foreign and Northern influence upon the architecture of the Old South. In March, 1834, an anonymous Baltimore builder announced plans to publish "The Carpenter's Own Book, or the Young Man's Self-Instructor," which was to include in sixteen monthly installments the orders of architecture, domes, arches, plans and elevations, perspective drawing and an architectural dictionary.[41] Though the proposed work was endorsed by important builders Jacob Small, Jr., George Milliman, Samuel Harris, James Curley and Robert Cary Long, Jr., there is no record that this work ever appeared.

One of the few architecture books issued anywhere in the South was *A Series of Select and Original Modern Designs for Dwelling Houses,* published at Baltimore in 1840.[42] Its author, James Hall, was born in Devonshire, England, in 1809, and worked as a draftsman, cabinetmaker, engraver and architect in Baltimore during 1834–35, Philadelphia in 1845–46, New York City in 1847 and again in Baltimore in 1848–55.[43] In September, 1840, Hall, describing himself as an architect, announced the opening of a school on North Gay Street to teach "Architectural, Orthographical, Isometrical, Scenographical and Ornamental Drawing."[44] Hall claimed that the designs in his *Dwelling Houses* were selected from buildings erected under his supervision in Baltimore and Philadelphia. The book's handsome engravings provide a record of city houses of the Greek Revival period—and, in particular, the Baltimore fondness for the subtle use of advancing and receding planes on façades. Instead of immense pedimented porticoes, the Greek Revival was expressed in Baltimore by squarer building profiles, parapets with denticulated cornices, trabeated doorways, one-story porticoes and heavy cast-iron or stone lintels.

The Charles Street Methodist Church was designed and built by Jacob Wall, Jr. (1800–1855), son of the veteran builder Jacob Wall, Sr. (1768–1823).[45] In February, 1843, the building committee, like that of Christ Church a few years earlier, resolved to visit Northern cities to inspect "approved specimens" of churches.[46] In May, 1843, the cornerstone was laid, and the Church was completed in 1844. Wall, Jr., also built and designed a house for Henry Tiffany on Madison Street in 1843,[47] another Methodist Church on Pennsylvania Avenue in 1844–45,[48] a house for Thomas Swann on Franklin Street in 1846–47, a house for William J. Ward on Lexington Street in 1849 and the German Reformed Church, Frederick City, in 1849–50.

Though Baltimore had been a cosmopolitan city and a leader of architectural innovation in the early 19th century, the Greek Revival, despite

Charles Street Methodist Church, Baltimore, 1843–44, a lithograph by E. Sachse, c. 1860. *Maryland Historical Society*

an early start, did not produce many great buildings in Maryland, because the 1820's and 1830's, the heyday of the Greek Revival in the upper South, were troubled times in the state. When peace and European competition were restored after the end of the Napoleonic wars, the trading patterns enjoyed by Baltimore exporters were disrupted. An 1819 panic, created by overproduction of cotton, speculative credit and controversy over the charter of the Bank of the United States, led to the failure of one hundred leading businesses in Baltimore and the eclipse of the older generation of civic leaders. Meanwhile, the wheat and corn lands of eastern and northern Maryland around the Chesapeake Bay were already exhausted, and farmers on the Eastern Shore began moving to western Maryland and beyond, to Tennessee, Kentucky, Alabama and Mississippi. The 1820's and 1830's were erratic years—a prolonged depression in the 1820's was followed by a panic in 1834, with the shocking collapse of the Bank of Maryland, which was followed by another panic in 1837.

But the foundations for future prosperity in the 1850's were also being laid in the 1820's and 1830's, as highways, canals and railroads—with trains first drawn by horses and then pulled by steam engines—offered wave after wave of technological progress to transport the wealth of produce from midwestern farms to the ships in Baltimore harbor. Construction of the Chesapeake and Delaware Canal, between the upper Chesapeake Bay and the Delaware River, and the Chesapeake and Ohio Canal, between the lower Potomac and upper Ohio rivers, had hardly begun before the Baltimore and Ohio Railroad, chartered in 1827, promised swifter communication between the coast and the Ohio River, 300 miles to the west.

Not surprisingly, the most imposing Greek Revival buildings of Maryland outside Baltimore were erected in cities through which the great Baltimore and Ohio Railroad was routed. By 1830, the B & O was opened fourteen miles between Baltimore and Ellicott City, where Robert Cary Long, Jr.'s Patapsco Female Institute was built in 1834–35. By 1832 the rails had reached sixty miles to Frederick City, where the Frederick Female Seminary on East Church Street was erected in 1843–45 by Connecticut-born Hiram Winchester, the first principal of the school. The Female Institute was enlarged in 1856, by adding a second portico connected to the original one by a recessed hyphen. In 1842 the rails reached Cumberland, where the Allegheny County Academy on Washington Street was erected in 1849–50. The railway finally reached the Ohio River at Wheeling, West Virginia, in 1853, twenty-five years after construction had commenced.

Female Seminary, Frederick, 1843–45, a lithograph showing the Seminary before its enlargement in 1856. *Maryland Historical Society*

Female Seminary, Frederick, 1843–45, as enlarged in 1856, a lithograph, c. 1860. *Maryland Historical Society*

Allegheny County Academy, Washington Street, Cumberland, 1849–50.

Baltimore County Courthouse, Towson, 1854–56.

IV. Romantic Styles

Design for a Gothic dog house, Ellicott City vicinity, 1810. *Maryland Historical Society*

The Gothic had been one of several exotic styles of architecture and decoration used in 18th-century England and, more sparingly, in colonial America. In March, 1761, Charles Digges of Annapolis was selling Gothic and Chinese wallpaper.[1] In 1794, the Annapolis architect Joseph Clark boasted that he was expert in "Tuscan, Doric, Ionic, Corinthian, Composite, Chinese, Attic, Cargatic, Arabesque, Moresque, Grotesque, Saracenic, Rustic, Antique, Antiquo-Modern [and] Gothic" design.[2] In 1799 the architectural amateur Nicholas Rogers and his builder Robert Cary Long, Sr., added Gothic parapets to their Baltimore Jail to give it an air of authority and permanence. In 1810 the house carpenter Abraham Lerew designed a Gothic dog kennel for Charles Sterett Ridgely's country seat, Oakland, south of Ellicott City.

Because of its association with the great cathedrals of the Middle Ages, Gothic architecture was often used for churches, though these were usually boxy neoclassical structures on which Gothic ornament had been applied like icing on a cake. Part of the problem was that Classical symmetry was still a prized ideal; another problem was a lack of correct knowledge of the details of Gothic design. When Benjamin Latrobe was preparing a preliminary Gothic design for the Baltimore Catholic Cathedral in February, 1805, he complained to his brother Christian that he was obliged to prepare his drawings from memories of Gothic churches at Bath, Bristol, Wells and Salisbury. "I cannot procure here a single technical account or representation of a Gothic building of any superior merit," he lamented.[3] Latrobe's Gothic design for the Cathedral was discarded in favor of a Classical one, because the taste for irregular Romantic buildings, as well as a correct knowledge of medieval architecture, would not come until some twenty years later.

The first Gothic building erected in Maryland was St. Mary's Chapel, designed by Latrobe's friend Maximilian Godefroy in March, 1806, for a Catholic seminary established at Baltimore in 1791. Looking at Godefroy's elegant presentation drawing, with its neat symmetry and

Design for the west front of the Baltimore Cathedral, the discarded Gothic design, by Benjamin H. Latrobe, 1805. *Archives of the Catholic Archdiocese of Baltimore*

The south front of the Baltimore Cathedral, the discarded Gothic design, by Benjamin H. Latrobe, 1805. *Archives of the Catholic Archdiocese of Baltimore*

A sectional view of the Baltimore Cathedral, the discarded Gothic design, by Benjamin H. Latrobe, 1805. *Archives of the Catholic Archdiocese of Baltimore*

St. Mary's Chapel, Baltimore, elevation by Maximilian Godefroy, 1806. *Maryland Historical Society; photograph from The Peale Museum, Baltimore*

St. Mary's Chapel, 600 North Paca Street, Baltimore, 1806.

dainty details, it is easy to understand why a contemporary visitor described the Chapel as "a little bijou" of a building: the 18th century's idea of a Gothic building. Godefroy carefully shaded the tower, as if shadowed by a passing cloud, to indicate that it was optional. In fact, a tower was not added until 1840, by Robert Cary Long, Jr. (This tower was removed in 1916.)

Completed in 1808, the Chapel design suffered several alterations made by its builders. The Chapel was built of brick rather than stone, a material more appropriate for a Gothic building. When the height of the nave was reduced to save more money, the upper façade became a sham supported by rear buttresses, giving the Chapel the melodramatic quality of a theatrical stage-set. The designer was then obliged to substitute niches for windows in the upper façade, and statues of the twelve Apostles intended to fill these niches were never installed. The limited skill of local builders obliged them to substitute stylized Roman columns for Gothic pillars, which were to flank the entrance. The rhetorical façade is further trivialized by completely bare side walls. In 1812 a simplified version of St. Mary's Chapel was used to build St. Thomas Church at Bardstown, Kentucky, for the same Catholic order.

Though Charles Harper, assisted by the architectural amateur John H. B. Latrobe, added Gothic windows, doors and porches when he remodeled an old overseer's cottage into a summer house about 1826,[4] the earliest truly Romantic house in Maryland—and probably in the United States—was built for Robert Gilmor near Baltimore in 1832–33. This Robert Gilmor, a country squire whose principal accomplishments were the creation of his magnificent house and fathering eleven children, should not be confused with his uncle Robert Gilmor, a famous early-19th-century Baltimore collector, or grandfather Robert Gilmor, the Scottish-born merchant who came to Baltimore in the 1760's and established the family fortune.[5] After graduating from Harvard, the third Robert Gilmor spent two years traveling in Europe. In August, 1830, carrying an introduction from the Duchess of Northumberland, he spent three days with Sir Walter Scott at Abbotsford, a sprawling mock-medieval castle that had been completed scarcely five years earlier. Gilmor was "delighted beyond description" with Abbotsford; Scott, lame since childhood, gave Gilmor one of his favorite walking sticks as a souvenir.[6]

Upon his return to America, the rich and romantic Gilmor purchased a 2500-acre farm north of Baltimore, which he called Glen Ellen. Imitating Scott, who had spent many years and more money than he could afford on the construction and decoration of Abbotsford, he commissioned the New York architects Ithiel Town and Alexander Jackson Davis to design

Design for Glen Ellen, Robert Gilmor House, north of Baltimore, by Ithiel Town and Alexander J. Davis, 1832. The two-story design, top, was revised as a one-story house, center. *The Metropolitan Museum of Art, Harris Brisbane Dick Fund, 1924. (24.66.17)*

A broadside announcing Robert C. Long, Jr.'s 1844 lectures at Baltimore's Mercantile Library, with Long's illustrations of Egyptian, Hindu, Mexican, Grecian, Roman, Romanesque, Saracenic and Gothic architecture. *Maryland Historical Society*

a Gothic house loosely copying the asymmetrical plan and projecting towers, turrets, crenellations and oriels of Scott's castle. Such a house was a revolutionary departure from the prim neoclassicism that had hitherto prevailed in Baltimore. In early October, 1832, A. J. Davis spent two days making plans and views of Gilmor's mansion and devoted a week of December to revisions.[7] In January, 1833, Davis went to Baltimore to confer with his client and remained there, off and on, until late May, 1833.[8] Gilmor must have realized that his eyes were bigger than his purse, for the original design was reduced by one story. Although the exterior bristled with Gothic finials and clustered chimney stacks, the plan featured a central neoclassical rotunda and a suave bow-fronted, Regency-inspired glazed conservatory. The house at Glen Ellen was acquired by the City of Baltimore in 1912 and, reduced to a ruin, was demolished in 1929.[9]

As we have already seen (pages 148–152), while he was in Maryland in early 1833, A. J. Davis designed a new hall for St. John's College at Annapolis. It was not until February, 1835, after a delay raising money, that the trustees decided to build—and then they selected a new design prepared by a different architect, Robert Cary Long, Jr., of Baltimore. Long (1810–1849), the son of the veteran Baltimore builder Robert Cary Long, Sr., was the beneficiary of great artistic gifts, sparked by intellectual ambition and enhanced by early training in New York City. Long's design for St. John's College was a Gothic hall containing fifty dormitory rooms for students, an apartment for a professor and his family, and a dining room and kitchen. This hall was built by a forty-year-old mechanic and pump maker named Elijah Wells in 1835–37.[10] Long, Jr., may have also provided the c. 1834 design for an eccentric Gothic house, Angelo Castle, perched on a hillside overlooking Ellicott City. When Long prepared a view of Ellicott City in 1834, he gave exaggerated importance to the Patapsco Female Institute, which he had designed in 1834, and Angelo Castle.

The modern rediscovery of Nile civilization had begun with Napoleon's expedition to Egypt in 1798–99. In addition to soldiers, he was accompanied by a small army of nearly two hundred surveyors, artists and scholars, who published sumptuous volumes illustrating the ancient monuments. The architecture of ancient Egypt, mother of philosophy and medicine, became a symbol of permanence, wisdom and healing. About 1815 Maximilian Godefroy, the French émigré, who may have seen the early French publications about these discoveries, essayed Egyptian design for five tombs in Baltimore's First Presbyterian churchyard.

In March, 1835, Robert Cary Long, Jr., submitted an eye-popping

Hall for St. John's College, Annapolis, 1835–37, a detail from a map of Annapolis, c. 1855. *Maryland Historical Society*

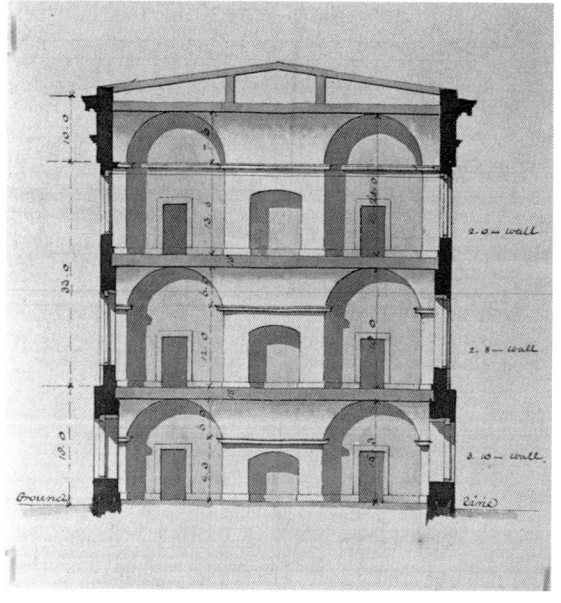
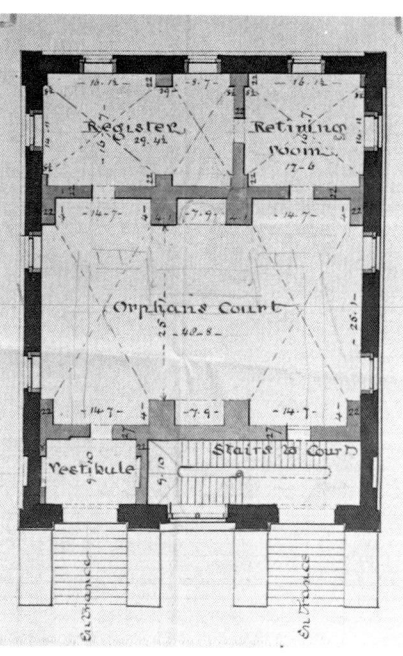
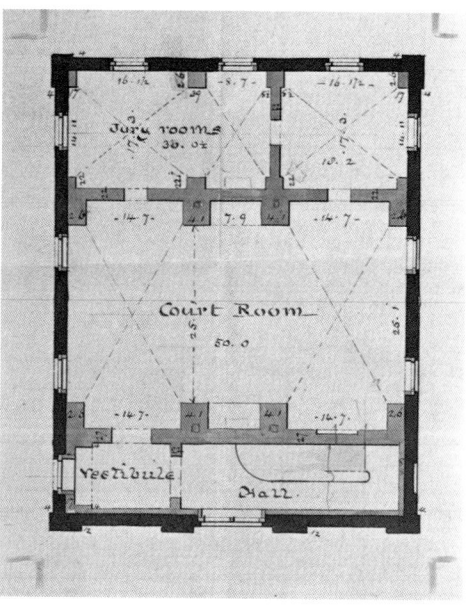

Record Office, Baltimore, Egyptian elevation, sectional view and plans by Robert C. Long, Jr., 1835. *Elevation from The Peale Museum, Baltimore, others from Baltimore City Archives*

Egyptian design for a new fireproof Record Office that was to be built for the city and county governments of Baltimore after the old Courthouse was damaged by fire. Long, Jr., probably got this idea by seeing the handful of Egyptian-style courthouses, hospitals and prisons in New York, New Jersey and Pennsylvania, where architects experimented with the style in the 1830's. The Record Office design featured giant columns with palm-tree capitals, a portico flanked by pylons, imitating the massive battered walls of ancient temples, and supported by a cavetto cornice, suggesting in stone the bushy tops of reeds spilling over the ancient mud brick walls through which they had been inserted for strength. As we have seen (page 153), the conservative building commissioners selected a conventional Grecian design.[11] R. C. Long, Jr.'s intellectual ambitions and his enthusiasm for exotic architecture were proclaimed in an immense broadside, illustrating Egyptian, Hindu, Mexican, Grecian, Roman, Romanesque, Saracenic and Gothic styles, which he sketched to promote lectures he gave at Baltimore's Mercantile Library Association in 1844.

The interior of Baltimore's Odd Fellows Hall on Gay Street was an Egyptian fantasy that *was* built. Erected for that mysterious fraternal order in 1830–31, the Hall was enlarged to the south in 1843 by William Quarle Caldwell (1807–1868).[12] Caldwell opened a drawing school in 1839 and announced his eagerness to design "all kinds of buildings" but no other works by him have been identified.[13] Caldwell replaced the original neoclassical front of the Odd Fellows Hall with tiers of Gothic windows, battlements and four octagonal towers containing fireplace flues and staircases. The building's glory was an Egyptian Saloon on the third story, fifty-one feet wide, sixty-four feet long and twenty-five feet high. Bright and glowing scenes on its walls depicted gods, mummies and seraphs from the temples at Thebes, "all strictly Egyptian and taken principally from the works of Belzoni"—Giovanni Battista Belzoni, an Italian-born adventurer, a weight-lifter who liked to play Apollo on the stage, a notorious looter of Egyptian tombs, among them the Tomb of Seti I in the Valley of the Kings, and author of *Narrative of the Operations and Recent Discoveries within the Pyramids* (London, 1820). On the Egyptian Hall's ceiling was a fantastic painting of five eagles surrounded by hieroglyphics and the convulsed elements of nature "in rainbow colors" on a sky-blue, star-studded background.[14] These decorations were created by a thirty-one-year-old Prussian-born artist named Ernest Dreyer, who had come to Baltimore about 1841. The Odd Fellows Hall was enlarged to the north in 1847–50 and again to the south by William H. Reasin in 1852.[15] The Hall was torn down in 1890.

Odd Fellows Hall, Baltimore, 1830–31, as remodeled in the Gothic style in 1843, an engraving by Samuel Sands. *Maryland Historical Society*

Perspective view of the Church of the Immaculate Conception, Baltimore, by Robert C. Long, Jr., 1842. *The Peale Museum, Baltimore*

Robert Cary Long, Jr., was also a pioneer in the ornamental and structural use of cast iron. His 1842 design for the Church of the Immaculate Conception, now known as St. Alphonsus Church, built on the northeast corner of Saratoga Street and Park Avenue in 1843–46, with a spire completed in 1854–55, is notable for the use of decorative window frames and sashes of cast iron and interior cast-iron pillars that support the tall roof.[16] An 1843 design by Long, Jr., for the Union Fire House on Balderston Street in Baltimore featured an eighty-five-foot-tall steeple supported by twelve cast-iron columns with capitals, cornices and images of griffins and other animals.[17] It is not known if this fantastic design was ever executed.

Cast iron was also employed for the Tudor windows and battlements of Long's 1844 design for the Franklin Street Presbyterian Church. The building committee also considered drawings and estimates submitted by William Minifee, an English-born artist and bookseller in Baltimore; by Samuel Harris, an architect from Delaware who was working in Baltimore; by Eugene LeBrun, a Philadelphia architect who worked for Thomas U. Walter.[18] The building committee later complained about Long's inattention, erroneous estimates, alterations and delays. As the Church finally neared completion in 1848, after four years of slow progress, an angry Long sued for full payment of his fees. Complaints from clients and self-righteous protests from Long, Jr., appear often in the architect's correspondence, for his ambition seems to have been matched by arrogance.

Franklin Street Presbyterian Church, Baltimore, 1844–48, a lithograph by Bowen and Trembly. *Maryland Historical Society*

Meanwhile, Long, Jr., was also establishing himself as a "correct" ecclesiastical architect, especially for the Episcopalians who required a more serious Gothic architecture than the Catholics or the Presbyterians. He joked derisively that a Gothic church was more than a plain square brick building of any size or proportions with pointed windows; he wrote that such an idea was as foolish as a schoolboy saying a man is an animal with two legs, a goose has two legs, and therefore a goose is a man![19] In the second quarter of the 19th century, reformers in England aspired to revive the Anglican church by purifying the liturgy and modeling new buildings on the style of medieval parish churches. These simple, solemn buildings were intended to symbolize in wood and stone a holier, less secular religious life, the traditions of the ancient church cleansed of 18th-century rationalism. In place of the boxy, light-filled neoclassical churches of the 18th and early 19th centuries, "correct" churches should be dark, narrow and mysterious. Upon its completion, Long's Mt. Calvary Episcopal Church, North Eutaw and Madison streets, 1844–46, was commended for its dark interior, timber-framed walnut ceiling, stone-colored walls and black-walnut pews: "The whole effect of the dark roof and pews and the tinted atmosphere thrown in by the colored glass is so different from what we have been accustomed to see in our churches."[20]

In 1844–46, Long, Jr., designed five similar small churches for the Episcopalians, each with a tall nave, bellcote over the front gable and separate chancel: St. Timothy's, Catonsville, 1844–45 (enlarged 1849–59); Trinity Church, Fell's Point, Baltimore, 1844–45 (demolished); the Church of the Ascension, Westminster, 1845–46; Trinity Church, Upper Marlboro, 1846 (entrance tower added in 1896);[21] and St. John's, Huntingdon, 1846–47 (burned in 1858).[22] The Maryland bishop, William R. Whittingham, heaped his most enthusiastic praise upon the two churches that have been demolished. Of Trinity Church, Fell's Point, he wrote: "This building, with its high pointed ceiling, long narrow windows, receding chancel and triple lancet window of stained glass, has a truly solemn and church-like air."[23] The Bishop called St. John's, Huntingdon, "the most strictly correct and chaste ecclesiastical edifice in the diocese."[24]

Robert Cary Long, Jr.'s domestic work was probably far more extensive than the meager list of his documented projects. About 1843, he designed a rambling house, half Greek and half Gothic, at the western outskirts of Baltimore for John H. B. Latrobe (son of the architect Benjamin Latrobe), who was the principal attorney for the Baltimore and Ohio Railroad. This house burned in 1850.[25] In 1846, Long, Jr., produced another suburban villa, Evesham, east of the York Road, for Joseph William Patterson, an iron merchant and president of the B & O. Evesham was demolished in 1961.[26]

Long, Jr.'s Roman Amphitheater, Franklin and Calvert streets, Baltimore, was built for a circus in a few short weeks during the summer of 1846 by Henry and Josiah Reynolds, who were also erecting a five-story commercial building by Long, Jr., for the banker Josiah Lee at the southeast corner of Baltimore and Calvert streets.[27] The Roman Amphitheater was a circular building, one hundred feet in diameter, with accommodations for 500 spectators and an adjacent stable for eighty horses.[28] A visitor to its opening in October, 1846, reported that the boxes and ceiling were decorated with splendid paintings of the ancient Olympic games by Ernest Dreyer and supported by sixteen cast-iron columns with spandrel arches. The Amphitheater, a frame building illuminated with gas, burned within less than a year.

In 1846 Long, Jr., designed a new Athenaeum, with rooms for the Maryland Historical Society, the Library Company and the Mercantile

St. Timothy's Church, Catonsville, 1844–45, after its enlargement in 1849–59. *Maryland Historical Society*

Church of the Ascension, Westminster, 1845–46.

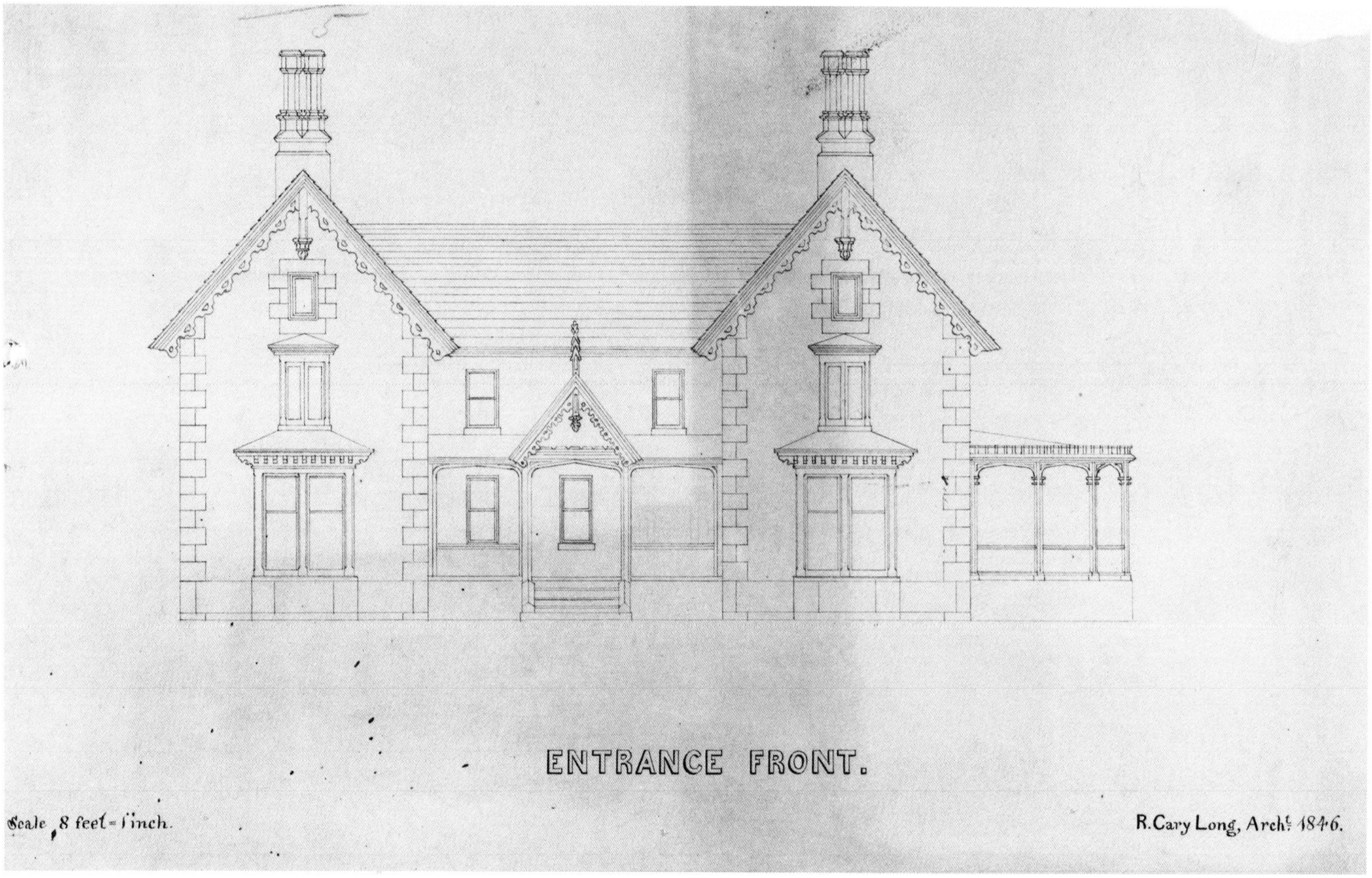

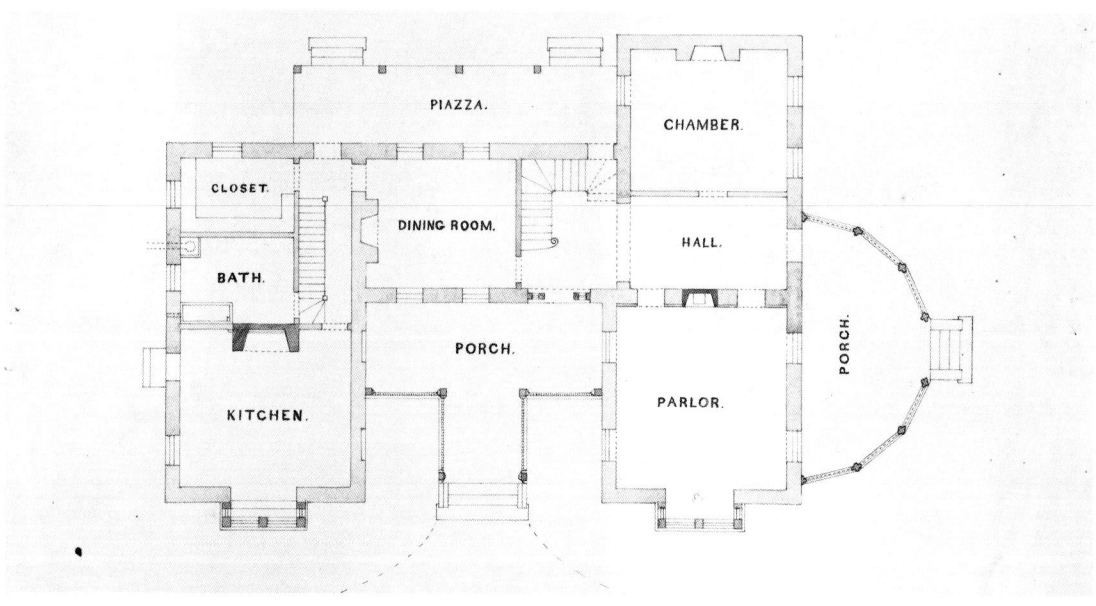

Elevation and plan for Evesham, Joseph William Patterson Villa, Baltimore, by Robert C. Long, Jr., 1846. *The Winterthur Library, Joseph Downs Collection of Manuscripts and Printed Ephemera, 68x198.55b/c*

Evesham, Joseph William Patterson Villa, Baltimore, 1846–47, before its demolition in 1961. *Private Collection*

Unidentified design for the wing of a Gothic house, drawn by Robert C. Long, Jr.
The Winterthur Library, Joseph Downs Collection of Manuscripts and Printed Ephemera, 68x198.54

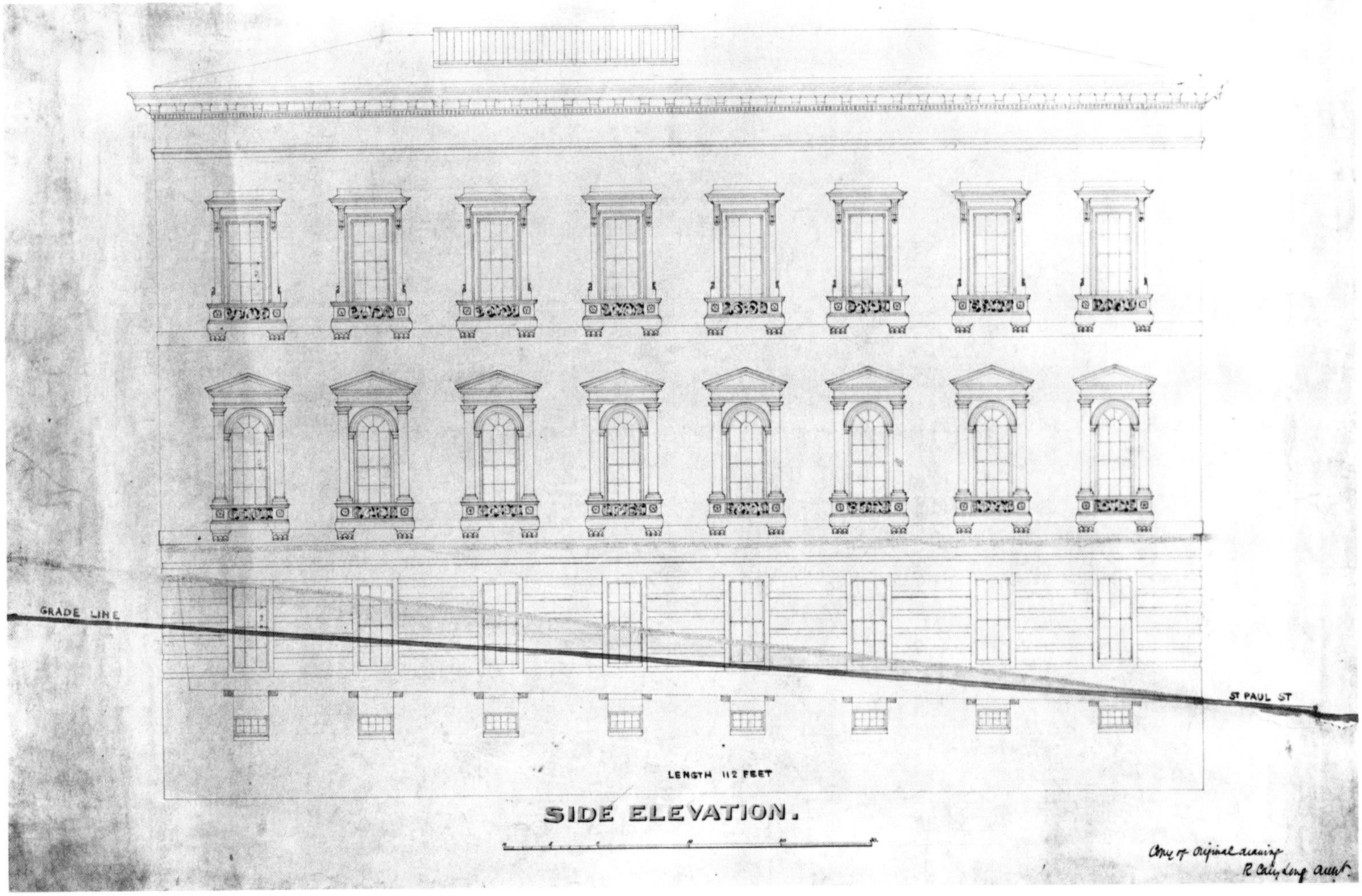

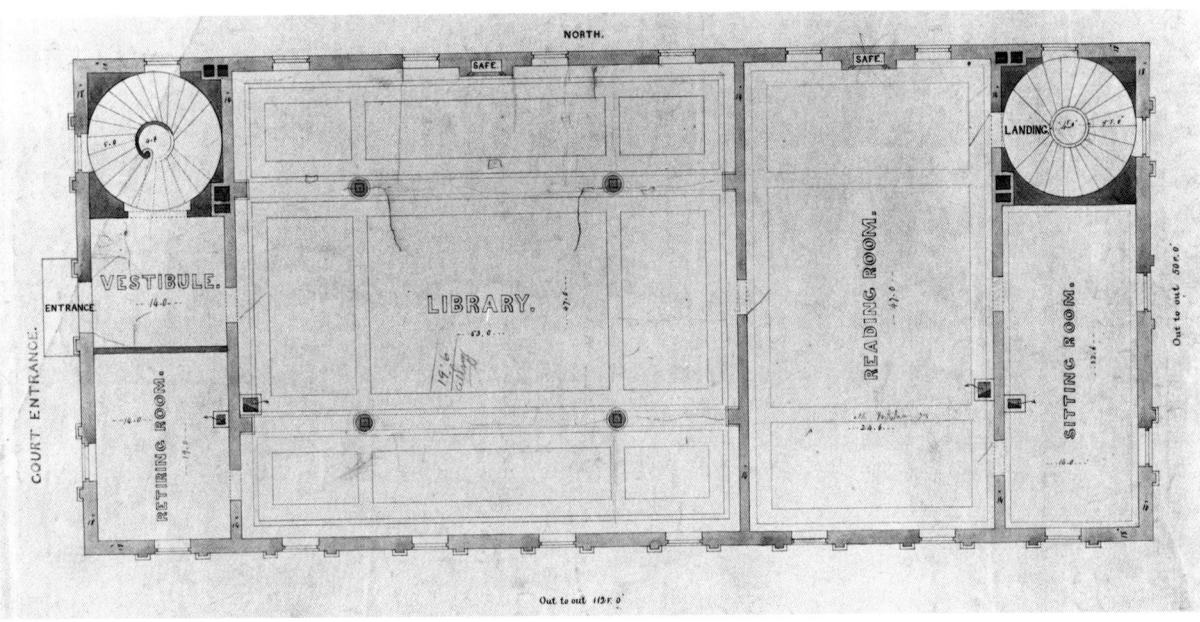

Side elevation and first-story plan of Athenaeum, Baltimore, 1847, by Robert C. Long, Jr. *Maryland Historical Society*

House at 204 West Lanvale Street, Baltimore, designed by Robert C. Long, Jr., in 1848. *Elevation by Michael Trostel and Peter Pearre*

Library, to be built on the northwest corner of St. Paul and Saratoga streets to replace the old Athenaeum on Lexington and St. Paul streets that had burned in 1835.[29] The new Athenaeum opened in October, 1848. The Library Company's quarters on the first story featured a screen of Corinthian columns painted to resemble sienna marble, octagonal reading tables and oak bookcases for 30,000 volumes.[30]

In September, 1848, the builder Henry Curley completed two brick houses on Lanvale Street designed by Long, Jr.[31] Another Long, Jr., building under construction in 1848 was the Baltimore American Office, 122–128 West Baltimore Street, featuring quatrefoils set into twin front gables.[32] In the fall the architect submitted drawings, specifications and estimates for St. Luke's Church, Baltimore. In October, 1848, Long moved to New York City, where he opened an office at 61 Wall Street and began work on the new Astor Library. Suddenly, in 1849, Robert Cary Long, Jr., died of cholera, too early in a most promising career.[33]

Though many talented Southerners would seek opportunity in the North after the Civil War, Long, Jr.'s move to New York was unusual for the antebellum period. More typically, Northern architects, in person or by mail, provided designs for important Southern buildings. In February, 1851, Thomas U. Walter of Philadelphia sent drawings to Maryland for Glenelg, a Gothic villa built in 1851–54 for the Pennsylvania-born lawyer and mine owner Joseph W. Tyson.[34] Walter (1804–1888) was born at Philadelphia, where he worked for his father, a bricklayer, and studied with the English-trained architect John Haviland. Walter's design for Glenelg incorporated parts of an earlier house within the rear wing. The design is also notable for the restraint of its Gothic exterior and for spacious interior planning, with four interconnecting parlors. The architect later listed the palindromical Glenelg among his fifty most important works outside Philadelphia.[35] Walter also designed a bank for J. I. Cohen and Brothers on Calvert Street, Baltimore, in 1834. In 1851 Walter was appointed supervisor of the U.S. Capitol at Washington, where he achieved his greatest fame as designer of its cast-iron dome, rushed to completion by President Lincoln during the Civil War as a symbol of national unity. Glenelg now houses a private school.

The Rt. Rev. William R. Whittingham, Episcopal Bishop of Maryland between 1840 and 1879, had been a great encourager of R. C. Long, Jr., and a man born and bred to be an ardent disciple of the anglophile, bookish, High Church reformers within the Anglican communion. Born in New York City of English parents, Whittingham was a sophisticated lover of ritual and a professor of church history with a library of 17,000 books. He was the only American bishop who was active in the 1848

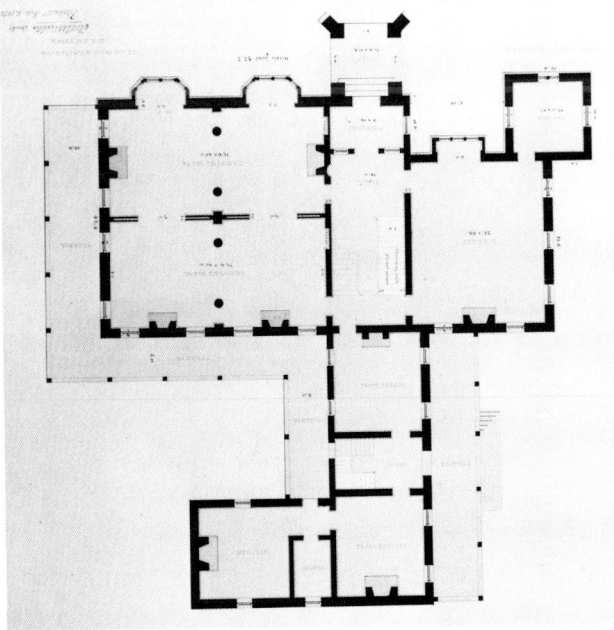

Glenelg, Joseph W. Tyson Villa, Howard County, 1851–54, a perspective view from Martinet's 1860 map of Howard County and Thomas U. Walter's plan of 1851. *Maryland Historical Society, The Athenaeum of Philadelphia*

founding of the New York Ecclesiological Society, which advocated simple rather than elegant Gothic architecture.[36] In particular, the Society prescribed asymmetrical design with provision for a separate chancel and the use of structurally functional materials, never lath and plaster. In March, 1850, the English-born Frank Wills of New York, one of the handful of architects endorsed by the Ecclesiologists, presented Bishop Whittingham with a copy of his new book, *Ancient Ecclesiological Architecture,* in which he proclaimed: "As in morals, so in architecture, honesty is the best policy. . . . Let us never be afraid of simplicity in building, and let us prefer a massive wall to a pretty moulding. . . . No house of God should be pretty!"[37] The design of Emmanuel Church, begun in 1849 on the ruins of an old fort on a hill overlooking the town of Cumberland, was adapted by John Notman of Philadelphia, another architect approved by the Ecclesiologists, from a view of St. Paul's, Brighton, published in the *New York Ecclesiologist,* edited by Wills.[38] The design of St. Mary's Episcopal Church, Emmorton, begun in 1851 for Bishop Whittingham's friend and official biographer, the Rev. William Francis Brand, was probably inspired by another illustration in the *Ecclesiologist*.

By inclination as well as necessity, Bishop Whittingham was an enthusiastic patron of church architects. In 1843, only three years after his election as bishop and five years before the founding of the Ecclesiological Society, he had visited the office of the architect Richard Upjohn in New York in pursuit of designs for churches. Upjohn (1802–1878) had come to America from England in 1829 at the age of twenty-seven. Trained as a cabinetmaker, surveyor and draftsman, Upjohn worked for the architect Alexander Parris of Boston in the 1830's. Upjohn's 1839 design for rebuilding Trinity Church, New York, erected in 1841–46, was a landmark of American architecture that established Upjohn's national reputation. In July, 1843, Upjohn sent Bishop Whittingham plans for "a small cheap church" followed by more details in August.[39] In November, 1844, architect was obliged to dun bishop for payment, which was not finally made until January, 1845.[40] Bishop Whittingham's cordial relations with Upjohn were well known, for in June, 1847, the Rev. Theodore P. Barker, Vermont-born rector of St. Philip's Church, Laurel, appealed to the bishop for help. Having received from Upjohn a design that was too expensive, Barker had asked further advice but received only an abrupt reply. Would Bishop Whittingham please visit Upjohn on his next trip to New York?[41] In October, 1849, Upjohn was made an honorary member of the New York Ecclesiological Society and in 1852 he was added to its list of approved architects.

In 1851, George S. Norris, a Baltimore hardware merchant, and his

St. Mary's Episcopal Church, Emmorton, 1851, an unsigned painting of the period. *Maryland Historical Society*

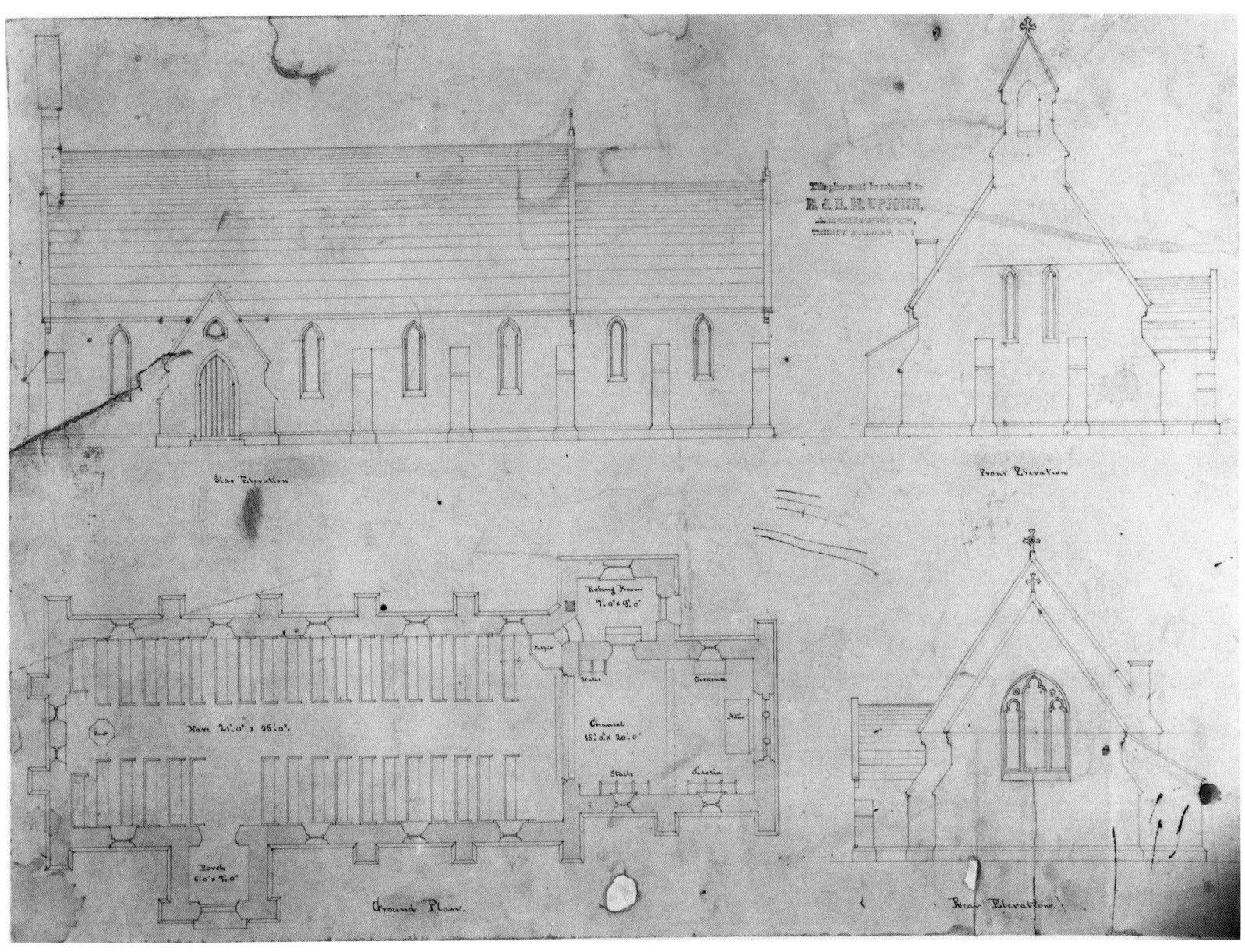

A design for the Church of the Holy Communion, Baltimore County, by Richard M. Upjohn, 1852. *Avery Architecture and Fine Arts Library, Columbia University*

brother Richard started a new church outside Reisterstown, giving the land on which the new Church of the Holy Communion was to be built and hiring Upjohn to design it. Upjohn prepared drawings in February, 1852, and specifications in March.[42] The design, with a "correct" tall nave, bellcote and separate chancel, proved too expensive.[43] A temporary frame church was erected in the spring of 1853 but this burned only eight months later; no permanent building was ever erected, and the congregation did not endure.

In June, 1851, the Rev. Henry V. D. Johns, rector of Christ Church, Baltimore, asked Upjohn for a design of a church to seat 1200 people, suggesting as a model the church Upjohn had designed in Brooklyn ten years earlier. When the Rev. Johns repeated his request in August, Upjohn declined to waste his time making drawings until money for construction had been raised.[44] Emmanuel Church was built at the southeast corner of Cathedral and Read streets, Baltimore, in 1853–54 with a design provided by two local architects, John R. Niernsee and James C. Neilson.

In the spring of 1851, Tench Tilghman, an important Talbot County planter, quarreled with the rector of Christ Church, Easton, and decided to start a new church at Oxford, which he asked Upjohn to design in September, 1851. Upjohn completed drawings and specifications for Holy Trinity Church, Oxford, by July, 1852, followed by details and a perspective view in August. The cornerstone was laid in April, 1853, and, though Tilghman confidently reported several times that masonry work would soon be completed, the Church was still unfinished when the Civil War interrupted construction.[45] The walls were left uncovered and overgrown with vines for several decades, and the building was not completed until the 1890's—and then without the tower projected by the architect. The Church was rebuilt with alterations after a fire in 1945.

Upjohn was often bothered by eager congregations too poor to pay for the drawings he delivered or to build his churches. Impatient with these wasteful claims on his time, Upjohn frequently replied abruptly to requests for help. To serve the needs of these fledgling parishes, in 1852 Upjohn published *Rural Architecture*, a brief but enthusiastic guide to country church-building. He explained how board-and-batten siding—boards laid vertically, their joints covered with thin slats, or battens—could be used to emphasize the verticality of the Gothic style and do so economically as well. The chapel at Hannah More Academy, a church-affiliated school for girls at Reisterstown, now known as St. Michael's Church, and St. Paul's Church, Hillsboro, 1853, are board-and-batten churches inspired by *Rural Architecture*.

St. Paul's Episcopal Church, Baltimore, perspective view of the exterior by Richard M. Upjohn, 1854. *Avery Architecture and Fine Arts Library, Columbia University*

St. Paul's Episcopal Church, Baltimore, perspective view of the interior by Richard M. Upjohn, 1854. *Avery Architecture and Fine Arts Library, Columbia University*

St. Paul's Episcopal Church, 233 North Charles Street, Baltimore, 1854–56.
Library of Congress

Design for Ninian Pinckney Villa, Easton, drawn by Richard M. Upjohn, 1860.
Avery Architecture and Fine Arts Library, Columbia University

In 1853 a young priest from Brooklyn, the Rev. Charles Seymour, was called to be rector of All Saints' Church at Frederick. Two days after his first sermon, Seymour wrote to Upjohn with a request for plans of a new building. Upjohn's drawings were approved by the vestry in May, 1854, and the building was erected in 1855–56.[46]

In late April, 1854, St. Paul's Church on North Charles Street in Baltimore burned.[47] In May, Upjohn was asked to come to Baltimore to plan its rebuilding.[48] In June, Upjohn sent a plan for a new church that incorporated the surviving walls of the original church, twenty-five feet high on the sides and thirty-five feet high on the east and west ends.[49] The Italianate exterior, with its loggia and corner tower, recalls a courthouse that Upjohn had designed for Dorchester County at Cambridge in 1852.[50] The Courthouse would not be completed until 1854. St. Paul's Church was consecrated in January, 1856, but the 150-foot-tall tower, the most dramatic feature of Upjohn's design, was never executed.[51]

In July, 1855, the Rev. Edmund B. Tuttle, a native of New York who had come to Baltimore two years earlier to run a mission for the poor and sick people on the northwest side of the city, wrote Upjohn for plans of a "Chapel" and "Church Home," but Upjohn's response, if any, has not been found.[52] In late 1855 Upjohn designed a new octagonal pulpit for St. Andrew's Church, High Street.[53] In November, 1856, the planter Richard Cooke Tilghman acknowledged receipt of plans for an Italianate reconstruction of his house, The Hermitage, at Centreville, which had been damaged in a fire.[54] In December, 1856, Charles Kemp, a thirty-four-year-old hardware importer of Baltimore, requested plans for a "plain but substantial dwelling house."[55]

Four years later, in 1860, Richard Mitchell Upjohn (1828–1903), who had come to the United States with his parents in 1829 and took over his father's office after the elder Upjohn's retirement, designed a villa at Easton for Ninian Pinckney, a forty-three-old naval surgeon. This English Gothic villa featured a mansard roof, sawnwork eaves cornice, long horizontal bands of polychromed brick laid into the walls and Tudor porches with striped roofs. The third story, roof and porches of Pinckney's villa burned in 1960.

Gothic design was also employed to represent military, governmental and intellectual authority. Institutional Gothic was a specialty of Delaware-born Thomas Dixon (1819–1886), who came to Baltimore in the late 1840's. In 1849, he produced the Indigent Women's Home on West Lexington Street. Dedicated in 1851, it was a three-story brick building devoted to the care of some thirty poor elderly women.[56] The basement contained a kitchen, dining room and pantries; the first and second sto-

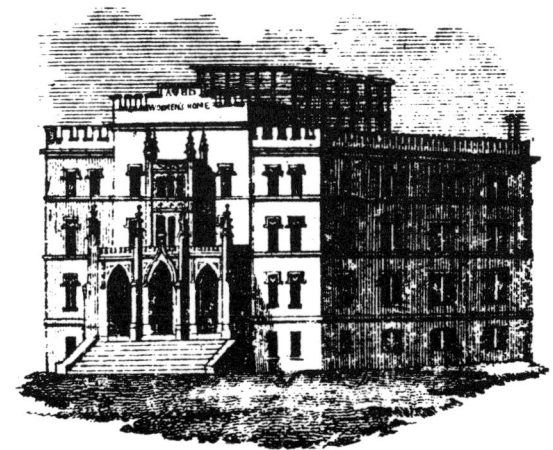

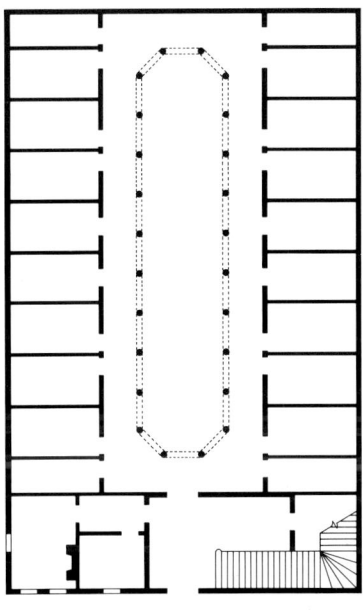

Indigent Women's Home, Baltimore, 1849–51, detail from the 1852 edition of Thomas H. Poppleton's map of Baltimore. *Library of Congress*

ries each provided fourteen chambers facing a central skylighted court; the third story was occupied by an infirmary. Dixon provided a similar design for the Aged Men's Home, built nearby in 1863–65. Both homes were demolished in 1959.

In the late winter of 1851, Thomas Dixon, who had been working with a builder named Wright, formed a new partnership with his brother James Dixon (1817–1863) and Scottish-born Thomas Balbirnie (born 1816). In 1851, Dixon, Balbirnie and Dixon produced designs for the First Presbyterian Church, Fayette and North streets,[57] stores for S. H. Norris, Joseph King and J. H. Carter on Baltimore Street,[58] and Waverley Terrace, a row of eleven houses on North Carey Street;[59] in 1852 they produced three rows of houses on Preston Street[60] and a store for Israel Griffith on Baltimore Street;[61] and in 1853 they produced St. Agnes Roman Catholic Church on the Frederick Road, six miles outside Baltimore.[62]

Female Seminary, Lutherville, 1854–55, and City Jail, Baltimore, 1858–60, institutional Gothic designs by the Dixon firm, seen in 19th-century lithographs. *Maryland Historical Society*

Dixon, Balbirnie and Dixon designed the Lutherville Female Seminary, which was built in 1854–55 as the centerpiece of a new community to the north of Baltimore projected by three Lutheran ministers. This commanding stone building was 126 feet long and 68 feet deep, with a cupola rising 96 feet. The center block contained apartments for teachers and dormitories for students; the wings contained classrooms.[63] Lutherville Female Seminary burned in 1911. The Dixon firm also designed the 1853 railroad station at Lutherville. Other projects included the Union Square Methodist Church, on the southeast corner of Lombard and Calhoun streets in Baltimore, in 1853[64] and the Baltimore County Courthouse and Jail, built at Towson in 1854–56 for the county government, which separated from the city in 1851. In 1856 the Dixon brothers formed a new partnership, leaving Thomas Balbirnie to open an office of his own.[65]

In 1858 the Dixon brothers revised the plan for a new City Jail that had been submitted by the Boston architect Gridley J. F. Bryant (1816–1899).[66] The new stone Jail, with 300 cells in each of two wings that flanked central offices, was completed in December, 1859, and the first 142 prisoners were moved into it in January, 1860.[67] Only a portion of the central block of the Jail remains standing. In February, 1859, the Dixon brothers submitted three plans for the workshops, hospital, infirmary and insane wards of a new city almshouse, featuring fire-resistant construction, hot and cold running water and steam heat for 334 men, 380 women and 68 children in the almshouse, plus an additional 158 men and 158 women in a nearby house of correction.[68] It is not known if the Dixon brothers' design was the one used to build the Bay View

City Jail, Baltimore, 1858–59. *Library of Congress*

Sheppard Asylum, Baltimore, designs by Calvert Vaux, 1861–62. *Sheppard and Enoch Pratt Hospital*

Asylum, which opened in 1866 at Canton, in Baltimore's eastern suburbs. In 1859 the Dixons were employed to design schools for Baltimore County.[69]

Upon his death in 1857, the Quaker merchant Moses Sheppard bequeathed funds for the construction of a mental hospital at Baltimore.[70] After purchasing a farm on the York Road north of the city, the trustees of the new Sheppard Asylum advertised in the newspapers of Baltimore, Washington, Philadelphia, New York and Boston, offering $300, $200 and $100 for the three best designs for a hospital with fireproof construction, gas lighting, mechanical heating and running water in two separate buildings for one hundred men and one hundred women. Having received twenty-one designs, the trustees awarded the prizes in December, 1859: $300 to Thomas and James Dixon of Baltimore, $200 to Samuel Sloan of Philadelphia and $100 to Richard Upjohn of New York.[71] However, the final plans were prepared in 1861–62 by Calvert Vaux of New York. Eleven years earlier, in 1850, Vaux (1824–1895), then twenty-six years old, had been hired in London by the American horticulturalist A. J. Downing and brought to New York. Vaux later collaborated with Frederick Law Olmsted on the design of New York's Central Park. The Asylum's Gothic buildings, with their intricate brickwork and colored roof tiles arranged in geometric patterns, are represented in the architect's perspective views. The extent to which he may have adopted features from the three prize-winning plans is unknown. The first building was begun in May, 1862, but, with Civil War disruptions and lack of money, the trustees had to work slowly with a dogged determination worthy of the pharaohs building their pyramids. The first patient was not admitted to the Sheppard Asylum until 1891!

Baltimore's John Rudolph Niernsee and his partner James Crawford Neilson were masters of Italianate design. Niernsee (1814–1887) was born in Vienna, studied architecture and civil engineering in Prague, sailed to the United States about 1838 and worked as a railroad engineer in Florida and Alabama before coming to Maryland in 1839.[72] Niernsee was described by his daughter as "an immense man, six and one-half feet tall . . . fair-haired, blue-eyed, with a ruddy complexion, erect carriage."[73] He worked as an office draftsman for the Baltimore and Ohio Railroad, and Niernsee's earliest documented work in Maryland was a house built on the west side of North Charles Street in 1846 for John H. B. Latrobe, attorney for the B & O.[74] Two years later, in 1848, Niernsee designed a store for Hamilton Easter and Company on Baltimore Street[75] and another nearby for Martin Lewis and Company, the latter with an Elizabethan façade and a seventy-foot-high dome.[76]

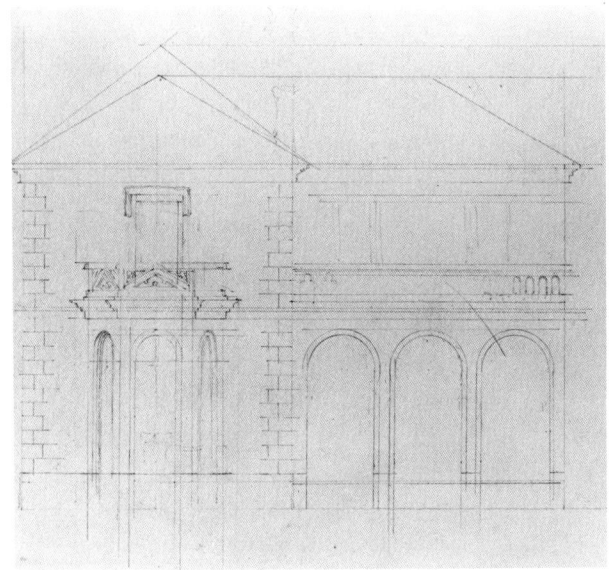

Italianate designs by James Crawford Neilson, c. 1855. *Maryland Historical Society*

Calvert Street Station, Baltimore, 1850. *Library of Congress*

In mid-1848 Niernsee formed a partnership with James Crawford Neilson. Born in Harford County, Maryland, Neilson (1817–1900) was trained as an engineer in Belgium and, like Niernsee, commenced his career as a railroad engineer, working for the Baltimore and Susquehanna Railroad. Early projects of the Niernsee-Neilson partnership included a three-story brick mansion for Dr. J. Hanson Thomas, with a Corinthian portico and a dome, on Mount Vernon Place and another for John S. Gittings on Monument and St. Paul streets in 1848;[77] James Williams Stores on Gay Street and the Romanesque-style synagogue on High Street in 1949;[78] the Romanesque-Gothic Second Presbyterian Church, East Baltimore and Lloyd streets,[79] four houses on Madison Street for John S. Gittings[80] and the Calvert Street Station for the Pennsylvania Railroad in 1850.[81] The Station, with its twin towers and tiers of round-headed windows, was demolished in 1950. Niernsee and Neilson also designed Grace Church, Park Avenue and Monument Street, in 1850–52.[82] This distinguished Gothic design, one of the earliest stone churches of Baltimore, was based on John Notman's 1848 St. Mark's, Philadelphia. The tower of Grace Church was never erected; the chancel was enlarged in 1903.[83]

Other Niernsee-Neilson projects in 1851 included St. Mark's Episcopal Church, a stone Gothic edifice on West Lombard Street,[84] and St. Luke's Church, Carey Street (St. Luke's was occupied in an incomplete state in late 1853 and completed in 1857–58 by John W. Priest of New York),[85] St. Michael's German Catholic Church, Pratt and Register streets (completed 1852),[86] a pair of houses for James Carroll on Howard and Monument streets;[87] in 1852 an extensive remodeling in the Italianate style of Clifton, home of the railroad promoter Johns Hopkins, and additions to the Baltimore Custom House;[88] in 1853 Emmanuel Church (completed in 1854 with an entrance tower added in the 1920's)[89] and a stuccoed Byzantine-style Central Presbyterian Church, on the southeast corner of Liberty and Saratoga streets (completed in 1854);[90] in 1855 houses for A. H. Schumacher and William E. Mayhew, Monument Street,[91] St. John the Evangelist Roman Catholic Church, Eager Street,[92] and the First Constitutional Presbyterian Church, Green and Monument streets.[93] In 1855 Niernsee and Neilson also submitted a design for the Baltimore and Ohio Railroad's Camden Street Station. Construction was completed by Joseph F. Kemp, a draftsman for the B & O who signed an 1858 lithograph of the building as its "architect." Sometime before the spring of 1855, Niernsee and Neilson designed a gate house for Thomas Winans, a New Jersey-born railroad engineer who had made a fortune building the first railroad in Russia in the early 1840's, suggesting that

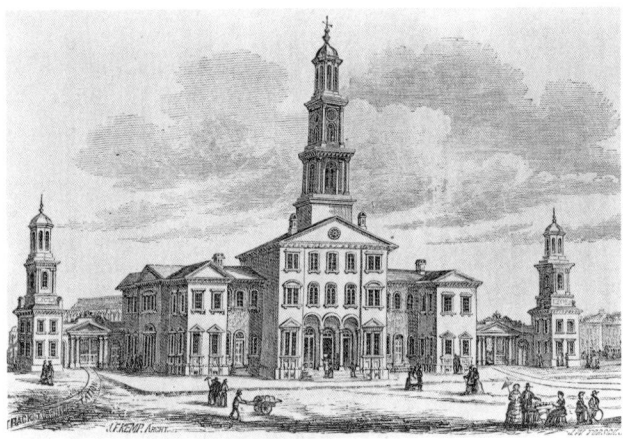

Camden Street Station, Baltimore, 1855–58.
Maryland Historical Society

Grace Episcopal Church, Park Avenue and Monument streets, Baltimore, begun 1850, interior view.

they probably designed the Winans villa, Alexandrofsky, which was demolished in 1928.[94]

In the spring of 1855 Niernsee went to South Carolina to supervise construction of the State House at Columbia, where he remained until the outbreak of the Civil War. In May, 1856, Neilson ("formerly of Niernsee and Neilson") designed the Italianate brownstone Bank of Baltimore on Baltimore Street, which was completed in July, 1857.[95] Other projects in 1857 included a cast-iron office on Hanover Street for H. M. Bash, the State Lunatic Asylum at Catonsville, six miles outside Baltimore,[96] the Union Protestant Infirmary on Mosher Street[97] and an unexecuted proposal for the Peabody Institute that was to be built on Mount Vernon Place.

Norris Gibson Starkwether (1818–1885), the son of a farmer who was also a carpenter and grist-mill owner, was born in Vermont.[98] In the spring of 1830, at the age of twelve, he was apprenticed to a master builder for the traditional term of seven years; making the customary progress from study to mastery, Starkwether worked for two years as a foreman, four years as a head foreman and then for two more years as a builder in Massachusetts during the 1840's. By 1850 Starkwether was established as an architect in Philadelphia. In 1854 Starkwether prepared the design for Baltimore's magnificent Gothic-style First Presbyterian Church on West Madison Street, and three years later he designed an Italianate manse next door for the Rev. John Backus.[99] The Church was completed in 1859, but the extraordinary spire, 273 feet tall and supported by the ingenious framework of sixteen cast-iron columns resting on stone piers buried eight feet below the basement, was not completed till 1874. Inside the Church, a series of groined arches across the ceiling form rows of bulbous cusped pendants. In 1856 Starkwether was busy with a new dormitory, Pinkney Hall, for St. John's College at Annapolis[100] and a wing for the Patapsco Female Institute at Ellicott City.[101] In 1855–57 he was also occupied adding extra floors, Italianate window lintels, cast-iron balconies and bracketed eaves to the City Hotel that had been built by William F. Small in 1825–27.

Of the Romantic styles, the Italian Villa style became the most popular for houses in the Old South, because it was easier to build than the Gothic and because its wide, overhanging eaves, long casement windows and shady loggias seemed better suited to the Southern climate. Inspired by the rural architecture of Tuscany in northern Italy, these buildings were generally irregular in plan, with a tall entrance tower, low roofs, wide eaves supported by sawnwork brackets, arcaded porches and bay windows, and round-headed windows grouped in twos and threes. In

Church of St. John the Evangelist, Baltimore, 1855, a mid-19th-century lithograph. *Maryland Historical Society*

Barnum's City Hotel, Baltimore, as remodeled by N. G. Starkwether in 1855–57, from a city directory of the period. *Maryland Historical Society*

First Presbyterian Church, West Madison Street, Baltimore, 1854–59, steeple completed 1874, a lithographed view of the exterior and photograph of the interior. *Lithograph from the Maryland Historical Society*

The Italianate front added to Trevanion, Uniontown vicinity, in 1855–56.

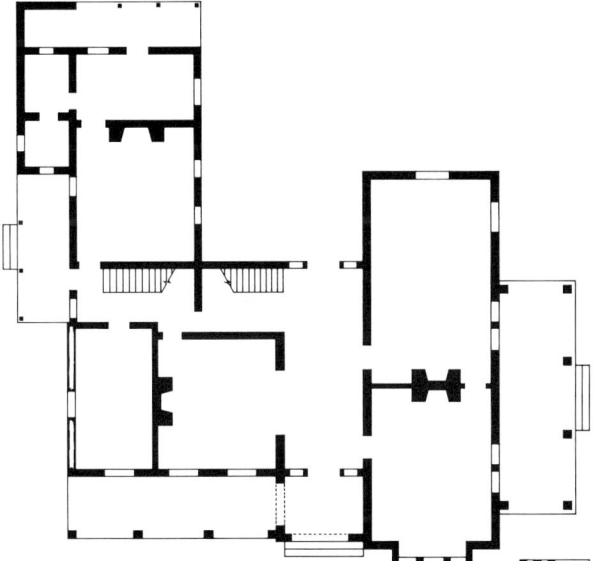

Anneslie, Frederick Harrison Villa, Towson, c. 1855.

1855–56 William Wallace Dallas commissioned a new Italianate front with most of these features for Trevanion, his 1817 house three miles northwest of Uniontown.

In 1855 Thomas Beale Dorsey, a jurist and reigning patriarch of a family that had been important landowners in Howard County since the early 18th century, died. After his property was divided among them, members of the family employed Norris Starkwether to design Italian villas. Thomas's son William H. G. Dorsey commissioned Wilton on his portion; Thomas's daughter Sally Elizabeth Dorsey commissioned El Monte on her property; a son-in-law, Dr. Arthur Pue, built a villa known as Temora; and Charles W. Dorsey's daughter Comfort Mackubin built Chatham. Wilton burned in 1939, and Chatham was demolished in the 1950's. Charles W. Dorsey, J. T. Dorsey, Reuben Meriweather Dorsey and William H. Dorsey were all members of the vestry of St. John's Church, west of Ellicott City, for whom Starkwether designed a new building in 1860.

Starkwether must have been well known among the country gentry for his villa designs. In 1857 he was hired to prepare drawings for Mrs. John Campbell White, the wealthy widowed daughter of John Carnan Ridgely of the Hampton Ridgelys. The design, though never executed, is preserved in a neatly bound album of spectacular presentation drawings.[102] A similar villa was produced by Starkwether for Richard Maynard, who lived at Grey Rock in the Pikesville vicinity of Baltimore County, in 1857–61.[103]

In early December, 1855, Starkwether hired a young assistant, Edmund G. Lind, to supervise construction of the First Presbyterian Church. Lind (1829–1909) was born on the outskirts of London, the son of an engraver of Swedish ancestry. After studying at the Government School of Design at Somerset House under Charles James Richardson, a pupil of Sir John Soane, Lind was apprenticed to John Blore, who designed a new façade for Buckingham Palace in the 1840's. Between 1852 and 1855, Lind worked in London, Sheffield and Yorkshire, and then he decided to sail to America. After spending his first month in New York, November, 1855, seeing the sights of the metropolis and looking for a job, Lind was finally hired by Starkwether, who had not interviewed Lind but was eager for an assistant. In early December, Lind was summoned to meet Starkwether in Baltimore. "My new master . . . rather disappointed to find me so young, feared I wouldn't suit, rather put out because I did not arrive a day or two earlier—business had worried him so much that little would have made him cross—live in hopes that he'll mend." Starkwether gave his new assistant only a brief tour around the

Italian villas by N. G. Starkwether for members of the Dorsey family in Howard County, details from the 1860 Martinet map: Wilton, El Monte and Chatham, c. 1856. *Maryland Historical Society*

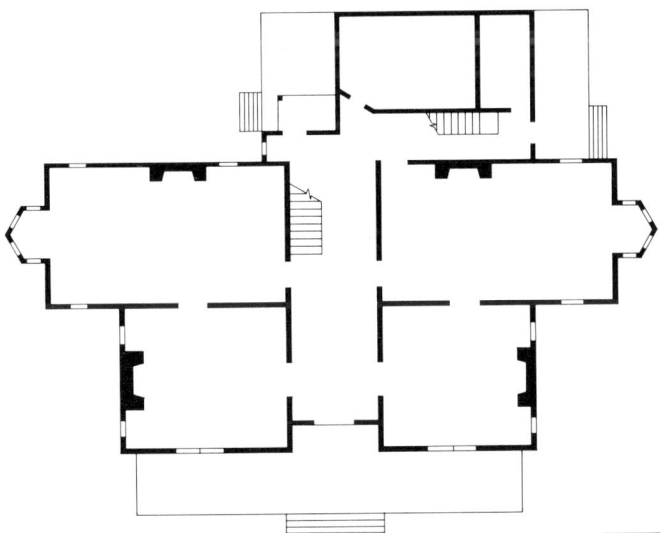

Temora, Dr. Arthur Pue Villa, Howard County, c. 1856.

This page and opposite: Elevations of a villa for Mrs. John Campbell White by N. G. Starkwether, 1857. *Maryland Historical Society*

This page and opposite: Elevations of a villa for Mrs. John Campbell White by N. G. Starkwether, 1857. *Maryland Historical Society*

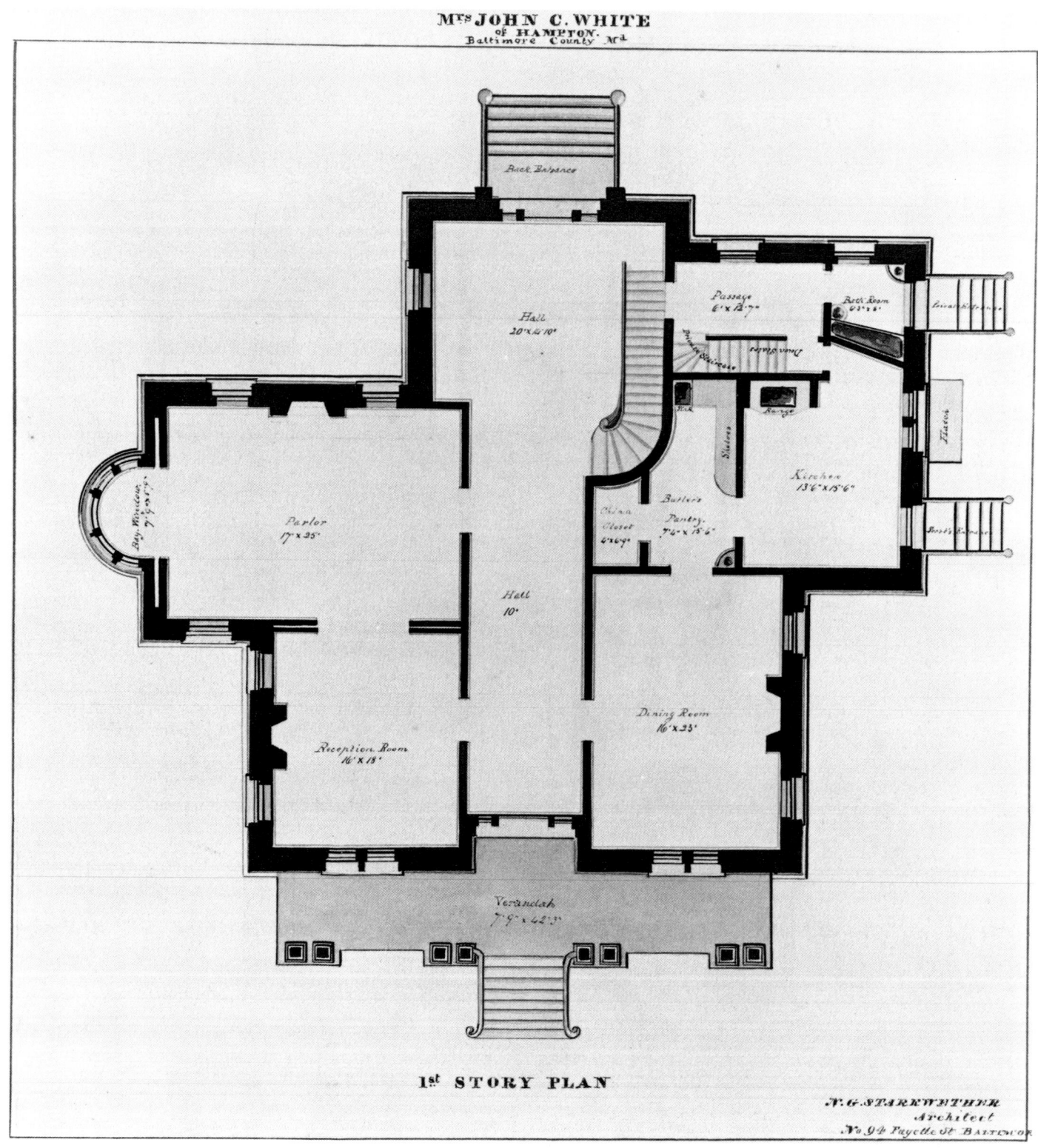

Plan of the villa for Mrs. John Campbell White by N. G. Starkwether, 1857. *Maryland Historical Society*

Grey Rock, Richard Maynard Villa, Baltimore County, 1857–61. *Maryland Historical Society*

five-foot-high walls of the First Presbyterian Church before returning hastily to Philadelphia, leaving his new assistant, Lind recalled, "like a babe in the Wood to get thru' brambles & briars as best I could."[104]

It must have been an unhappy association, for Lind formed a new partnership only six months later with William T. Murdoch, a twenty-nine-year-old draftsman who was also working in Starkwether's office, described by Lind as "quite green at his profession but with plenty of Yankee go-aheadedness." They remained partners until 1860. Lind prepared a catalogue of his works: some 118 buildings in Maryland between 1856 and 1861.[105] In 1856, Lind and Murdoch designed a French neoclassical, marble-fronted store for the furniture dealer James Corlan at 216–218 Baltimore Street.[106] In 1857 they produced three stores for the attorney Charles R. Carroll.[107] In 1857–58 they devised a large Italian villa, Guilford, for William McDonald, the wealthy, pleasure-loving son of a Scottish-born merchant and land speculator.[108] This design featured an irregular plan, front-facing gables with wide, bracketed eaves, bay windows, hood moldings and a six-story tower. Guilford was demolished in 1914.

Lind and Murdoch's surviving masterwork is Baltimore's Peabody Institute on Mount Vernon Place. In 1857 George Peabody, the Massachusetts-born, London-based international banker, endowed the Institute, a temple of the arts for the citizens of Baltimore, where he had laid the foundations of his vast fortune after the War of 1812. The archives of the Peabody Institute preserve the most complete record of the design and construction of a major public building in the Old South.[109] In March, 1857, the trustees of the Institute advertised in the newspapers of Boston, New York, Philadelphia, Washington and Baltimore, offering prizes of $500, $300 and $200 for the best designs sent to them. The trustees specified that they wanted a two-story building with a brownstone façade (later changed to marble), containing a library for 100,000 volumes, a lecture hall to seat 1500 people, an art gallery, a concert hall and rooms for the historical society. Because the trustees had dreams larger than their purse, each architect was instructed to submit two designs: the first, a 75-foot-wide building that would be erected immediately, and a second, 150 feet wide, that would be a harmonious enlargement of the first. In May, the trustees further challenged their architects by selecting a site on Mount Vernon Place. This was a prestigious location, but it was also an awkward one that sloped wildly downhill in two directions. Respecting the chaste Monument and decorous town houses on Mount Vernon Place, the trustees decreed that the style of architecture could not be Gothic.

Perspective view of Guilford, William McDonald Villa, Baltimore, by Edmund G. Lind and William T. Murdoch, 1857–58. *Maryland Historical Society*

By November, 1857, the building committee had received at least thirty-four designs from more than seventeen architects, including William Baldwin Stewart, Joseph C. Wells, John Bolton, Lawrence B. Volk and Mettam and Burke of New York; A. von Steinwehr of Albany, New York; T. H. Williamson, professor of civil and military engineering at Virginia Military Institute at Lexington, Virginia; and from R. Snowden Andrews, Thomas Balbirnie, Augustus Frosberg, Louis L. Long, James C. Neilson, W. Angelo Powell, W. H. Reasin and Norris G. Starkwether (submitted by his German-born draftsman Anton Pohl) of Baltimore, as well as by Lind and Murdoch. Other inquiries were received from William Pratt, Henry and Josiah Reynolds and Horace B. Volk of Baltimore, Charles Harkins of Washington, William S. Andrews, Stephen Decatur Button and Samuel Sloan of Philadelphia, Bernard Lockwood of Newburgh, New York, C. Anderson, F. Diaper and Richard Upjohn of New York, Gridley Bryant, H. W. Hartwell, Charles Kirby, Paul Shulze and John Small of Boston, Charles Hartshorn of Providence, Rhode Island, Rankin and Jones of Chicago and J. L. Foster of Concord, New Hampshire.

Though the trustees had offered three prizes of $500, $300 and $200 for the three best designs, they decided in December, 1857, after the designs had been submitted and judged, to change the rules and award $125 to each of nine entrants. The nine winners were William Baldwin Stewart and Mettam and Burke of New York, and Angelo Powell, Augustus Frosberg, J. C. Neilson, N. G. Starkwether (Anton Pohl), Lind and Murdoch, R. Snowden Andrews and Louis L. Long of Baltimore. Richard Snowden Andrews (1830–1903), a Washington-born architect who had worked for Niernsee and Neilson, scolded the trustees for changing the rules and refused his award.[110] Considering the elegance of several of the other designs, particularly those submitted by William Baldwin Stewart, and the crudeness of their own effort, it is surprising that Lind and Murdoch were hired to prepare the final drawings for the Peabody Institute. Propinquity, personalities and politics must have played a part in the selection. The building committee approved Lind and Murdoch's design in April, 1858, commending its dignified appearance. The Institute's cornerstone was laid in April, 1859; construction of the first building was completed in 1861 under the supervision of Joseph Kemp, a former draftsman with the Baltimore and Ohio Railroad; the long anticipated additions were made in 1874–76.[111]

In 1858 Lind and Murdoch produced a house at 153 St. Paul Street for the dry goods merchant William F. Murdoch, a "villa residence" in Baltimore County for the attorney Elisha R. Sprague and a depot for the

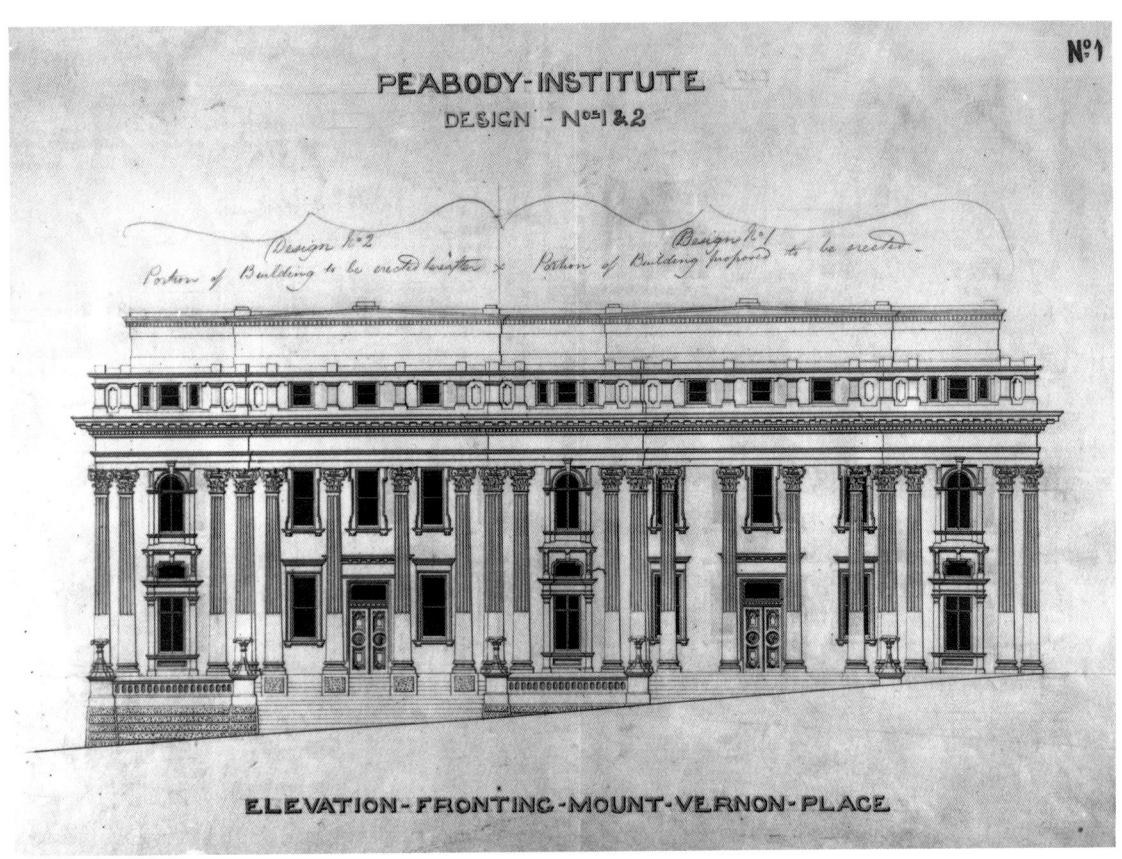

Designs for the Peabody Institute, Baltimore, 1857, submitted by Edmund G. Lind and William T. Murdoch (top) and William B. Stewart (bottom). *Peabody Institute*

Designs for the Peabody Institute, Baltimore, 1857, submitted by William Baldwin Stewart (top) and Mettam and Burke (bottom). *Peabody Institute*

Design for the Peabody Institute, Baltimore, 1857, submitted by James C. Neilson (top) and a perspective view of the final design by Edmund G. Lind and William T. Murdoch, 1858 (bottom). *Peabody Institute*

Memorial Church, Bolton Street, Baltimore, 1860, a 19th-century lithograph. *Maryland Historical Society*

Northern Central Railroad. In 1859 they produced a bank and another commercial building on Baltimore Street for Alexander Brown and two dwellings at 124 St. Paul Street for the stockbroker William Fisher and one of his sons.

In 1860, the final year of their partnership, Lind and Murdoch designed another "villa residence" for James Howard McHenry, grandson of Washington's Secretary of War, south of Pomona in Pikesville; a hotel and cottages for a "watering place" to be built on four hundred acres owned by William Cost Johnson at Point Lookout; the Fourth Presbyterian Church, Franklin Square, and Memorial Church, Bolton Street, Baltimore.[112] The McHenry villa was never completed according to the drawings because of the Civil War; the hotel at Point Lookout became a Federal army hospital during the War. Memorial Church honored the Rev. Henry V. D. Johns, the longtime rector of Christ Church who had died in 1859. The vestry received Lind and Murdoch's drawings in March, 1860; the cornerstone was laid in July; and the Church was opened in July, 1864, though the tower shown in the architects' perspective view was never erected. In 1860 Murdoch formed a new partnership with William T. Richards, the former chief draftsman in the Lind-Murdoch office, and Lind continued to practice independently.[113]

We have often observed how, in an era before professional schools and when country builders had virtually no opportunity to see the great buildings of the world, books were responsible for spreading a knowledge of sophisticated architectural styles. Early-19th-century books, like those of Asher Benjamin and Minard Lafever, had been little more than illustrated dictionaries, containing pictures of the Classical orders, details of the capitals, columns and entablatures of ancient temples, with solutions to geometrical problems for the construction of stairs and roofs, a selection of designs for doors, windows, chimneypieces and moldings, and a very small group of sample elevations and plans for a few houses and one or two churches. By the mid-19th century, authors and publishers were creating more elaborate books to serve the needs of an expanding profession. These larger and more comprehensive works featured plans, details and perspective views for many model buildings in many styles—Greek, Gothic, Italian, Swiss and Oriental—and all were specific and complete, with suggestions for landscaping, painting, furnishing, costs and even moralistic essays on virtuous styles. At first the publishing pace was established by English works like John Loudon's *Encyclopedia of Cottage, Farm & Villa Architecture*, a massive 1138-page compendium of designs by several architects for houses, interiors and gardens first published in London in 1833 but so popular that the work appeared in twelve different editions. In April, 1836, just three years after its first publication, Loudon's *Encyclopedia* was offered for sale by the Baltimore bookseller Fielding Lucas, and a copy belonged to the amateur Baltimore architect William Howard.[114]

In the 1850's, Andrew Jackson Downing, the horticulturist and architectural theorist from Newburgh, New York, became the principal tastemaker of American houses. It was not without significance that Romantic architecture in America first blossomed in the Hudson River Valley of New York, a center of landscape painting and rhapsodic writings inspired by the natural world in the early 19th century. Downing's idea was to create houses that appeared to spring naturally, sympathetically from their pastoral surroundings. In February, 1855, a writer in the Baltimore *Sun*, perhaps the architect William H. Reasin whose country houses were being praised in the article, mused: "A good deal of attention is now being given to the architecture of suburban and country houses. . . . We hope the time is not far distant when our people will cease building in the country those three-story town houses which Mr. Downing complains of, disfiguring the face of nature, looking as if lifted out of a three-story row in a well packed city street, and suddenly dropped in the midst of a green field in the country, full of wonder and contempt!" Downing's books, *A Treatise on the Theory and Practice of Landscape Gardening*, 1841, which included an extensive discussion of rural architecture, *Cottage Residences*, 1842, and *The Architecture of Country Houses*, 1850, provided inspiration and specific instruction for country builders.

In August, 1845, Tench Tilghman, the influential Talbot County landowner and senior warden of Christ Church, Easton, asked Richard Upjohn in New York to draw plans for a Gothic cottage similar to an illustration of a one-and-one-half-story gate house from Downing's *Landscape Gardening*.[115] Tilghman had discovered the illustration in a review of the second edition of Downing's work published in the January, 1845, issue of *The Cultivator*, a monthly journal devoted to agriculture, horticulture and farm life.[116] The design had originated with Alexander Jackson Davis, who had published it in his own book, *Rural Architecture*, in 1837. Tilghman may have hoped to use the design—intended for a New York estate—for the new rectory of Christ Church, which was built to a different Upjohn plan in 1851–52.

In late 1860 Norris G. Starkwether designed a parsonage for the Church of the Redeemer in the northern outskirts of Baltimore. His conception of a Gothic cottage with an unusual front verandah was adapted from an unmistakable source, Design II of Downing's *Cottage Resi-*

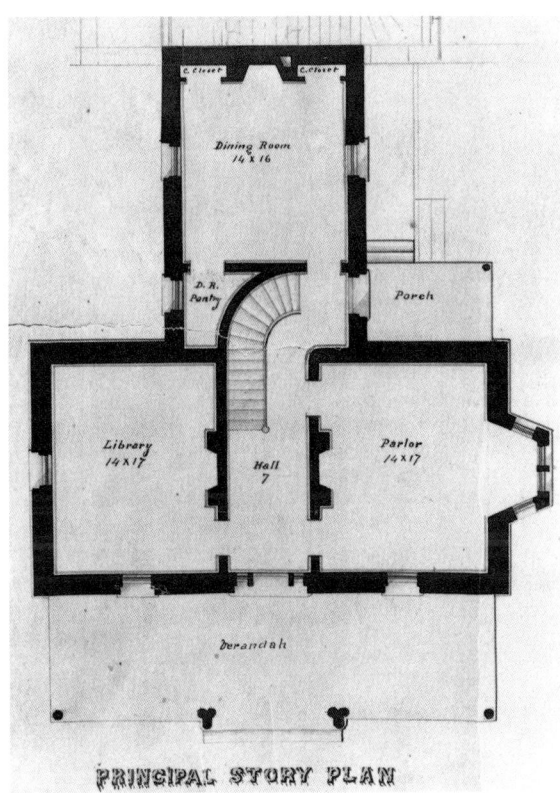

Plan of the parsonage for the Church of the Redeemer, Baltimore vicinity, by N. G. Starkwether, 1860. *Maryland Historical Society*

224

Top: Parsonage for the Church of the Redeemer, Baltimore vicinity, 1860, with its model, Design II of A. J. Downing's *Cottage Residences* (New York, 1842).
Bottom: Fairy Knowe, John H. B. Latrobe House, Baltimore vicinity, 1850, with its model, Design XXV of Downing's *The Architecture of Country Houses* (New York, 1850). *Church of the Redeemer; Private Collection; Maryland Historical Society; Private Collection*

Top: Albert C. Greene Villa, Frostberg, c. 1853, with its model, Design XX of A. J. Downing's *Country Houses*. Bottom: Charles Trail House, Frederick, 1855, with its model, Design XXI of Samuel Sloan's *The Model Architect* (Philadelphia, 1852–53). *Photograph of Greene Villa by Van Jones Martin; photograph of Trail House by Jeff D. Goldman; book illustrations from private collection*

dences. In May, 1861, James Harrison was employed to build the parsonage; in 1863, after delays caused by wartime shortages of men and material, Harrison was discharged and replaced by a builder named A. H. Bucher, who completed the work in February, 1864.[117]

John H. B. Latrobe, born in Philadelphia in 1803, son of the architect Benjamin Latrobe, was an inventor, bibliophile and architectural connoisseur as well as a railroad lawyer. He was also an artist of considerable skill, who had worked in his father's office and been sent to West Point because it offered the only engineering school in the United States before the Civil War. His summer house of Fairy Knowe, near the Baltimore and Ohio rail line in the western suburb of Baltimore known as Lawyers' Hill, burned in 1850. Within days, after a consultation over the weekend with a builder, perhaps the carpenter A. L. McNeal who had built the earlier house, Latrobe selected an illustration in Downing's newly published *Country Houses* and completed construction in just fifty-four working days.[118] Except for the addition of an exuberant corner tower, the new house, with its two front-facing gables and board-and-batten siding, resembled Downing's Design XXV, "A Plain Timber Cottage-Villa."

In the early 1850's, Albert C. Greene, the superintendent of a coal mine in western Maryland, built an Italian villa outside the town of Frostburg, soon after he arrived there from Providence, Rhode Island. Greene selected as his model Design XX, a "Villa in the Italian Style," in Downing's *Country Houses*.

Another luxurious architecture book was *The Model Architect* by the Philadelphian Samuel Sloan, published there in 1852–53. Sloan's Design VI was the model for an Italian villa built in Talbot County in 1853–54 for the Baltimore banker Richard France. This villa was demolished in 1954. Sloan's Design XXI was the model for Charles E. Trail's 1855 Italianate mansion at Frederick.

Larger and more lavish designs were featured in another mid-19th-century pattern book, William H. Ranlett's *The Architect,* published at New York in 1847–49. Junius Brutus Booth, the English-born actor who was for thirty years, despite a fondness for drink, the greatest tragic actor of his time, came to America in 1821 and purchased a farm at Bel Air, Maryland, the following year. About 1850, only two or three years before his death, Booth built a little Gothic cottage modeled on Design XVII of Ranlett's book. Junius Brutus Booth was the father of two actors, Edwin Booth and the infamous John Wilkes Booth, who shot President Lincoln in the closing days of the Civil War.

Design XVII of William H. Ranlett's *The Architect* (New York, 1847–49), the model for Tudor Hall. *Private Collection*

Tudor Hall, Junius Brutus Booth Villa, Bel Air, c. 1850.

Design XXVIII of A. J. Downing's *The Architecture of Country Houses* (New York, 1850), the model for William Wyman Villa, Baltimore. *Private Collection*

One of the most arresting and popular designs in Downing's *Country Houses* was Design XXVIII, an Italian villa that had been designed in 1845 by Richard Upjohn for Edward King at Newport, Rhode Island. Versions of the King villa were built at Richmond, Virginia; Marion, Alabama; and Baltimore. In 1851, only a few months after the publication of *Country Houses*, William Wyman, a Baltimore merchant, asked his brother-in-law, the New York lawyer Herman D. Aldrich, to visit Upjohn's office, because he wished to build a villa based on Design XXVIII. In June, 1851, Aldrich reported on his visit with the architect: "I have seen Mr. Upjohn & he thinks Mr. King's cottage as built cost about $20,000.... Mr. Upjohn would be very glad to make your plans ... Mr. King's or any other of his which you might decide on. He showed me some of his designs which I like full as well or better than Mr. King's. He has a great many plans and designs in his office."[119] Soon thereafter, Wyman and Aldrich returned to Upjohn's office, but, in the architect's absence, his assistant pretended he could not locate the drawings. Aldrich observed of architects: "They are very careful not to let others take ideas from them if they can prevent it."[120] In spite of Aldrich's earnest advice to hire a proper architect, Wyman began construction in the fall of 1851 with a local builder copying the Upjohn design from Downing's book; after a few weeks Wyman was again begging architectural advice from his relatives. At the end of 1851, Wyman asked his cousin, George H. Cary of Boston, to procure construction details from Francis Wilbar, the Newport carpenter who had built King's villa.[121] In December, Wilbar visited the house; the owner was not at home, so Wilbar bluffed his way inside, wandered around the premises, refreshing his memory and taking notes—and even taking a sample of leftover molding—later sending sketches and instructions for Wyman's builder in Baltimore.[122] Wyman's villa was completed in 1853 and demolished in 1955.

Octagons had a modest place in 18th- and early-19th-century Maryland architecture. Joseph Clark built an octagonal privy beside the State House at Annapolis and Joseph Horatio Anderson built an octagonal stable at Whitehall, outside Annapolis, in the 1770's. Sometime before 1798 members of the Carroll family built a one-story frame octagonal house, twenty-four feet in diameter, at The Caves, ten miles north of Baltimore. One of Robert Mills's early designs for the Baltimore Washington Monument was a seven-story-high octagon. An octagonal brick toll house, facing the old national highway, was erected in Cumberland County in 1836.

However, the interest in octagons received a new urgency in the writings of Orson Squire Fowler, a phrenologist, vegetarian, teetotaler, sex

William Wyman Villa, Baltimore, 1851–53. *The Peale Museum, Baltimore*

educator and publisher whose exotic, quixotic architectural ideas appealed to the emotional and idealistic age in which he lived. In his treatise *A Home for All, or the Gravel Wall and Octagon Mode of Building*, published in 1853, Fowler looked to the natural world for inspiration. Like Nature's own favorite shapes—fruits, eggs, nuts, seeds and tree trunks—Fowler believed that house plans should be circular—or, next best, octagonal. Almost singlehandedly, Fowler popularized a new gimmick in American domestic architecture, but it was only a passing fad, for these octagonal buildings were architectural mules with a strange ancestry and no hope of offspring.

We have counted two or three octagons in each of the states from Virginia to Louisiana, but Maryland, the most northern of the Southern states, had the most. Octagonal houses were built at Lutherville for the Rev. William Heilig, a second for the Jewett family on the western outskirts of Darlington and a third, a three-story frame octagon, for the tailor Henry T. Scott at Hyattsville. In 1854 Charles Calvert, an ardent agricultural reformer who was the grandson of Henri Stier, builder of Riversdale mansion near Bladensburg, won the Maryland Agricultural Society's annual award with his plan for an octagonal cattle barn. The barn was two stories high, one hundred feet in diameter, with a glass dome and paved gutters for urine and manure.[123] Thomas and James Dixon designed a four-story brick octagonal dormitory and classroom building, two hundred feet in diameter, for the Mount Washington Female College in 1856.[124]

Despite the region's reputed antipathy toward industry, manufacturing had a long and honorable history in Southern life—and more in Maryland than in any other state of the Old South.[125] In the 1730's members of the Carroll family erected an iron furnace on the south bank of the Patapsco River near the Jones Falls; Maryland began shipping iron as well as tobacco to England; and by 1756 there were six ironworks in Baltimore County. The greatest 19th-century Maryland manufacturer of cast iron, Bartlett and Hayward, began operations in the 1830's. Iron beams were used for structural support in William F. Small's 1830 Maryland Penitentiary. In May, 1833, the Baltimore booksellers Carey, Hart and Company offered Thomas Tredgold's *Practical Essay on the Strength of Cast Iron* and Turnbull's *Treatise on the Strength and Dimension of Cast Iron Beams*, two obscure books on industrial technology. The 1830's began a period of railroad construction, and by the Civil War the Baltimore and Ohio Railroad built seventy-one iron bridges.[126]

In the 1840's and 1850's, prosperity returned to Baltimore. Shipping, especially the South American trade, flourished, but more important

Charles Calvert's octagonal cattle barn at Riversdale, 1854, an illustration in *American Farmer* that same year. *Maryland Historical Society*

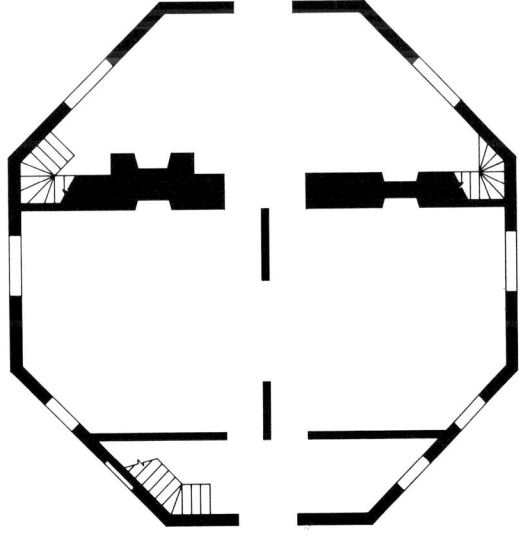

Jewett Family Octagon, Darlington vicinity, c. 1855.

was the completion of the railroads, symbolizing Baltimore's reliance on steam-powered manufacturing and the iron industry in particular. Though Romantic styles were in part a reaction against industrialization, the elaborate ornament in wood and metal so necessary to create Gothic and Italianate decorations were facilitated by steam-powered sawmills and iron foundries. Romanticism and industrialization, at first glance so antithetical, came to England at the same time, the end of the 18th century, and developed side by side as the two most important factors of 19th-century English life. Romantic architecture came to Maryland on a tide of industrial prosperity. Perhaps industrial backwardness in other parts of the South was one reason Romantic architecture, and the Gothic Revival particularly, did not flourish there.

In the early 1840's, nearly fifty tons of cast iron were used for the window frames, sashes and exterior moldings of Robert Cary Long, Jr.'s Church of the Immaculate Conception, and the same architect's 1848 Athenaeum featured cast-iron balconies and lintels.[127] A visitor to the new Baptist Church, rising at the corner of Saratoga and Paca streets in Baltimore in 1846, observed the conspicuous use of cast iron: "The uses to which cast iron is now applied appear to be steadily on the increase. . . . Now it is used for pillars, beams, doors and windows and is fast usurping hewn stone in furnishing building ornaments, cornices, &c."[128] "Almost every day shows some fresh innovation of cast iron upon the hitherto right of wood and stone."[129] The Baltimore City Hall proposed in 1860 by George A. Frederick (1842–1924), an architect who had worked for Lind and Murdoch, featured a dome with gigantic cast-iron Corinthian columns.

In the late 1840's, manufacturers discovered that cast iron was not only easy to use for ornament but that it was stronger, lighter and cheaper than masonry construction, also allowing more light and air into a building. Arunah S. Abell, proprietor of the *Sun* newspaper of Baltimore, had been born in Rhode Island and worked in Providence, Boston and New York before coming to Maryland in 1837. An irrepressible innovator, Abell had used the Pony Express, carrier pigeons, the telegraph and rotary printing presses to speed the news. In 1850 he employed James Bogardus (1800–1875), a New York inventor who had recently introduced the use of cast iron for the construction of tall buildings, to design the structure of a cast-iron building for the *Sun* newspaper in Baltimore. Though Bogardus was responsible for the cast-iron structure, the general architects of the Sun Building were Robert G. Hatfield (1815–1879) of New York and William H. Reasin (c. 1820–1867) of Baltimore.[130] Reasin was the architect of the 1851 Maryland Institute on

Center Street, an Italianate public market and exhibition hall built for a society promoting the mechanical arts.[131] Reasin also designed the Byzantine-style house for Henry James on Paca and Lombard streets, 1853,[132] added a campanile to the Independent Fire Company, 1853, and designed Apollo Hall—with Venetian Gothic arches and iron columns manufactured by Bartlett and Hayward—on Baltimore Street in 1852[133] and the Swedenborgian Church, Orchard Street, in 1860.[134]

The Sun Building rose at a corner of Baltimore and Charles streets in 1850–51.[135] The façade displayed tiers of arches and twenty-three cast-iron statues of American patriots. The girders, floors, pillars and façade were cast iron. Cast iron for the windows and doors of the first story was produced by Daniel Badger, a Massachusetts-born industrialist who had worked for three years, 1818–21, as a jeweler's engraver in Savannah, Georgia, before becoming the principal manufacturer of cast iron in New York. Badger produced cast iron for at least three other commercial buildings in Baltimore: the Canfield Brothers store,[136] the Joseph King store designed by Dixon, Balbirnie and Dixon,[137] and the Adam Company store, Baltimore Street, designed by William H. Reasin in 1852.[138] The columns and castings for the upper façade of the Sun Building were manufactured by Benjamin S. Benson of Baltimore; interior columns were produced by Adam Denmead of Baltimore; and construction was supervised by the veteran builders Henry and Josiah Reynolds. The first story of the Sun Building contained shops; the second story was occupied by a telegraph company; the newspaper's editorial and composing rooms and job printing office were on the third story; two underground stories, extending beneath the sidewalks, lighted by glass pavements and ventilated by hollow iron pipes, were occupied by presses and storerooms. The Sun Building was destroyed in a fire that swept downtown Baltimore in 1904.

In 1861, when the Sun Building was eight years old, Maryland's iron manufacturers began casting cannon for the Civil War. Despite its history as a slave state and considerable pro-Southern sentiment, Maryland did not leave the Union to join the Confederacy—and the cannon were sent to the Northern army.

Sun Building, Baltimore, 1850–51, seen on a sheet music cover. *Maryland Historical Society*

Notes

The following notes record the author's debt to other writers in place of an extended bibliography and also suggest further reading. The place to begin studying Maryland architecture is at the Maryland Historical Trust, Annapolis, which maintains extensive files of National Register properties and county surveys of historic buildings throughout Maryland.

I. THE COLONY

1. Clayton Colman Hall, *Narratives of Early Maryland, 1633–1684* (New York, 1910), 21–22, 94–95, 98–99.
2. Maryland Historical Society, *The Calvert Papers*, III (Baltimore, 1899), 21.
3. *Calvert Papers*, I (Baltimore, 1889), 174.
4. Garry Wheller Stone, "Society, Housing and Architecture in Early Maryland: John Lewger's St. John's," Ph.D. dissertation, University of Pennsylvania, 1982; William Hand Browne, *Archives of Maryland*, IV (Baltimore, 1887), 422–424.
5. *Ibid.*, 189.
6. Michael G. Kammen, "Maryland in 1699: A Letter from the Rev. Hugh Jones," *Journal of Southern History*, XXIX (1963), 362–372.
7. *Archives of Maryland*, X (Baltimore, 1891), 213–214.
8. *Ibid.*, 301–302.
9. *Archives of Maryland*, I (Baltimore, 1883), 538–539.
10. *Archives of Maryland*, II (Baltimore, 1884), 138.
11. *Ibid.*, 405–406.
12. *Archives of Maryland*, V (Baltimore, 1887), 266.
13. Peter Sluyter and Jaspar Danckaerts, *Journal of a Voyage to New York & A Tour in Several of the American Colonies in 1679–80* (Brooklyn, 1867), 173.
14. Cary Carson et al., "Impermanent Architecture in the Southern American Colonies," *Winterthur Portfolio*, XVI (1981), 135–196.
15. Susan Myers Kingsbury, *The Records of the Virginia Company of London* (Washington, 1906–35), IV, 259.
16. Henry F. Thompson, "Maryland at the End of the Seventeenth Century," *Maryland Historical Magazine* (henceforth abbreviated *MHM*), II (1907), 163–171; Gloria L. Main, *Tobacco Colony: Life in Early Maryland* (Princeton, 1982). The volumes of *MHM* are numbered in roman numerals to XLIX (1954) and with Arabic numerals from 50 (1955).
17. Thomas Hollyday, "Readbourne Manor Revisited: Gleanings from an Eighteenth-Century Journal," *MHM*, 85 (1990), 44–50. The quoted sentence, on page 44 of the published journal, differs slightly from my transcription, which was made from a xerox of the original supplied by Michael F. Trostel.
18. John Christensen and Charles Bohl, *McDowell Hall at St. John's College in Annapolis, 1742–1989* (Annapolis, 1989).
19. *Ibid.*, 9.
20. Rev. Andrew Burnaby, *Travels through the Middle Settlements in North-America* (London, 1775), 66.
21. J. Reaney Kelley, "Tulip Hill, Its History and Its People," *MHM*, 60 (1965), 349–403.
22. Cary Carson, "Mulberry Fields, St. Mary's County, Maryland," typescript, Maryland Historical Trust files.
23. *Maryland Gazette*, Annapolis, May 22, 1751.
24. *Ibid.*, January 31, 1760.
25. *Ibid.*, November 1, 1774.
26. *Ibid.*, February 14, 1771; see also Alfred Coxe Prime, *The Arts & Crafts in Philadelphia, Maryland and South Carolina* (n.p., 1929).
27. The author is indebted to the research files at Sotterley mansion.
28. Vestry Minutes, St. Andrew's Church, April–May, 1766, Hall of Records, Annapolis, microfilm.
29. Charles Scarlett, Jr., "Governor Horatio Sharpe's Whitehall," *MHM*, XLVI (1951), 8–26.
30. *Ibid.*, 12.
31. Aubrey C. Land, "The Familiar Letters of Governor Horatio Sharpe," *MHM*, 61 (1966), 61.
32. The author is indebted to Mrs. F. Leif Eareckson of Annapolis for information about Upton Scott House.
33. "Chinese" stairs appear at Sotterley and Bushwood in St. Mary's County, Paca House, Bohemia in Cecil County, and Oak Lawn, c. 1783, in Caroline County.
34. Orlando Ridout IV, "The James Brice House, Annapolis, Maryland," M.A. thesis, University of Maryland, 1978; James Brice's accounts, quoted extensively in the thesis, are at the Hall of Records in Annapolis.
35. Michael F. Trostel, *Mount Clare* (Baltimore, c. 1981).
36. *Ibid.*, 34.
37. Joseph Kennedy, stucco worker, mentioned his work at Mount Clare in his advertisement, *Maryland Journal*, Baltimore, October 6, 1789.
38. Ann C. Van Devanter, *Anywhere So Long as There Be Freedom, Charles Carroll of Carrollton, His Family & His Maryland* (Baltimore, 1975).
39. Ralph D. Gray and Gerald E. Hartdagen, "A Glimpse of Baltimore Society in 1827: Letters by Henry D. Gilpin," *MHM*, 69 (1974), 266–268.
40. Rosamond Randall Beirne, "The Chase House in Annapolis," *MHM*, XLIX (1954).

41. Rosamond Randall Beirne and John Henry Scarff, *William Buckland* (n.p., 1958); Barbara Allston Brand, "William Buckland, Architect in Annapolis" in Mario di Valmarana, *Building by the Book* (Charlottesville, 1986), 65–100.

42. Buckland's inventory described in *MHM*, XLI (1946), 217–218.

43. Morris L. Radoff, *The State House at Annapolis* (Annapolis, 1972).

44. Rosamond Randall Beirne, "Two Anomalous Annapolis Architects: Joseph Horatio Anderson and Robert Key," *MHM*, 55 (1960), 183–200.

45. Morris L. Radoff, "Charles Wallace as Undertaker of the State House," *MHM*, 51 (1956), 50–53.

46. Joseph Towne Wheeler, "Reading and Other Recreations of Marylanders," *MHM*, XXXVIII (1943), 171–75.

47. Advertisement for further repairs to State House, *The Maryland Journal and Baltimore Advertiser*, Baltimore, May 11, 1792.

II. THE FEDERAL ERA

1. Fred W. Dumschott, *Washington College* (Chestertown, 1980).

2. *Ibid.*, 41.

3. Maynard Pressley White, Jr., "An Account of the First College Edifice of Washington College, Chestertown, Maryland, 1783–1827," M.A. thesis, University of Delaware, 1966.

4. Kym Snyder Rice, "Joseph Clark, Maryland Architect," *Antiques*, CXV (1979), 552–555.

5. Quoted in *Ibid*.

6. *Maryland Gazette*, Baltimore, April 7, 1785.

7. Jeanne F. Butler, *Competition 1792: Designing a Nation's Capitol* (Washington, 1976).

8. *Maryland Journal and Baltimore Advertiser*, Baltimore, January 17, 1794.

9. Gregory A. Stiverson and Phoebe R. Jacobson, *William Paca: A Biography* (Baltimore, 1976).

10. *Maryland Journal and Baltimore Universal Daily Advertiser*, Baltimore, January 1, 1795.

11. Lynne Dakin Hastings, *A Guidebook to Hampton National Historic Site* (Towson, 1986).

12. Records for family building projects, including Hampton, are in Ridgely Family Papers, MS 692 and MS 692.1, at Maryland Historical Society.

13. Jehu Howell drowned in 1787, *Maryland Journal*, Baltimore, November 27, 1787.

14. Edwin Wolff, 2d, "The Library of Edward Lloyd IV," *Winterthur Portfolio*, V (1969), 87–121.

15. John Tilden Howard, "The Doctor Gustavus Brown" in *Annals of Medical History*, New Series, IX (1937), 437–448.

16. *The Cultivator*, 5 (October, 1839), 148.

17. Ruthella Page Andrews, "The City of Baltimore, 1797–1850" in Clayton Colman Hall, *Baltimore, Its History and Its People* (New York, 1912).

18. Extensive documentation for the construction of a house on Pleasant Street, Baltimore, for Judith C. Riddell by John Donaldson, 1810–12, can be found in Pleasants Papers, MS 194, Maryland Historical Society.

19. *Maryland Journal*, Baltimore, August 10, 1792.

20. *Federal Intelligencer & Baltimore Daily Advertiser*, Baltimore, October 3, 1795.

21. *Federal Gazette & Baltimore Daily Advertiser*, Baltimore, March 12, 1817.

22. Judge William Cranch to Benjamin H. Latrobe, quoted by Latrobe, 1817, John C. Van Horne, *The Correspondence and Miscellaneous Papers of Benjamin Henry Latrobe*, III (New Haven, 1988), 972.

23. *Maryland Gazette or the Baltimore General Advertiser*, Baltimore, November 14, 1783.

24. *Ibid.*, February 21, 1786.

25. *Ibid.*, January 16, 1787.

26. *Baltimore Daily Intelligencer*, Baltimore, June 10, 1794.

27. *Federal Intelligencer and Maryland Daily Gazette*, Baltimore, January 14, 1795.

28. A pioneering survey of early architects in Baltimore is Claire Wittler Eckels, "Baltimore's Earliest Architects," Ph.D. dissertation, Johns Hopkins University, 1950.

29. *Maryland Journal or Baltimore Advertiser*, December 28, 1784.

30. Jeanne F. Butler, *op. cit.*, describes the submissions of Hart and Diamond; Diamond announces that he has invented an instrument to measure "the right line, distance, bearing and size of any object" by sight only, *Maryland Gazette or the Baltimore General Advertiser*, Baltimore, April 29, 1785; most of the competition drawings are at the Maryland Historical Society.

31. *Maryland Journal and Baltimore Advertiser*, Baltimore, August 19, 1791.

32. J.H.B. Latrobe, *Picture of Baltimore* (Baltimore, 1832), 81, 91; Milliman's obituary, *American and Commercial Daily Advertiser*, Baltimore, December 9, 1850.

33. Latrobe, who often criticized craftsmen-builders, praised Steuart as "a scholar as well as a workman."

34. *Federal Intelligencer and Baltimore Daily Advertiser*, Baltimore, October 3, 1795.

35. *Federal Intelligencer and Baltimore Daily Advertiser*, July 22, 1795; *American*, Baltimore, November 29, 1832.

36. The author is indebted to Barry Kessler, Decorative Arts Curator, Carroll Mansion, City Life Museums, Baltimore, for his guidance; Helen Straw

Whitmore, "The Carroll Mansion . . . An Historical and Architectural Study," M.S. thesis, University of Maryland, 1969.

37. *Federal Gazette*, Baltimore, July 29, 1797.

38. *American and Daily Advertiser*, Baltimore, April 4, 1801.

39. *Federal Gazette*, Baltimore, July 29, 1796.

40. *Federal Journal*, Baltimore, April 5, 1793.

41. *Federal Intelligencer and Baltimore Daily Advertiser*, Baltimore, August 18, 1795.

42. *Maryland Journal*, Baltimore, April 20, 1784.

43. The Maryland Historical Society has manuscript and printed catalogues of the Library Company of Baltimore; catalogues were published in 1797, 1798, 1802, 1809, 1823.

44. Robert L. Raley, "The Baltimore Country House," M.A. thesis, University of Delaware, 1959.

45. Stiles Tuttle Colwill, *Francis Guy, 1760–1820* (Baltimore 1981).

46. Godfrey T. Vigne, *Six Months in America* (London, 1832), I, 129.

47. "Sales at Auction of the Personal Estate of Col. John E. Howard at Belvidere House . . . 1827," Maryland Historical Society.

48. Thomas W. Griffith, *Annals of Baltimore* (Baltimore, 1824), 154–155, says Willow Brook was built by Scroggs, Robert Steuart and James Mosher, "erected on a plan furnished by himself [Thoroughgood Smith]."

49. Robert Gilmor, Jr., "Memoir in Sketch of the History of Robert Gilmor of Baltimore," 30, Maryland Historical Society.

50. J. Gilman Paul, "Montebello, Home of General Samuel Smith," *MHM*, XLII (1947), 253–260.

51. Eugene Calvert Holland, "Riversdale, the Stier-Calvert Home." *MHM*, XLV (1950), 281.

52. The author is indebted to William Elder, Baltimore Museum of Art, for pointing out Birch's possible role in designing Montebello.

53. The author is indebted to Susan Tripp, Homewood House, for opening her research notebooks, from which the information in this paragraph has been extracted; the original documents are at the Maryland Historical Society and the Historical Society of Pennsylvania; Susan Gerwe Tripp, "Homewood in Baltimore, Maryland," *Antiques*, CXXXIII (1988), 248–257; Mendell, Mesick, Cohen, White, "Homewood, A Historic Structures Report," Johns Hopkins University, 1983.

54. Ralph D. Gray and Gerald E. Hartdagen, "A Glimpse of Baltimore Society in 1827: Letters by Henry D. Gilpin," *MHM*, 69 (1974), 263.

55. Robert L. Alexander, "Nicholas Rogers, Gentleman Architect of Baltimore," *MHM*, 78 (1983), 85–105.

56. In his *Picture of Baltimore*, J. H. B. Latrobe says Long, Sr., designed the Baltimore County Jail.

57. *American and Commercial Daily Advertiser*, Baltimore, October 2, 1835.

58. Robert L. Alexander, "The Union Bank by Long after Soane," *Journal of the Society of Architectural Historians*, XXII (1963), 135–138.

59. The manuscript records of the Library Company are at the Maryland Historical Society.

60. Nicholas Rogers to Rev. James Kemp, February 2, 1814, Archives of the Episcopal Diocese of Maryland.

61. Latrobe mentions that Godefroy had been asked to prepare a design for the Medical College, John C. Van Horne, *op. cit.*, 282.

62. Thomas W. Griffith, *Annals of Baltimore* (Baltimore, 1824).

63. Carol Eaton Herner, *Rembrandt Peale, 1778–1860, A Life in the Arts* (Philadelphia, 1985); Wilbur Harvey Hunter, Jr., *The Story of America's Oldest Museum Building* (Baltimore, 1952); Hunter, *Rendezvous for Taste, Peale's Baltimore Museum* (Baltimore, 1956); Hunter, *The Peale Family and Peale's Baltimore Museum* (Baltimore, 1965).

64. Nicholas Rogers to Rev. James Kemp, February 2, 1814, Archives of the Episcopal Diocese of Maryland. The author is exceedingly grateful to F. Garner Ranney, the distinguished Archivist, for pointing out this document.

65. *Federal Gazette and Baltimore Daily Advertiser*, Baltimore, March 12, 1817.

66. Gwynn was writing anonymously in the Delphinians' *The Red Book* (Baltimore, 1819), 55–65.

67. John Earle Uhler, "The Delphinian Club," *MHM*, XX (1925), 305–346.

68. *American and Commercial Daily Advertiser*, Baltimore, July 11, 1817.

69. Latrobe to Maximilian Godefroy, July 19, 1815, in Van Horne, *op. cit.*, 674.

70. Latrobe to Godefroy, January, 1807, in *Ibid.*, II (New Haven, 1986), 359.

71. Latrobe to Richard Caton, May 25, 1817, in *Ibid.*, III, 882.

72. Latrobe to Godefroy, October 10, 1814, in *Ibid.*, III, 579.

73. The author is indebted to Margaret Law Callcott for her great generosity in sharing typescripts of Stier family letters relating to the design and construction of Riversdale; Margaret Law Callcott, *Mistress of Riversdale, The Plantation Letters of Rosalie Stier Calvert, 1795–1821* (Baltimore, in press).

74. The author is indebted to Alfons Bousse of Belgium for providing the xerox copies used to re-create Latrobe's lost drawing of Riversdale.

75. Latrobe to Bishop John Carroll, March, 1806, Van Horne, *op. cit.*, II, 210.

76. Latrobe to Carroll, December 13, 1806, *Ibid.*, 324.

77. Proposals requested to build foundations of the new portico, *The Sun*, Baltimore, June 14, 1841.

78. Godefroy's own catalogue of his works, "*Indication des Pièces Justificatives*," was published by Caroline V. Davison, "Maximilian Godefroy," in *MHM*, XXIX (1934), 175–212. See Robert L. Alexander, *Maximilian Godefroy* (Baltimore, 1974).

79. *Federal Gazette and Baltimore Daily Advertiser*, Baltimore, February 24, 1809.

80. Paul F. Norton, "The Architect of Calverton," *MHM*, 76 (1981), 113–123.

81. House at Calverton described as "a large Mansion House, built of stone . . . three stories in height . . . a basement, containing kitchen, pantries, servants apartments, &c., &c., the first floor . . . of four rooms, two circular 26 feet in diameter, two square . . . and a hall 14 feet wide. . . . The exterior is rough cast of a straw color, the window sills and facings of marble and free stone," *American and Commercial Daily Advertiser*, Baltimore, March 11, 1820; another ad appeared in the same paper, January 12, 1821.

82. Talbot Hamlin, *Benjamin Henry Latrobe* (New York, 1955), 489.

83. Latrobe asked Godefroy to collaborate in June, 1815; the design was accepted in February, 1816; they quarreled in the summer of 1816.

84. These quoted sentences have been reordered for literary purposes: Latrobe to John Spear Smith, "director of the Exchange," June 6, 1816, in Van Horne, *op. cit.*, III, 785.

85. *American and Commercial Daily Advertiser*, Baltimore, February 29, 1820, June 2, 1820.

86. "You were so pleased with the Church that I have designed the building in the same taste." Latrobe to Samuel Ringgold, March 10, 1817, Van Horne, *op. cit.*, III, 867.

87. Robert Goodloe Harper to Latrobe, May 30, 1817, *Ibid.*, 883–884.

88. Latrobe to Maximilian Godefroy, October 10, 1814, *Ibid.*, 580.

89. Michael Xavier Evans, "The Daily Journal of Robert Mills, Baltimore, 1816," *MHM*, XXX (1935), 257–269.

90. Robert McCleery Account Book, 1814–16, Maryland Historical Society.

91. Robert Mills to John Hoffman, July 19, 1817, Maryland Historical Society.

92. House of Industry Records, 1817–23, RG 19, Baltimore City Archives, document this project. By March 18, 1818, the committee had purchased a lot on the east side of the Jones Falls from Martin Rivers and plans had been prepared by the same date.

93. Robert L. Alexander, "William F. Small, Architect of the City," *Journal of the Society of Architectural Historians*, XX (1961), 63–77.

94. *American and Commercial Daily Advertiser*, Baltimore, October 9, 1824.

95. All three of these public buildings are illustrated in John H. B. Latrobe's *Picture of Baltimore*.

96. W. Ray Luce, "The Cohen Brothers of Baltimore: From Lotteries to Banking," *MHM*, 68 (1973), 288–308.

97. *American and Commercial Daily Advertiser*, Baltimore, January 6, 1830.

98. *Ibid.*, June 1, 1831.

III. THE GREEK REVIVAL

1. *American and Commercial Daily Advertiser*, Baltimore, November 15, 1839.

2. *An Account of the Grand Celebration of the Independent Order of Odd-Fellows for the Dedication of the New Hall* (Baltimore, 1831), 51.

3. *American and Commercial Daily Advertiser*, Baltimore, May 5, 1830, June 3, 1831, and June 26, 1832.

4. The construction date for the McKim Free School has often been given as 1821–22, a mistake. Though there was another McKim school that opened nearby, the Grecian building was a decade later. The first building is mentioned in *American and Commercial Daily Advertiser*, Baltimore, February 28, 1821; Charles Varle in his *Complete View of Baltimore* (Baltimore, 1833), says McKim Free School is "a splendid edifice not yet finished . . . now building," 31; W. H. Corwin, *A Guide to the City of Baltimore* (Baltimore, 1869), 91, gives the date as 1833.

5. Obituary for William Howard, *American and Commercial Daily Advertiser*, Baltimore, August 29, 1834.

6. *Catalogue of the Splendid Library and Philosophical, Chemical and Astronomical Apparatus of the late Dr. William Howard* (Baltimore, 1834).

7. A. J. Davis, Diary, 37, Metropolitan Museum of Art.

8. A. J. Davis, Daybook, 145, New York Public Library.

9. A. J. Davis, Daybook, 148, New York Public Library; *American and Commercial Daily Advertiser*, Baltimore, January 17, 1833.

10. A plan, "City Residence for Robert Gilmor," at Avery Library, Columbia University, New York, is different from the Metropolitan Museum elevation.

11. A. J. Davis, Daybook, 131, 153, New York Public Library.

12. A. J. Davis, Daybook, 131, New York Public Library.

13. Tench Francis Tilghman, "An Early Victorian College, St. John's, 1830–1860," *MHM*, XLIV (1949), 251–268.

14. *American and Commercial Daily Advertiser*, Baltimore, May 14, 1833.

15. Hector Humphries to A. J. Davis, May 11, 1833, Davis Collection, Avery Architecture and Fine Arts Library.

16. *Baltimore Gazette and Daily Advertiser*, Baltimore, January 3, 1834, and January 7, 1835.

17. R. C. Long, Jr., to [Thomas B.] Dorsey, February 28, 1834, discusses fees and planning, Patapsco Female Institute Papers, Maryland Historical Society.

18. Trustees advertised for designs on November 21, 1833, *American and Commercial Daily Advertiser*, Baltimore.

19. *Ibid.*, April 9, 1834.

20. *Ibid.*, July 4, 1835, and July 24, 1835.

21. Extensive records of construction of Record Office are in Court House Commissioners Papers, 1835–37, RG-10, City Archives, Baltimore. George Milliman was named superintendent of repairs to the damaged courthouse; the agreement is dated April 28, 1835.

22. Robert Mills to Solomon Etting, April 7, 1835, and April 14, 1835, in Court House Commissioners Papers, Baltimore City Archives.

23. R. C. Long, Jr., to Solomon Etting, April 17, 1836; in Court House Commissioners Papers; William Strickland to Solomon Etting, November 7, 1836, February 12, 1837, February 18, 1837, March 20, 1837, all in Court House Commissioners Papers.

24. Thomas U. Walter to Solomon Etting, June 4, 1838, in Court House Commissioners Papers.

25. *American and Commercial Daily Advertiser*, Baltimore, December 2, 1835.

26. The Record Office was nearly complete on November 27, 1839, *The Sun*, Baltimore.

27. *American and Commercial Daily Advertiser*, Baltimore, November 15, 1839; *The Sun*, Baltimore, November 16, 1839; *Baltimore Clipper*, Baltimore, November 18, 1839.

28. *The Sun*, Baltimore, November 24 and November 27, 1845. Saul E. Zalesch, "Synagogue Building in Baltimore during the Nineteenth Century," M.A. thesis, University of Delaware, 1984. The enlarged Synagogue is described in *The Sun*, September 15, 1860.

29. *The Sun*, Baltimore, May 23, 1843, October 11, 1843.

30. *Ibid.*, August 30, 1843, December 15, 1843. The church was built by Episcopalians in 1815–20 and acquired by the Methodists in 1828.

31. *Ibid.*, July 12, 1843.

32. *Ibid.*, February 27, 1846.

33. *Ibid.*, December 1, 1848.

34. Vestry Minutes, Christ Church, I, 118–119, Maryland Historical Society. The builder was Henry Little of Philadelphia.

35. Anna Wells Rutledge, *The Pennsylvania Academy of the Fine Arts, Cumulative Record of Exhibition Catalogues* (Philadelphia, 1955), 217.

36. "Sales of the Effects of Jos. Robinson, at his Store . . . December 8, 1850," City Archives, Baltimore.

37. *American and Commercial Daily Advertiser*, Baltimore, October 13, 1830.

38. *Ibid.*, March 24, 1831.

39. *Ibid.*, April 20, 1833.

40. *Ibid.*, September 3, 1835.

41. *Ibid.*, March 4, 1834.

42. Hall also published *Cabinet Maker's Assistant* (Baltimore, 1840) and *A New and Concise Method of Handrailing* (Baltimore, 1840).

43. Robert C. Smith, "John Hall, A Busy Man in Baltimore," *Antiques* 92 (1967), 360–366.

44. *The Sun*, Baltimore, September 17, 1840.

45. *Ibid.*, May 18, 1843, March 26, 1844, July 27, 1849.

46. *Ibid.*, February 11, 1843.

47. *Ibid.*, April 21, 1843.

48. *Ibid.*, September 2, 1844.

IV. ROMANTIC STYLES

1. *Maryland Gazette*, Annapolis, March 5, 1761.

2. *Maryland Journal and Baltimore Advertiser*, Baltimore, January 17, 1794.

3. Latrobe to his brother Christian, February 6, 1805, in Talbot Hamlin, *Benjamin Henry Latrobe* (New York, 1955), 234.

4. They "turned the windows, doors, porches, &c. into Gothic." Henry Gilpin to his father, September, 1827, Ralph D. Gray and Gerald E. Hartdagen, "A Glimpse of Baltimore Society in 1827: Letters by Henry D. Gilpin," *MHM*, 69 (1974), 261.

5. Robert Gilmor of Glen Ellen inherited some of his uncle's pictures. *Catalogue of Rare and Valuable Oil Paintings, Engravings, &c. . . . of the late Robert Gilmor . . . at Glen Ellen* (Baltimore, 1875).

6. Robert Gilmor, Travel Diary, MS 387, Maryland Historical Society.

7. Davis went to Baltimore in June, 1831, as part of "a Tour of observation in the South." A. J. Davis, Daybook, 118, New York Public Library; Davis returned to Baltimore in June, 1832, A. J. Davis, Daybook, 135, New York Public Library; October, 1832, work, A. J. Davis, Diary, 31, Metropolitan Museum of Art, and Daybook, 141, New York Public Library.

8. A. J. Davis, Daybook, 147, New York Public Library.

9. Davis left Baltimore in early summer of 1833. His only subsequent project in Maryland was a September, 1835, "sketch of a Pavillion in Moorish style" for a Mr. Cameron of Baltimore. A. J. Davis, Daybook, 201, New York Public Library; Diary, 62, Metropolitan Museum of Art.

10. March 29, 1833, Board of Visitors of St. John's College resolved to build "a boarding house" for a steward, his family and lodgings for forty students and delegated the selection of a site and management of construction to the Principal; finally resolved to build after a delay raising money, February, 1835 (Proceedings of Visitors and Governors of St. John's College, 115, 135, Hall of Records Annapolis); *An Account of the Ceremony of Laying the Corner Stone of the New Building at St. John's College* (Annapolis, 1835); receipts to Elijah Wells for building the new college building begin April, 1835, and extend at least through January, 1837 (Treasury Department of Records, St. John's College, Hall of Records); Elijah Wells prepared estimate for outfitting library in the new building, April, 1837 (Humphries Correspondence, 1831–57, St. John's College Papers, Hall of Records).

11. In the late 1830's Long, Jr., proposed Egyptian entrance gates to Green Mount Cemetery, but again the authorities selected an alternate—Gothic—design. Thomas U. Walter also designed Egyptian gates for a Baltimore cemetery. "An elegant perspective view of the lodges and iron railings . . . in the Mount Orange Cemetery . . . of the Egyptian style," *The Sun*, Baltimore, February 13, 1839.

12. *The Sun*, Baltimore, August 28, 1843.

13. *Ibid.*, October 11, 1839; advertisement for school, *Ibid.*, October 11, 1839; further ad for school teaching carpentry and architecture, *Republican Daily Argus*, Baltimore, January 3, 1851; obituary, *The Sun*, Baltimore, April 8, 1868.

14. *The Sun*, Baltimore, August 28, 1843.

15. *Ibid.*, November 26, 1850, and April 27, 1852.

16. R. C. Long, Jr., "Gothic Architecture: A New Look" in *U.S. Catholic Magazine*, 2 (May, 1843), 297–304; St. Alphonsus Church steeple was completed by Louis L. Long, *The Sun*, Baltimore, October 15, 1855.

17. *The Sun*, Baltimore, July 12, 1843.

18. Vestry Minutes, Franklin Street Presbyterian Church, August 26, 1844, Maryland Historical Society.

19. R. C. Long, Jr., "Gothic Architecture," 297; in February, 1844, a circular was printed describing a plan for a new church to be built on Franklin Street by R. C. Long, Jr., Circular in Pamphlets VII, 37, Archives of the Episcopal Diocese of Maryland.

20. *The Sun*, Baltimore, March 15, 1845, February 19, 1846, January 7, 1848.

21. Drawings for Trinity Church, Upper Marlboro, were completed, R. C. Long, Jr., to Bishop William R. Whittingham, January 12, 1846, Archives of the Episcopal Diocese of Maryland.

22. Vestry approved plans for St. John's, Huntingdon, in May, 1846; construction began April, 1847; completed, November, 1847. *Journal of the Sixtieth Annual Convention of the Protestant Episcopal Church in Maryland* (Baltimore, 1848), 22.

23. *Journal of the Fifty-Seventh Convention of the Protestant Episcopal Church in Maryland* (Baltimore, 1845), 38.

24. *Journal of the Sixtieth Annual Convention of the Protestant Episcopal Church in Maryland* (Baltimore, 1848), 22. Long also designed a 150-foot-tall steeple for Christ Church, Gay and Fayette streets, Baltimore, in 1845, *The Sun*, Baltimore, August 29, 1845.

25. J.H.B. Latrobe's c. 1843 house at Fairy Knowe was illustrated in *The American Farmer*, I, 2 (August, 1845), 49–50, with a note that he had been the object of admiration "for the last two years."

26. Bryden Bordley Hale, "Evesham, A Baltimore Villa," *MHM*, 52 (1957), 202–209. Long's drawings had not turned up when this article was written.

27. Johnson and Lee building, *The Sun*, Baltimore, April 22, 1846, and September 9, 1846.

28. *Ibid.*, September 29, 1846, and October 21, 1846.

29. Foundations for the Athenaeum begun, *Ibid.*, October 1, 1846.

30. *Ibid.*, September 21, 1848.

31. *Ibid.*, September 12, 1848.

32. Baltimore American Building illustrated, George W. Howard, *The Monumental City* (Baltimore, 1873), 55.

33. "He [Long, Jr.] was said to have been stricken with cholera while journeying to New York City and was hastily removed from the train at some point near New Brunswick, N.J., and there died in an outhouse," George Frederick, Reminiscences, 5, Maryland Historical Society.

34. Walter's plan for Glenelg is dated February 5, 1851.

35. Thomas U. Walter to John A. McAllister, November 26, 1860, Letterbook, Walter Collection, Athenaeum of Philadelphia. The author is indebted to Bruce Laverty for pointing out this interesting document.

36. R. Ralston Cox, corresponding secretary, wrote to Bishop Whittingham, March 27, 1848, to

announce the foundation of the New York Ecclesiological Society and invite him to become a patron and founding member, Archives of the Episcopal Diocese of Maryland.

37. Wills first wrote Whittingham seeking employment on December 13, 1847, and presented books to Whittingham, March 7, 1850, Archives of the Episcopal Diocese of Maryland.

38. Samuel M. Semmes, treasurer of building committee, mentions Notman's visit to Cumberland and the architect's suggestion of adding a gallery, Semmes to Bishop William R. Whittingham, June 23, 1851, Archives of the Episcopal Diocese of Maryland.

39. Bishop William R. Whittingham to Richard Upjohn, "St. James Day, 1843," Upjohn Collection, New York Public Library.

40. Upjohn to Whittingham, July 21, 1843, August 2, 1843, November 21, 1844, and January 22, 1845, Archives of the Episcopal Diocese of Maryland.

41. Rev. Theodore P. Barker to Bishop William R. Whittingham, June 18, 1847, Archives of the Episcopal Diocese of Maryland.

42. Specifications for a frame church "near the city of Baltimore" for G. S. Norris, March 1852, Upjohn Collection, New York Public Library.

43. G. S. Norris to Richard Upjohn, March 15, 1853, Upjohn Collection, New York Public Library.

44. Rev. Henry V. D. Johns to Upjohn, July 4, 1851, August 30, 1851, December 1, 1851, and January 5, 1853.

45. Tench Tilghman to Bishop William R. Whittingham, November 9, 1853, Archives of the Episcopal Diocese of Maryland; other letters from Tilghman to Upjohn, September 30, 1851, October 7, 1851, July 12, 1852, July 13, 1852, July 27, 1852, August 17, 1852, September 27, 1852, March 29, 1853, November 23, 1853, November 28, 1854, and specifications, July, 1852, Upjohn Collection, New York Public Library.

46. Drawings for All Saints' Church, Frederick, are at Avery Library, D-4, 1–4.

47. *The Sun*, Baltimore, May 1, 1854.

48. George S. Norris to Richard Upjohn, May 1, 1854, Upjohn Collection, New York Public Library.

49. Surviving walls incorporated in new building, *The Sun*, Baltimore, January 11, 1856.

50. Specifications for courthouse, August, 1852, Upjohn Collection, New York Public Library.

51. Other letters relating to St. Paul's in Upjohn Collection, New York Public Library, include June 19, 1854, January 29, 1855, and September 4, 1855.

52. Rev. E. B. Tuttle to Upjohn, July 4, 1855, Upjohn Collection, New York Public Library.

53. *The Sun*, Baltimore, December 22, 1855.

54. R. C. Tilghman to Upjohn, September 19, 1856, Upjohn Collection, New York Public Library.

55. C. D. Kemp to Upjohn, December 8, 1856, Upjohn Collection, New York Public Library.

56. *The Sun*, Baltimore, September 18, 1849, June 4, 1850, October 29, 1851; *The Annual Report of the Baltimore Humane Impartial Society and Aged Women's Home for the Year 1852* (Baltimore, 1852).

57. *The Sun*, Baltimore, August 13, 1851.

58. *American*, Baltimore, August 29, 1851.

59. *The Sun*, Baltimore, September 30, 1851.

60. *Ibid.*, March 24, 1852, and March 5, 1853.

61. *Ibid.*, January 25, 1852.

62. *Ibid.*, April 15, 1853.

63. *Ibid.*, May 20, 1853.

64. *Ibid.*, September 27, 1853.

65. Balbirnie's first independent work was a Methodist Church on Madison Avenue in late 1856. *Ibid.*, December 17, 1856, and December 22, 1858.

66. *Ibid.*, June 16, 1857.

67. *Ibid.*, December 14, 1859, and January 11, 1860.

68. Thomas and J. M. Dixon to Mayor and City Council of Baltimore, February 22, 1859, Doc. 338, City Archives, Baltimore.

69. Dixon brothers designed Richard Colvin Office, 105–107 North Gay Street, c. 1860, *Ibid.*, October 13, 1860.

70. Research files at Sheppard and Enoch Pratt Hospital; Henry M. Hurd, *The Institutional Care of the Insane in the United States and Canada* (Baltimore, 1916) II, 560.

71. *The Sun*, Baltimore, January 4, 1860.

72. John Niernsee, Diary, 1838–41, Niernsee Collection, Maryland Historical Society.

73. Recollections of Emma Atkinson, Niernsee Collection, Maryland Historical Society.

74. *The Sun*, Baltimore, April 17, 1846.

75. *Ibid.*, August 10, 1848.

76. *Ibid.*, March 1, 1848.

77. *Ibid.*, December 14, 1848, and January 24, 1851.

78. *Ibid.*, February 15, 1849, and July 12, 1849.

79. *Ibid.*, June 19, 1850.

80. *Ibid.*, October 18, 1850.

81. Randolph W. Chalfont, "Calvert Station: Its Structure and Significance," *MHM*, 73 (1978), 11–22.

82. *The Sun*, Baltimore, July 22, 1850, and December 3, 1852.

83. Niernsee and Neilson designed chapel at Green Mount Cemetery, *American*, Baltimore, March 28, 1851.

84. *Ibid.*, July 18, 1851; *The Sun*, Baltimore, July 18, 1851.

85. *American*, Baltimore, November 1, 1851, September 9, 1852, August 31, 1853, January 19, 1859.

86. *Ibid.*, January 12, 1852.

87. *Ibid.*, January 22, 1852.

88. *Ibid.*, February 3, 1853.

89. *Ibid.*, February 5, 1853, and October 19, 1854.

90. *Ibid.*, March 21, 1854, and November 3, 1854.

91. *Ibid.*, January 24, 1855.

92. *Ibid.*, May 30, 1855.

93. *Ibid.*, July 9, 1855.

94. The Baltimore architect George A. Frederick, who had worked for Lind and Murdoch in 1856–60, recalled in his memoirs that Niernsee and Neilson built Alexandrofsky, Frederick Reminiscences, 19, Maryland Historical Society; but Marion M. Lind Laird, daughter of E. G. Lind, said Lind was architect of Alexandrofsky. Since Lind was not in America in 1853–54 when Alexandrofsky was built, she may have heard that Lind designed the additions of 1870–80.

95. *The Sun*, Baltimore, May 5, 1856, and July 9, 1857.

96. *Ibid.*, January 13, 1858, September 1, 1860, December 10, 1860.

97. *Ibid.*, October 14, 1857.

98. Kenneth T. Gibbs, "The Architecture of Norris G. Starkweather [sic]," M.A. thesis, University of Virginia, 1972. The author is indebted to Pamela Scott for calling this thesis to his attention. Starkwether signed his name "Starkwether." Some biographical information is contained in Starkwether's letter of March 12, 1877, to A. J. Bloor, AIA Library, Washington, D.C.

99. *The Sun*, Baltimore, November 14, 1855, reported that the architect of the First Presbyterian Church as "V. G. Starkweather [sic], an architect of Philadelphia."

100. See "Bills and Financial Receipts, 1857–58," St. John's College Papers, Hall of Records.

101. Contract for construction of 1856 Starkwether wing, Patapsco Female Institute Papers, Maryland Historical Society.

102. Related plans can be found in Ridgely Papers, MS 692, Box 12, Maryland Historical Society.

103. "After an erratic career, he [Starkwether] moved to New York." George Frederick: Reminiscences, 22, Maryland Historical Society.

104. The author is indebted to Phoebe Stanton for sharing a copy of Lind's fragmentary journal-autobiography.

105. "List of Works designed and executed by me, E. G. Lind, since commencing business in Baltimore, Md. in the year 1856," Maryland Historical Society.

106. *The Sun*, Baltimore, May 25, 1857.

107. The stores were completed in 1859, *Ibid.*, January 29, 1859.

108. J. Gilman D'Arcy Paul, "A Baltimore Estate: Guilford," *MHM*, 51 (1956), 14–26.

109. The author is indebted to Elizabeth Scharf, Archivist, for making the trustees minutes, building committee reports and drawings from the Institute's collections so available.

110. Andrews designed the Church of the Redeemer, Baltimore, in 1856. Vestry Minutes, Church of the Redeemer, 25, MS 247, Box 4, Maryland Historical Society.

111. *The Sun*, Baltimore, April 26, 1858, and April 20, 1859.

112. Lind and Murdoch's design for Memorial Church is described in *The Sun*, Baltimore, April 4, 1860. Lind and Murdoch presented their plan, Vestry Minutes, Memorial Church, March 1, 1860, Microfilm M-1408, Hall of Records.

113. Lind designed Trinity Church, Towson, in 1869. The Maryland Historical Society has receipts for its construction. Lind moved to Atlanta in 1883.

114. *American and Commercial Daily Advertiser*, Baltimore, April 9, 1836.

115. Tench Tilghman to Richard Upjohn, August 22, 1845, Upjohn Collection, New York Public Library.

116. *The Cultivator*, II (1845), 84.

117. "Receipts and Expenditures on Account of the Parsonage, Church of the Redeemer, 1861–65," Church of the Redeemer Papers, MS 247; see also the treasurer's receipts, 1854–86, vestry minutes, and specifications.

118. J. H. B. Latrobe wrote, "I sent to town for an architect, and he came . . . Sunday. We had a consultation . . . and determined upon a plan. On Monday I had a superintending carpenter, and the cellar was begun, and . . . the present dwelling was erected in fifty-four working days, papered, supplied with water, gas, speaking tubes, and all the modern arrangements for comfort." John E. Semmes, *John H. B. Latrobe and his Times* (Baltimore, 1917).

119. Herman D. Aldrich to William Wyman, June 19, 1851, Wyman Collection, Maryland Historical Society.

120. H. D. Aldrich to Wyman, December 16, 1851, Wyman Collection, Maryland Historical Society.

121. G. H. Cary to Wyman, October 3, 1851, and January 15, 1851 [or 1852?], Wyman Collection, Maryland Historical Society.

122. Francis Wilbar to Wyman, May 22, 1852, Wyman Collection, Maryland Historical Society.

123. Charles B. Calvert, "Essay on Farm Buildings," *The American Farmer*, IX (1854), 369–371.

124. *The Sun*, Baltimore, April 28, 1856.

125. David G. Wright, *Baltimore City Cast Iron* (New York, 1978).

126. *The Sun*, Baltimore, October 4, 1860.

127. *Ibid.*, February 19, 1845.

128. *Ibid.*, November 4, 1846.

129. *Ibid.*, February 5, 1848.

130. Hatfield's obituary, *American Architect and Building News*, March 1, 1879.

131. *American and Commercial Daily Advertiser*, Baltimore, August 13, 1851; *The Sun*, Baltimore, June 28, 1851. The Maryland Institute was 355 feet long, the open market on the ground story featured fifty-four arches, the second-story hall was 265 feet long, 54 feet wide and 32 feet high, with a 6-foot-wide gallery around all four walls; the Hall burned in 1904.

132. *The Sun*, Baltimore, August 4, 1853.

133. *Ibid.*, October 2, 1852.

134. *Ibid.*, August 25, 1860.

135. Sun Building described, *American and Commercial Daily Advertiser*, Baltimore, September 30, 1851, and October 30, 1851.

136. *American and Commercial Daily Advertiser*, Baltimore, May 17, 1851; *The Sun*, Baltimore, May 17, 1851.

137. *American and Commercial Daily Advertiser*, Baltimore, August 21, 1851.

138. *The Sun*, Baltimore, August 28, 1852.

Index

Abbotsford, Scotland (Sir Walter Scott residence), 172–75
Abell, Arunah S., 232
Adam, Robert, 93; *Works in Architecture* (with J. Adam), 94
Adam Company store, Baltimore, 233
Aged Men's Home, Baltimore, 196
Aldrich, Herman D., 228
Alexandrofsky (Thomas Winans villa), Baltimore, 203
Allegheny County Academy, Cumberland, 162, 164
Allegheny County Courthouse, at Cumberland, 158
Allison, Robert, 74
All Saints' Church, Frederick, 195
All Saints Episcopal Church, Baltimore, 137
American Builder's Companion, The (book; Benjamin), 158
Ancient Ecclesiological Architecture (book; Wills), 188
Anderson, C., 218
Anderson, Joseph Horatio, 64–73, 228
Andrei, Giovanni, 122, 123
Andrews, R. Snowden, 218
Andrews, William S., 218
Angelo Castle, Ellicott City, 175
Anglican Church, 16, 28–30, 179
Annapolis, 28–30; city plan, 30
Anneslie (Frederick Harrison villa), Towson, elevation and plan, 207
Antiquities of Athens (book; Stuart), 94, 142, 146
Antiquities of Ionia (book; Society of the Dilettanti), 146
Apollo Hall, Baltimore, 233
Architect, The (book; Ranlett), 226, 226
architects: English, 93; Northern, 186. *See also* Balbirnie, Thomas; Bryant, Gridley J. F.; Clark, Joseph; Davis, Alexander Jackson; Dixon, James; Dixon, Thomas; Godefroy, Maximilian; Howard, William; Latrobe, Benjamin Henry; Lind, Edmund G.; Long, Robert Cary, Jr.; Lovering, William; Mills, Robert; Murdoch, William T.; Neilson, James Crawford; Niernsee, John Rudolph; Reasin, William H.; Rogers, Nicholas; Small, William F.; Starkwether, Norris Gibson; Strickland, William; Town, Ithiel; Upjohn, Richard; Upjohn, Richard Mitchell; Wall, Jacob, Sr.
architectural styles, designs derived from books, 223–28. *See also* Egyptian style; Federal style; Gothic style; Greek Revival; Italian Villa style; Palladian style; romantic styles
architecture: books on, 85, 94–95, 158–61, 222–30; as profession, 84–85, 133; public vs. domestic, 123; Southern, influences on, 161
Architecture Hydraulique (book; Belidor), 94
Architecture of Country Houses, The (book; Downing), 223, 224, 225, 226, 228, 228
Ariss, John, 42
Ashton, Alexander, houses, Baltimore, 141
Assembly Rooms, Baltimore (1795), 103, 103; improvements to, 153
Astor Library, New York City, 186
Athenaeum, Baltimore (1824), 141, 186
Athenaeum, Baltimore (1848), 152, 180–86, 232; elevation and plan, 185

Bachelor's Hope (William Hammersley house), Chaptico vicinity, 48; elevation and plan, 49
Backus, John, manse, Baltimore, 203
Badger, Daniel, 233
Baker, Andrew, 13
Baker, Elias, house, Altoona, Pa., 157
Balbirnie, Thomas, 196, 218
Baltimore, Cecil, 2nd Lord, 12
Baltimore, 73, 84–141; culture of, 113; growth of, 84
Baltimore American Office, Baltimore, 186
Baltimore and Ohio Railroad, 162, 199, 201
Baltimore Cathedral (Catholic), 88, 116–22, 119, 121, 166; elevation and plan, 116, 117, 118; proposed Gothic design, 167, 168, 169; sectional view, 120
Baltimore County Courthouse, Towson, 165, 196
Baltimore County Jail (1799), Baltimore, 103
Baltimore Courthouse (1768), 88
Baltimore Courthouse (1806), 89, 90, 153
Baltimore Custom House, 201
Baltimore Exchange, 90, 123, 125–30, 135, 158; studies for, 126, 127, 128, 141
Baltimore Jail, 166, 196, 197
Baltimore Museum, 107–11, 111, 123, 145
bank, design by A. J. Davis, 148, 148
Bank of Baltimore, 135, 203
Bank of Pennsylvania, Philadelphia, 158
Bank of the United States, William Small drawings for, 141
Baptist Church (1846), Baltimore, 232
Barker, Theodore P., 188
Barnes, James, 42, 64
Barnum's City Hotel. *See* City Hotel
Bartlett and Hayward (iron works), 230, 233
Bash, H. M., office, 203
Bayard, James, house. *See* Great House
Bayley, Samuel, 64
Baylor, Richard, house. *See* Kinloch
Bay View Asylum, Canton, 196–99
Beech Hill (Robert Gilmor, Jr., house), Baltimore, 96, 98
Belidor, Bernard, *Architecture Hydraulique*, 94
Belvidere (John Eager Howard house), Baltimore, 94, 95
Belzoni, Giovanni Battista, *Narrative of the Operations and Recent Discoveries within the Pyramids*, 177
Benjamin, Asher, 222; *The American Builder's Companion*, 158; *Practical House Carpenter*, 146, 158
Benson, Benjamin S., 233
Beverly (Littleton Dennis house), Pocomoke City vicinity, 32, 37
Bindley, Robert, *Compendium of Civil Architecture*, 158
Birch, William, 98
Bladen, Thomas, 30
Bladen's Folly. *See* Governor's Mansion, Annapolis
Blore, John, 208
board-and-batten churches, 190
Bogardus, James, 232
Bohemia (George Milligan house), Earleville vicinity, 47, 48; elevation and plan, 46
Bolton, John, 218
Bolton (George Grundy house), Baltimore, 95, 95

Bonaparte, Jerome N., house, Baltimore, 157
Book of Architecture (book; Gibbs), 30, *30*, 42, 85, 87
Booth, Junius Brutus, house. *See* Tudor Hall
Botts, Joshua, 73
Boudier, J. J., 84, 90
Boulton, Richard, 42–48
Bounds, Jonathan, house (Bounds Lott), Allen vicinity, 16, *17*, 18
Bowles, John, house. *See* Sotterly
Brampton, William, 53
Brand, William Francis, 188
Breze, Luke, 22
Brice, James, house, Annapolis, 53, 59; elevation and plan, *58*
brick houses, 18–22, 83
bricks, brick making, 13
bridge, Jones Falls, 88
British Architect, The (book; Swan), 53, 59, 74, 85
British Carpenter (book; Price), 94
British Palladio (book; Pain), 94
Britton, John, *Illustrations of Public Buildings in London* (with A. Pugin), 146
Brown, Alexander, commercial buildings, Baltimore, 222
Brown, Gustavus, house. *See* Rose Hill
Brunner, John, house. *See* Schiefferstadt
Bryant, Gridley J. F., 196, 218
Buchanan, Colonel, house, Baltimore, 135
Buchanan, James, houses, Baltimore, 90
Bucher, A. H., 226
Buckland, James, 63
Buckland, William, 63, 63–64
builders, 84–93; from England, 42–48. *See also* Buckland, William; Harbaugh, Leonard; Long, Robert Cary, Sr.; Milliman, George; Rohrback, George; Small, Jacob, Sr.
Builder's Assistant, The (book; Haviland), 158
Builder's Jewel, The (book; T. and B. Langley), 85
Builder's Pocket Treasure or Palladio Delineated (book; Pain), 94
building materials. *See also* bricks, brick making; cast iron; timber-frame construction
Burnaby, Andrew, 30

Bushwood, Leonardtown vicinity, 42, *42*
Button, Stephen Decatur, 218

Caldwell, William Quarle, 177
Callis, John, 64
Calvert, Charles, 230
Calvert, Leonard, house, St. Mary's, 13
Calvert family, 12, 16
Calverton (Dennis Smith house), Baltimore, 125; elevation and plan, *125*
Calvert Street Station, Baltimore, 200, 201
Camden Street Station, 201, *201*
Campbell, Colin, *Vitruvius Britannicus*, 146
Campbell, Matthew, 84; plan of house by, *84*
Canedy, Cornelius, 13
Canfield Brothers store, Baltimore, 233
Capitol, U.S., 77, 90, 116, 133, 186; designs for, 88
Carlisle, Henry, 78
Caroline County, courthouse and prison, 64
"Carpenter" (book; Nicholson and Pain), 85
Carpenter & Joiner's Instructor (book; Martin), 158
Carpenter's and Joiner's Repository (book; Pain), 94
Carpenter's New Guide (book; Nicholson), 158
"Carpenter's Own Book, or the Young Man's Self-Instructor" (unpublished; anonymous), 161
Carroll, Charles, Jr., 95, 103; house (*see* Homewood)
Carroll, Charles, of Annapolis, 64
Carroll, Charles, of Carrollton, 60–63, 98; houses (*see* Carroll Mansion; Doughoregan Manor)
Carroll, Charles, of Doughoregan, 63
Carroll, Charles ("the Barrister"), house. *See* Mount Clare
Carroll, Charles R., stores, Baltimore, 216
Carroll, James, houses, Baltimore, 201
Carroll, John, Archbishop, 116
Carroll family, 60–63; iron works, 230; octagonal house, at The Caves, Baltimore vicinity, 228
Carroll Mansion (Robert Lawson

house), Baltimore, 90–93, *91*, *92*; plan, *90*
Carter, J. H., store, Baltimore, 196
Carter family, Richmond County, 63–64
Cary, George H., 228
casement windows, 14
cast iron, 179, 230–33
Catholic Archbishop's Residence, Baltimore, 141
Catholic Cathedral, Baltimore. *See* Baltimore Cathedral
Catholic settlers, 12, 28
Caton, Richard, house. *See* Carroll Mansion
cattle barn, octagonal (by C. Calvert), 230, *230*
Cedar Park (Richard Galloway II house), Galesville, 16
Central Park, New York City, 199
Central Presbyterian Church, Baltimore, 201
Chambers, Robert, *Treatise on the Decorative Part of Civil Architecture*, 146
Chambers, William, *Treatise on Civil Architecture*, 94
Chambray, Roland Fréart de, *Parallèle de l'Architecture*, 146
Charles Street Methodist Church, 161, *161*
Chase, Samuel, house. *See* Chase-Lloyd House
Chase, Thorndike, house, Baltimore, 135
Chase-Lloyd House, Annapolis, 63–64, 65, 66, 67, 68; plan, *64*
Chatham (Comfort Mackubin house), Howard County, 208, *208*
Chesapeake and Delaware Canal, 116, 133, 162
Chesapeake and Ohio Canal, 162
Cheston, James, house. *See* Ivy Neck
Chevalier, Augustin, 90, 113
Christ Church (Church of the Messiah), Baltimore, 157–58; plan, *159*
Christ Church, Easton, 158, 223
church architecture, 179–80, 186–95; board-and-batten, 190; Gothic, 166–72
Churchman, George, 28
Churchman, John, house, Calvert vicinity, 27, 28; plan, *28*
Church of the Ascension, Westminster, 180, *181*

Church of the Holy Communion, Baltimore County, proposed design, 189, 190
Church of the Immaculate Conception (St. Alphonsus Church), Baltimore, 178, 179, 232
Church of the Redeemer, Baltimore vicinity, 223, 224; plan, 223
Circular Congregational Church, Charleston, 135
City Hall, Baltimore, 145; proposed, by G. A. Frederick, 232; proposed, by R. C. Long, Jr., 153–57
City Hotel (Barnum's), Baltimore, 141, 203, 203
Civil War, 233
Claiborne, William, 12
Clark, Joseph, 228; career, 74–78; State House, Annapolis, 73, 77; styles, 166; Wye Hall, 77–78
Clarke, John Attaway, house. *See* Mulberry Fields
Clifton (Johns Hopkins house), Baltimore, 201
Cockerell, Samuel Pepys, 113
Cohen, Benjamin, house, Baltimore, 141
Cohen, J. I., and Brothers, bank, Baltimore, 186
Cohen, Joshua, 145; house, Baltimore, 140, 141
colonial architecture, 12–73; builders, 42–48
Commercial and Farmers Bank, Baltimore, 122, 123
Commercial Exchange. *See* Baltimore Exchange
Compendium of Civil Architecture (book; Bindley), 158
Connolly, John F., 122
Convenient and Ornamental Architecture (book; Cruden), 146
Convenient and Ornamental Designs (book; Cruden), 85
Corlan, James, store, Baltimore, 216
Cornwallis, Thomas, house, St. Mary's, 12–13
Cottage Residences (book; Downing), 223, 224
cottages and huts, 12, 14–16
Country Builder's Assistant, The (book; anonymous), 85
Country Gentleman's Architect (book; Miller), 85
Courthouse: Allegheny County, at Cumberland, 158; Baltimore (1768), 88; Baltimore (1806), 89, 90, 153; Baltimore County, at Towson, 165, 196; Caroline County, 64; Dorchester County, at Cambridge, 195; Prince George's County, at Upper Marlboro, 115; St. Mary's County, at Leonardtown, 141, 141; Talbot County, at Easton, 123; Washington County, at Hagerstown, 130, 130
craftsmen: early colonial, 12; English, 42; indentured, 85; itinerant, 32
Cranch, William, 85
Crouch, Henry, 42
Cruden, John: *Convenient and Ornamental Architecture*, 146; *Convenient and Ornamental Designs*, 85
Curley, Henry, 186
Curley, James, 161

Dakin, James, 148
Dallas, William Wallace, house. *See* Trevanion
Dalrymple, John, 88
Danckaerts, Jaspar, 14
Davidge, John B., 107
Davis, Alexander Jackson: Glen Ellen, 172–75; *Rural Architecture*, 223; St. John's College, Annapolis, college hall, 148–52
Deavour, John, 32
Denmead, Adam, 233
Dennis, Littleton, house. *See* Beverly
Desgodetz, Antoine, *Edifices Antiques de Rome*, 94
Deshon, Christopher, house. *See* Carroll Mansion
Designs in Architecture (book; Soane), 94
Diamond, James, 88
Diaper, F., 218
Diffenderffer, Michael, 88
Digges, Charles, 166
Dixon, Balbirnie and Dixon, 196, 233
Dixon, James, 196, 199, 230
Dixon, Thomas, 195–99, 230
Dorchester County Courthouse, at Cambridge, 195
Dorsey, Charles W., 208
Dorsey, J. T., 208
Dorsey, Reuben Meriweather, 208
Dorsey, Sally Elizabeth, house. *See* El Monte
Dorsey, Thomas Beale, 208
Dorsey, William H., 208
Dorsey, William H. G., house. *See* Wilton

Doughoregan Manor (Charles Carroll of Carrollton house), Howard County, 60–63, 63
Downing, Andrew Jackson, 199, 223; *The Architecture of Country Houses*, 223, 224, 225, 226, 228, 228; *Cottage Residences*, 223, 224; *A Treatise on the Theory and Practice of Landscape Gardening*, 223
Dreyer, Ernest, 177, 180
Druid Hill (Nicholas Rogers house), Baltimore, 103, 103
Dugan, Cumberland, house, Baltimore, 90
Dulaney, Daniel, the Younger, 64
Durand, Jean N. L., *Précis des Leçons d'Architecture*, 146

Easter, Hamilton, store, Baltimore, 199
Eccleston, John, house. *See* Yarmouth
Eden, Robert, house, Annapolis, 64
Edifices Antiques de Rome (book; Desgodetz), 94
Edwards, Robert and William, 98
Egyptian style, 175–77
El Monte (Sally Elizabeth Dorsey house), Howard County, 208, 208
Elsam, Richard, *Essay in Rural Architecture*, 94
Emmanuel Church, Baltimore, 190, 201
Emmanuel Church, Cumberland, 188
Encyclopedia of Cottage, Farm and Villa Architecture (book; Loudon), 146, 222–23
English architects, influence of, 93
Episcopal Church, East Baltimore Street, Baltimore, 88
Episcopalians, 179–80, 186–95
Essay in Rural Architecture (book; Elsam), 94
Essay on British Cottage Architecture (book; Malton), 94
Essays on Gothic (book; Warton), 94
Etting, Solomon, 153
Evans, Thomas, 157
Evesham (Joseph William Patterson house), Baltimore, 180, 183; elevation and plan, 182

Fairy Knowe (John H. B. Latrobe house), Baltimore vicinity, 224, 226
farmers, tobacco, 16–18
Federal style, 74, 93

Female Seminary, Frederick, 162, *162*, *163*
Female Seminary, Lutherville, 196, *196*
fireproof houses, 83
First Baptist Church, Baltimore, 135, *136*; plan, *137*
First Constitutional Presbyterian Church, Baltimore, 201
First English Lutheran Church, Baltimore, 146
First Presbyterian Church, Baltimore, 88, *88*, 196, 203, *204*, *205*, 208–16; tombs in churchyard, *175*
First Unitarian Church, Philadelphia, 135
Fisher, William, houses, Baltimore, 222
five-part houses, 32, 78, 83–84
Folly Quarter (John McTavish house), Howard County, 144, *145*; elevation and plan, *143*
Foster, George, 53
Foster, J. L., 218
Four Books of Architecture (book; Palladio), 30, 94
Fourth Presbyterian Church, Baltimore, 222
Fowler, Orson Squire, 228–30; *A Home for All*, 230
France, Richard, villa, Talbot County, 226
Franklin Row, Philadelphia, 135
Franklin Street Presbyterian Church, 179, *179*
Franzoni, Giuseppe, 123
Frederick, George A., 232
Frederick, Maryland, 28
Freeman, W. B., school, Baltimore, 135
French builders, 90
Frosberg, Augustus, 218
Fuller, William, 78

Galloway, John, 32
Galloway, Richard, II, house. *See* Cedar Park
Galloway, Samuel, house. *See* Tulip Hill
gate house, Baltimore, 201–3
German Evangelical Reformed Church (Otterbein Church), Baltimore, 88
German Lutheran Church, Baltimore, 88
German Reformed Church, Baltimore, 85, *87*, 88

German Reformed Church, Frederick City, 161
German settlers, 22–28
Gibbs, James, 64, 83; *Book of Architecture*, 30, *30*, 42, *85*, *87*
Gilmor, Robert, 95, 172
Gilmor, Robert, Jr., 98, 172; house (*see* Beech Hill); proposed house, Baltimore, 148, *150*
Gilmor, Robert, III, 172–75; estate (*see* Glen Ellen)
Girard College, Philadelphia, 153
Gittings, John S., houses, Baltimore, 201
Glenelg (Joseph W. Tyson house), Howard County, 186; elevation and plan, *187*
Glen Ellen (Robert Gilmor III house), Baltimore vicinity, 148, *149*, 172–75; elevation and plan, *173*
Godefroy, Maximilian, 115; and B. H. Latrobe, 122–25; St. Mary's Chapel, 166–72; style, 175; Unitarian Church design, 130–33; Washington Monument design, 142
Goldsborough, Howes, house. *See* Pleasant Valley
Gothic house, unidentified, by R. C. Long, Jr., elevation, *184*
Gothic style, 166–75, 179–80; churches, 166–72; institutional, 195–96; villas, 195
Governor's Mansion, Annapolis (Bladen's Folly), 30, 77; elevation, *31*
Grace Church, Baltimore, 201
Grace Episcopal Church, Baltimore, 202
Gray, Francis, 13
Great House (James Bayard house), St. Augustine, 28, 29; elevation and plan, *28*
Greek Revival, 142–65
Greene, Albert C., villa, Frostberg, *225*, 226
Green Mount (Robert Oliver country house), Baltimore vicinity, 103, *107*
Greenwood (Philip Rogers house), Baltimore vicinity, 103
Grey Rock (Richard Maynard villa), Baltimore County, 208, *215*
Griffith, Israel, store, Baltimore, 196
Grundy, George, 95; house (*see* Bolton)
Guilford (William McDonald villa), Baltimore, 216, *217*

Gunston Hall, Alexandria vicinity, Va., 63
Guy, Francis, 95, *96*, 98
Gwynn, William, house. *See* Tusculum, The

Hager, John, house, Hagerstown, *25*, 28
Halfpenny, William, 95; *Modern Builder's Assistant*, 133; *Useful Architecture*, 48, *48*
Hall, Acquilla, house. *See* Sophia's Dairy
Hall, James, *A Series of Select and Original Modern Designs for Dwelling Houses*, 160, *161*
Hall, Thomas, 64
Hammersley, William, house. *See* Bachelor's Hope
Hammond, John, 14
Hammond, Mathias, house, Annapolis, 64, *64*; elevation and plan, *69*, *70*
Hampton (Charles Ridgely house), Towson vicinity, 78; elevation and plan, *79*
Handy, Isaac, house. *See* Pemberton Hall
Hannah More Academy, chapel, Reisterstown, 190
Hannan, John and James, 88
Hanson, Alexander, 77
Harbaugh, Leonard, 85–88
Harbine, Thomas, 130
Harkins, Charles, 218
Harper, Charles, summer house, Baltimore, 172
Harper, Robert Goodloe, 130; country house (*see* Oaklands)
Harris, Samuel, 161, 179
Harrison, Frederick, villa. *See* Anneslie
Harrison, James, 226
Hart, Philip, 88
Hartshorn, Charles, 218
Hartwell, H. W., 218
Harvey, Thomas, 53
Hatfield, Robert G., 232
Haviland, John, 153, 186; *The Builder's Assistant*, 158
Hayden, John, 122
Hayward and Bartlett, 230, 233
Heilig, William, octagon house, Lutherville, 230
Henning, Thomas, 130
Hermann, Augustin, 22

Hermitage, The (Richard Cooke Tilghman house), Centreville, 195
Herring, Ludwig, 88
Hicks, Nicholas, 74
Hillen, John, 122
Hoban, James, 133
Hoffman, David, 113
Hogan, James, 88
Holliday Street Theater, Baltimore, 107, *107*
Hollins, John, house, Baltimore, 90
Hollyday, Henry, house. *See* Ratcliff Manor
Hollyday, James, house. *See* Readbourne
Holly Hill, Friendship vicinity, *15*, 16, *16*, 18; plan, *14*
Holy Trinity Church, Oxford, 190
Home for All, A (book; Fowler), 230
Homeland (David M. Perrine house), Baltimore vicinity, 157; elevation and plan, *154*, *157*
Homewood (Charles Carroll, Jr., house), Baltimore, 98–103, *101*, *102*; elevation and plan, *100*
Hope (Peregrine Tilghman house), Easton vicinity, 83, *83*
Hopkins, Johns, house. *See* Clifton
Hose, John F., 145
hotel, design by A. J. Davis, *148*
House of Industry, Baltimore, 137; elevation and plan, *139*
houses: brick, 18–22, 83; early colonial cottages, 12, 14–16; fireproof, 83; five-part, 32, 78, 83–84; octagon, 115, 228–30; three-part, 48; timber-frame, 12
Howard, John Eager, 95; house (*see* Belvidere)
Howard, William, 142, 146, 223; house, Baltimore, 146
Howell, Jehu, 78
Hudson River school, 223
Humphries, Hector, 148–52
hyphens, architectural, 78

Ichnographic Distribution for Small Villas (book; Peacock), 94
Illustrations of Public Buildings in London (book; Britton, Pugin), 146
indentured craftsmen, 85
Independent Fire Company, Baltimore, 233
Indigent Women's Home, Baltimore, 195–96; elevation and plan, *195*

industrialization, 230–33
iron industry, 230–33
Italian Villa style, 203–8
Ivy Neck (James Cheston house), Annapolis vicinity, 88

James, Henry, house, Baltimore, 233
Jefferson, Thomas, 133
Jennings, Thomas, 73
Jewett family, octagon house, Darlington vicinity, 230; elevation and plan, *231*
Johns, Henry V. D., 190, 222
Johnson, William Cost, hotel, Point Lookout, 222
Jones, Hugh, 13
Jones, Richard Ireland, house. *See* Kennersley
Jones Falls, bridge, 88
Jordan, John Morton, 64

Kemp, Charles, 195
Kemp, James, 111
Kemp, Joseph F., 201, 218
Kennersley (Richard Ireland Jones house), Centreville vicinity, 83; elevation and plan, *82*
Kent Island, 12
Keplinger, Michael, 98
King, Edward, villa, Newport, R.I., 228
King, Joseph, store, Baltimore, 196, 233
Kinloch (Richard Baylor house), Essex County, Va., 157
Kirby, Charles, 218
Krafft, Johann Karl, *Recueil d'Architecture Civile*, 146

Lafayette triumphal arch, William Small drawings for, 141
Lafever, Minard, 222; *Modern Builder's Guide*, 146, 158
Lane, Samuel, 133
Langley, Batty, 64, 85
Langley, Thomas, *Builder's Jewel, The* (with B. Langley), 85
Lanphier, Robert Goin, 115–16
Latrobe, Benjamin Henry, 113–33, 226; and architecture profession in America, 133; Baltimore Cathedral, 88, 116–22, 166; Baltimore Exchange, 125–30; career, 113–15, 133; commercial buildings, 123;

and Godefroy, 122–25; Library Company designs, 130; Masonic Hall, 123–25; opinions of, 84, 113–15; Stier house design, 115; and W. Strickland, 158; style of, 142; U.S. Capitol, 116; and W. Small, 137–41
Latrobe, John H. B., 88, 103, 172, 226; country house (*see* Fairy Knowe); house, Baltimore, 180, 199
Law Institute, Baltimore, 90, 113
Lawson, Robert, house. *See* Carroll Mansion
Leaman, Thomas, 94
LeBrun, Eugene, 179
Lee, Josiah, office building, 180
Lerew, Abraham, 113, 166
Letherbury, Peregrine, house, Baltimore, 85, *86*; elevation and plan, *85*
Lewger, John, house, St. Mary's, 12–13
Lewis, Martin, store, Baltimore, 199
Library Company of Baltimore, proposed building: design by B. H. Latrobe, 113, *129*, 130; design by Robert Mills, 137, *137*
Light Street Meeting House, 88
Lincoln, Abraham, 186
Lind, Edmund G., 208–22; and W. T. Murdoch, 216; Peabody Institute, 216–18, *219*; and N. G. Starkwether, 208–16; villa designs, 218–22
Lloyd, Edward, IV, houses. *See* Chase-Lloyd House; Wye House
Lloyd Street Synagogue, *156*, 157
Lockwood, Bernard, 218
Long, Louis L., 218
Long, Robert Cary, Sr., 107–13, 145, 175; Assembly Rooms, 103; Baltimore Jail, 166; Baltimore Museum, 107–11; churches, 111; craftsmen associated with, 90; Library Company design, 130; and R. C. Long, Jr., 152; Medical School, 107; public buildings by, 107–13; skill of, 85; Union Bank, 107, 123
Long, Robert Cary, Jr., 161, 175–86; Athenaeum, 152–53, 180–86; Baltimore Cathedral, 122; cast iron, use of, 232; City Hall design, 153–57; Gothic churches, 179–80; houses, 186, *186*; lectures on architecture, 174, 177; miscellaneous buildings, 157; Patapsco Female In-

stitute, 152, 162; Record Office, 153, 175–77; St. Mary's Chapel, 172; style of, 142
Long Hill (John Stewart house), Wetipquin vicinity, 18, 21; elevation and plan, 20
Loudon, John, *Encyclopedia of Cottage, Farm and Villa Architecture*, 146, 222–23
Lovering, William, 115–16
Lucas, Fielding: bookstore, 148; store, Baltimore, 135

McCleery family, builders (Andrew, Henry, Robert), 135–37
McCutchan, George, 88
McDonald, William, villa. *See* Guilford
McHenry, James Howard, villa, Pikesville, 222
Mackenheimmer, John, 88
McKim Free School, Baltimore, 146, 147
Mackubin, Comfort, house. *See* Chatham
McNeal, A. L., 226
McTavish, John, house. *See* Folly Quarter
Male and Female School, Baltimore, 145
Male School Number One, Baltimore, 145, 145
Male School Number Three, Baltimore, 145, 145
Malton, James, *Essay on British Cottage Architecture*, 94
Mantle, Michael and Frederick, 53
Maryland: boundaries, 28; colonial history, 12–73; eastern and tidewater, 28, 162; economic conditions, 32, 162, 230–32; immigration into, 22–28; western, 28
Maryland Institute, Baltimore, 232–33
Maryland Penitentiary, Baltimore, 141, 230
Mason, Henry M., 158
Masonic Hall, Baltimore, 123, 123–25, 124
Mayhew, William E., house, Baltimore, 201
Maynard, Richard, villa. *See* Grey Rock
Medical College, Baltimore, 107, 108, 109

Memorial Church, Baltimore, 222, 222
Merchants Exchange, New York City, 152
Methodist Church, Pennsylvania Avenue, Baltimore, 161
Mettam and Burke (N.Y.), 218, 220
Middleton, Charles, *Picturesque and Architectural Views for Cottages, Farm Houses and Country Villas*, 94
Miller, John, *Country Gentleman's Architect*, 85
Milligan, George, house (*see* Bohemia)
Milliman, George, 88–90, 161
Mills, Robert, 133–37, 153; Commercial Exchange, 125; and B. H. Latrobe, 116; Library Company design, 130, 137; miscellaneous projects and designs, 135–37; Washington Monument, 133, 142, 228
Mills, Thomas, 133
Minifee, William, 179
Mitchell, Robert, *Plans and Views in Perspective*, 94
Model Architect, The (book; Sloan), 225, 226
Modern Builder's Assistant (book; Halfpenny), 133
Modern Builder's Guide (book; Lafever), 146, 158
Montebello (Samuel Smith house), Baltimore, 98; elevation and plan, 98, 99
Montpelier (Thomas Snowden house), Prince George's County, 64; elevation and plan, 71
Monumental Church, Richmond, 135
Morris, Robert, 95; *Select Architecture*, 30, 30, 48, 48
Mosher, James, 88, 90, 107
Mount Airy (Tayloe family house), Richmond County, 64
Mt. Calvary Episcopal Church, 179–80
Mount Clare (Charles Carroll the Barrister's house), Baltimore, 60, 61, 62; elevation and plan, 60
Mount Washington Female College, design for dormitory, 230
Mulberry Fields (John Attaway Clarke house), Beauvue vicinity, 32
Murdoch, William F., house, Baltimore, 218
Murdoch, William T.: and E. G. Lind, 216–22; Peabody Institute, 219

Narrative of the Operations and Recent Discoveries within the Pyramids (book; Belzoni), 177
Neilson, James Crawford, 218; churches, 190; miscellaneous designs by, 199; Peabody Institute design, 221; projects with J. R. Niernsee, 199–203
neoclassicism, 93
New Vitruvius Britannicus, The (book; Richardson), 146
New York Ecclesiological Society, 188
Nicholson, Francis, 28–30
Nicholson, Peter: "*Carpenter*" (with W. Pain), 85; *Carpenter's New Guide*, 158; *Principles of Architecture*, 94, 146
Niernsee, John Rudolph: churches, 190; projects with J. C. Neilson, 199–203
Noke, William, 64, 83
Norris, George S., 188–90
Norris, Richard, 190
Norris, S. H., store, Baltimore, 196
Northern Central Railroad, depot, Baltimore, 222
Notman, John, 188, 201

Oakland (Charles Sterett Ridgely house), Baltimore, 113; elevation and plan, 112; Gothic dog kennel, 166, 166
Oaklands (Robert Goodloe Harper country house), 142
Oakley (Levi Pierce house), Baltimore, 95–98, 96
Octagon House (William Thornton house), Washington, D.C., 115
octagon houses, 115, 228–30
Odd Fellows Hall, Baltimore, 145, 177, 177
Oliver, Robert: country house (*see* Green Mount); house, Baltimore, 103, 103, 107
Olmsted, Frederick Law, 199
Otterbein Church, Baltimore, 88
Overton (architectural writer), 83
Oxen Hill, Prince George's County, 40

Paca, William: house, Annapolis, 53, 53, 56, 57; house, Queen Anne's County (*see* Wye Hall)
Pain, William: *British Palladio*, 94; *Builder's Pocket Treasure or Palladio Delineated*, 94; "*Carpenter*"

(with P. Nicholson), 85; *Carpenter's and Joiner's Repository*, 94; *Practical Builder*, 85
Paine, James, *Plans, Elevations and Sections of Noblemen's and Gentlemen's Houses*, 94
Palladian style, 30, *30*, 48, 53, 78, 95
Palladio, Andrea, 83; *Four Books of Architecture*, 30, 94
Palladio Londinensis (book; Salmon), 85, 86
Parallèle de l'Architecture (book; Chambray), 146
Parris, Alexander, 188
Patapsco Female Institute, Ellicott City, 152, *152*, 162, 175, 203
Patterson, Joseph, estate, Baltimore vicinity, 90
Patterson, Joseph William, house. *See* Evesham
Patuxent Manor, Lower Marlboro, 13, 16–18
Peabody, George, 216
Peabody Institute, Baltimore, 216–18; designs, 203; elevations, *219*, *220*, *221*
Peacock, James, *Ichnographic Distribution for Small Villas*, 94
Peale, Charles Willson, 107
Peale, Rembrandt, 107
Pemberton Hall (Isaac Handy house), Salisbury vicinity, 18, 19; elevation and plan, *18*
Pennsylvania, 28; settlers from, 22–28
pent eaves, 28
Perrine, David M., house. *See* Homeland
Picturesque and Architectural Views for Cottages, Farm Houses and Country Villas (book; Middleton), 94
Pierce, Levi, house. *See* Oakley
Pinckney, Ninian, villa, Easton, *194*, 195
Pinckney Hall, St. John's College, Annapolis, 203
Plans, Elevations and Sections of Noblemen's and Gentlemen's Houses (book; Paine), 94
Plans and Views in Perspective (book; Mitchell), 94
Plater, George, III, 42, 48
Pleasant Valley (Howes Goldsborough house), Easton vicinity, 32, *38*, *39*
Pohl, Anton, 218

Potts family, house, Frederick, 135; elevation and plan, *138*
Powell, W. Angelo, 218
Practical Builder (book; Pain), 85
Practical Builder or Workman's General Assistant, The (book; anonymous), 85
Practical Essay on the Strength of Cast Iron (book; Tredgold), 230
Practical House Carpenter (book; Benjamin), 146, 158
Pratt, William, 218
Précis des Leçons d'Architecture (book; Durand), 146
Preston Street, houses by Dixon, 196
Price, Francis, *British Carpenter*, 94
Priest, John W., 201
Prince George's County Courthouse, at Upper Marlboro, 115
Principles of Architecture (book; Nicholson), 94, 146
privy, octagonal, Annapolis, 228
Public Record Office, Charleston, 153
Pue, Arthur, house. *See* Temora
Pugin, Augustus, 146
puncheon buildings, 16

Quigly, John, 14

railroads, 230. *See also* Baltimore and Ohio Railroad
railroad stations: Baltimore, 200, 201; Lutherville, 196
Rakestraw, Joseph, 74
Ramée, Joseph Jacques, 125
Randall, John, 64
Rankin and Jones (Chicago), 218
Ranlett, William H., *The Architect*, 226, *226*
Ratcliff Manor (Henry Hollyday house), Easton vicinity, 32; elevation and plan, *36*
Rawlings, John, 42, 64
Readbourne (James Hollyday house), 18, 22
Reasin, William H., 218; Odd Fellows Hall, 177; Sun Building, 232–33; villa designs, 223
Record Office, Baltimore, 153, 158, 177; plans, *153*, *158*, *176*
Recueil d'Architecture (book; Krafft), 146
Revett, Nicholas, 94, 142, 146
Reynolds, Elija, 74

Reynolds, Henry and Josiah, 180, 218, 233
Richards, William T., 222
Richardson, Charles James, 208
Richardson, George: *The New Vitruvius Britannicus*, 146; *Series of Designs for Country Seats or Villas*, 94
Ridgely, Charles, house. *See* Hampton
Ridgely, Charles Sterett, house. *See* Oakland
Ridgely, John Carnan, 208
Ridout, John, 48
Ringgold, Samuel, 130
Riversdale (Henri Joseph Stier house), Riverdale, 98, 115–16; elevation and plan, *116*
Rogers, Nicholas: Baltimore Jail, 95, 166; house (*see* Druid Hill); and R. C. Long, Sr., 107; Temple of Divine Worship (design), 111
Rogers, Philip, house. *See* Greenwood
Rohrback, George, 85, 88, 122
Rohrer, Jacob, 28
Roman Amphitheater, Baltimore, 180
Romantic styles, 166–233
Rose Hill (Gustavus Brown house), Port Tobacco vicinity, elevation and plan, *80*, 83
Rose Hill (Thomas Owen Williams house), Williamsport vicinity, 104, *105*
row houses, 135, 196
Ruins of Balbec (book; Woods), 146
Rumsay House, Joppa vicinity, 28
Rural Architecture (book; Davis), 223
Rural Architecture (book; Upjohn), 190

St. Agnes Roman Catholic Church, Baltimore vicinity, 196
St. Alphonsus Church. *See* Church of the Immaculate Conception, Baltimore
St. Andrew's Church, Baltimore, 142, 195
St. Andrew's Church, Leonardtown vicinity, 42–48, *44*, *45*
St. Anne's Church, Annapolis, 30
St. John's Church, Ellicott City vicinity, 208
St. John's Church, Huntingdon, 180
St. John's College, Annapolis, 30, 77; college hall, 148–52, *151*, 175, *175*; Pinckney Hall, 203

St. John's Episcopal Church, Baltimore, 137
St. John's Episcopal Church, Washington D.C., 130
St. John's Methodist Church, 157
St. John the Evangelist Roman Catholic Church, Baltimore, 201, 203
St. Luke's Church, Baltimore, 186, 201
St. Mark's Church, Philadelphia, 201
St. Mark's Episcopal Church, Baltimore, 201
St. Mary's, Maryland, 12–14, 28–30
St. Mary's Chapel, Baltimore, 166–72, 171; elevation, 170
St. Mary's College, Ellicott City vicinity, 141
St. Mary's County Courthouse, at Leonardtown, 141, 141
St. Mary's Episcopal Church, Emmorton, 188, 188
St. Mary's Female Seminary, St. Mary's City, 157
St. Michael's Church, Reisterstown, 190
St. Michael's German Catholic Church, Baltimore, 201
St. Paul's Church, Baltimore, 195
St. Paul's Church, Brighton, 188
St. Paul's Church, Hillsboro, 190
St. Paul's Episcopal Church, Baltimore, 111, 111, 145, 191, 192, 193
St. Peter's Roman Catholic Church, 157
St. Philip's Church, Laurel, 188
St. Thomas Church, Bardstown, Ky., 172
St. Thomas Manor, Port Tobacco, 30–32; elevation, 31
St. Timothy's Church, Catonsville, 180, 180
Salmon, William, *Palladio Londinensis*, 85, 86
Samson Street Baptist Church, Philadelphia, 135
Schiefferstadt (John Brunner house), Frederick, 26, 28
school, design by R. C. Long, Jr., elevation and plan, 155
school buildings, 145–46
School for the Deaf and the Blind, Staunton, Va., 157
Schumacher, A. H., house, Baltimore, 201
Scott, Henry T., octagon house, Hyattsville, 230

Scott, Sir Walter, 172
Scott, Upton, house, Annapolis, 53, 55; elevation and plan, 54
Seamen's Bethel, Baltimore, 141, 141
Second Bank of the United States, New York City, 152
Second Presbyterian Church, Baltimore, 90, 90, 201
Select Architecture (book; Morris), 30, 30, 48, 48
Series of Designs for Country Seats or Villas (book; Richardson), 94
Series of Select and Original Modern Designs for Dwelling Houses, A (book; Hall), 160, 161
Seymour, Charles, 195
Shannon, Michael, 78
Sharpe, Horatio, 64; house (see Whitehall)
Sheppard, Moses, 199
Sheppard Asylum, Baltimore, 198, 199
Shulze, Paul, 218
Sinclair, Robert, 84
Sketches in Architecture (book; Soane), 94, 107
Sloan, Samuel, 199, 218; *The Model Architect*, 225, 226
Sluyter, Peter, 14
Small, Jacob, Sr., 137; Otterbein Church, 88
Small, Jacob, Jr., 137, 161; Commercial Exchange, 125, 130; houses built by, 90; Masonic Hall, 123
Small, John, 218
Small, William F.: Baltimore Museum, 111; and B. H. Latrobe, 137–41; Maryland Penitentiary, 230; Masonic Hall, 123; school buildings, 145–46
Smith, Dennis, house. See Calverton
Smith, Samuel, 95; house (see Montebello); house, Baltimore, 90
Smith, Samuel W., house, Baltimore, 157
Smith, Thoroughgood, 95; house (see Willow Brook)
Smith, William, 14, 74
Snowden, Thomas, house. See Montpelier
Soane, John, 208; *Designs in Architecture*, 94; *Sketches in Architecture*, 94, 107
Society of the Dilettanti, *Antiquities of Ionia*, 146
Sophia's Dairy (Acquilla Hall house), Belcamp, 32–42, 41

Sotterly (John Bowles house), Hollywood vicinity, 42, 42, 43
Southern architecture, influences on, 161
Sprague, Elisha R., villa, Baltimore County, 218
stable, octagonal, Annapolis vicinity, 228
stairs, 32–42, 48
Starkwether, Norris Gibson, 203–16, 218; First Presbyterian Church, 203; style, 223; villas, 203–16
State House, Annapolis (1696; 1704), 28–30
State House, Annapolis (1769), 64–73, 73, 77; elevation and plan, 72
State House, Columbia, S.C., 203
State House, St. Mary's, 14
State Lunatic Asylum, Catonsville, 203
Sterret, Benjamin, house, Baltimore, 135
Steuart, William, 90, 107, 130
Stewart, John, house. See Long Hill
Stewart, William Baldwin, 218, 219, 220
Stier, Henri Joseph, 230; house, proposed (design by B. H. Latrobe), 114, 115; house (see Riversdale)
stone work, 28
Strickland, William, 153; Christ Church, 157–58; Commercial Exchange, 125; and B. H. Latrobe, 116
Stuart, James, *Antiquities of Athens* (with N. Revett), 94, 142, 146
Sun Building, Baltimore, 232–33
Swan, Abraham, 64, 83; *The British Architect*, 53, 59, 74, 85; *Town and Country Builder's Assistant*, 85
Swann, Thomas, house, Baltimore, 161
Swedenborgian Church, Baltimore, 233
Sympson, Paul, house, 14
synagogue, High Street, Baltimore, 201

Talbot County Courthouse, at Easton, 123
Tayloe, John, 63
Tayloe family, 63–64; house (see Mount Airy)
Temora (Arthur Pue house), Howard County, 208; elevation and plan, 209

Temple of Ceres (folly; A. J. Davis), 148; elevation and plan, *149*
Temple of Divine Worship, design by N. Rogers, 110, *111*
Tennessee State Capitol, Nashville, 158
Thomas, J. Hanson, house, Baltimore, 201
Thompson, Martin, 152
Thornton, William, house. *See* Octagon House
Tiffany, Henry, house, Baltimore, 161
Tilghman, Peregrine, house. *See* Hope
Tilghman, Richard Cooke, house. *See* Hermitage, The
Tilghman, Tench, 190, 223
Timanus, Charles, 152, 153
timber-frame construction, 12–16
toll house, octagonal, Cumberland County, 228
tombs, First Presbyterian Church, Baltimore, 175
Town, Ithiel: Glen Ellen, 172–75; partnership with A. J. Davis, 148–52
Town and Country Builder's Assistant (book; Swan), 85
Towson, Thomas, 107
trade and shipping, 84
Trail, Charles E., house, Frederick, 225, *226*
Treatise on Civil Architecture (book; Chambers, W.), 94
Treatise on the Decorative Part of Civil Architecture (book; R. Chambers), 146
Treatise on the Strength and Dimension of Cast Iron Beams (book; Turnbull), 230
Tredgold, Thomas, *Practical Essay on the Strength of Cast Iron*, 230
Trevanion (William Wallace Dallas house), Uniontown vicinity, 206, *208*
Trinity Church, Fell's Point, 180
Trinity Church, New York City, 188
Trinity Church, Upper Marlboro, 180
Tuck, William, 53
Tudor Hall (Junius Brutus Booth house), Bel Air, 226, *226*, *227*
Tulip Hill (Samuel Galloway house), Galesville vicinity, 32, *34*, *35*; elevation and plan, *33*

Turnbull, *Treatise on the Strength and Dimension of Cast Iron Beams*, 230
Tusculum, The (William Gwynn house), Baltimore, 111–13
Tuttle, Edmund B., 195
Tyson, Joseph W., house. *See* Glenelg

Union Bank, Baltimore, 90, *106*, *107*, 123
Union Engine House, Baltimore, 157
Union Fire House, Baltimore, 179
Union Protestant Infirmary, Baltimore, 203
Union Square Methodist Church, Baltimore, 196
Unitarian Church, Baltimore, 130–33, *131*; elevation and plan, *133*; sectional view, *132*
Upjohn, Richard, 199, 218, 228; church buildings, 188–95; *Rural Architecture*, 190; style, 223
Upjohn, Richard Mitchell, 195
Useful Architecture (book; Halfpenny), 48, *48*

Vaux, Calvert, 199
villas, 98, 203–8
Vitruvius, 146
Vitruvius Britannicus (book; Campbell), 146
Volk, Horace B., 218
Volk, Lawrence B., 218
von Steinwehr, A., 218

Walker, James, 84
Wall, George, 88
Wall, Jacob, Sr., 88, 161
Wall, Jacob, Jr., 161
Wallace, Charles, 73
Walter, Thomas U., 153, 179, 186
Ward, William J., house, Baltimore, 161
Ware, Isaac, 53, 64
Warton, Thomas, *Essays on Gothic*, 94
Washington, George, 73, 74, 77
Washington College, 74; elevation, *75*
Washington County Courthouse, at Hagerstown, 130, *130*
Washington Monument, Baltimore, designs for, 133–35, *134*, *142–45*, 228
Washington Monument, Washington, D.C. (R. Mills, 1815), 133–35, *134*, *142–45*; (R. Mills, 1845), *137*
Waterloo Row, Baltimore, 135, *135*
Waverley Terrace, Baltimore, 196
Wells, Elijah, 175
Wells, Joseph C., 218
West, Cornelius, 123
West, Philip, 13
White, George, 42
White, Mrs. John Campbell, proposed house, 208, *210*, *211*, *212*, *213*; plan, *214*
Whitehall (Horatio Sharpe house), Annapolis vicinity, 48–53, *51*, *52*, 64; elevation and plan, *50*
Whitelaw, John, 122
Whittingham, William R., 180, 186
Wilbar, Francis, 228
Wilford, Thomas, 14
Williams, J., house, Baltimore, 135
Williams, James, stores, Baltimore, 201
Williams, Thomas Owen, house. *See* Rose Hill
Williamson, T. H., 218
Willow Brook (Thoroughgood Smith house), Baltimore, 95–98, *96*, *97*; plan, *98*
Wills, Frank, 188; *Ancient Ecclesiological Architecture*, 188
Wilson, Henry, house. *See* Carroll Mansion
Wilton (William H. G. Dorsey house), Howard County, 208, *208*
Winans, Thomas: gate house, Baltimore, 201–3; villa (*see* Alexandrofsky)
Winchester, Hiram, 162
windows, casement, 14
Wood, Robert, *Ruins of Balbec*, 146
Works in Architecture (book; R. and J. Adam), 94
Wye Hall (William Paca house), Queen Anne's County, 77–78; elevation and plan, *76*
Wye House (Edward Lloyd IV house), Easton vicinity, 78–83; elevation and plan, *81*
Wyman, William, villa, Baltimore, 228, *229*

Yarmouth (John Eccleston house), Bucktown vicinity, 22, *23*, *24*; elevation and plan, *22*